YOU CAN GO HOME AGAIN

YOU CAN
GO HOME
AGAIN

RECONNECTING

WITH YOUR FAMILY

MONICA McGOLDRICK

W. W. NORTON & COMPANY

NEW YORK LONDON

Lines from "Willie" reprinted from *And Still I Rise* by Maya Angelou.
Copyright © 1978 by Maya Angelou.
Reprinted by permission of Random House, Inc.

The text of this book is composed in Caledonia
with the display set in Garamond Titling
Composition and manufacturing by The Maple-Vail Book Manufacturing Group.
Book design by Chris Welch

Library of Congress Cataloging-in-Publication Data
McGoldrick, Monica.
You can go home again : reconnecting with your family / Monica
McGoldrick.
p. cm.
Includes bibliographical references and index.
1. Family—Psychological aspects.   2. Family assessment.
3. Genealogy.   I. Title.
HQ518.M38   1995
306.87—dc20   93-48812

ISBN 0-393-03494-1
ISBN 0-393-31650-5 pbk.

W. W. Norton & Company, Inc.
500 Fifth Avenue, New York, N.Y. 10110
www.wwnorton.com

W. W. Norton & Company Ltd.
Castle House, 75/76 Wells Street, London W1T 3QT

5 6 7 8 9 0

For my mother, who taught me that you can go home again, even though it is never the place you left behind. Perhaps it is not so much our mothers who have let us down as the yardsticks by which we have been measuring them.

CONTENTS

ILLUSTRATIONS

Photographs

Genograms and Figures

PREFACE

This book has been many years in the writing. It grew out of my own efforts "to go home again"—efforts which began more than twenty years ago, when I first learned of Murray Bowen's ideas about family systems and began to try to change my role in my family. Through exploring our family history, I came to love my powerful and vulnerable mother more deeply. I came to acknowledge my sweet, brilliant, funny father's limitations in ways that did not make me love him less but did enable me to love my mother more. I spent many years doing genealogical research on my family as well as tracking down relatives from Wyoming to "the Glen" near Ballybofey, in Donegal, and Leap near Skibbereen. My personal journey made me realize that I am a part of all that has come before and that my generation must pay attention to the legacy we leave to our children and their children.

For twenty-three years I have been teaching family therapy and trying to enrich others with the ideas of systems theory that have made so much difference to me. I have become so enamored of genograms that I can never read a book without doing the genogram of the characters. I hope the readers of this book will be as fascinated and inspired as I have been by the stories of the famous families described here.

So that readers have some idea of the person who is talking to them, I want to say a bit about my own history. I am the middle of three sisters and a fourth-generation Irish American. Born in Brooklyn in 1943 (and raised on the Brooklyn Dodgers), I grew up from age six on a farm in Solebury, Pennsylvania. My mother, one of the most interesting women I have ever known, with whom I struggled for all the years of my childhood, adolescence, and young adulthood, was a graduate of Barnard, class of '34. She gave up a successful career in public relations for marriage and family when she met my father, whom she adored for all of their thirty-seven years together. My father was a well-known reform politician in New York City and also a lawyer and a teacher. In fact, I come from a family of teachers (including both my sisters, all the in-laws, and all but one of the members of my parents' generation). My adored caretaker, Margaret-Margaret Pfeiffer Bush, an African American from Asheville, North Carolina, who because of racism did not learn how to read until after I did—ran the family along with my mother and was the person to whom I was closest throughout childhood. My father was a beloved visiting dignitary on weekends.

I benefited a great deal from my extended family. My aunt Mamie was our "Santa Claus"; my aunt Mildred, who wanted to adopt me, taught several generations of children in Brooklyn Public Schools and taught me to draw. My uncle Raymond shared with me his enjoyment of Russian and music and was thrilled that I brought another physicist into the family (my husband).

I also had a wonderful informal family, including Marie and Elliot Mottram, who went to school with my father and were like godparents to us. My mother's mother could charm us with her piano rendition of "Golliwog's Cake Walk," but it was not until later that I found many connections with our other extended family, including my dear cousin Hughie and the other McGoldricks. From them I learned several important family secrets, which helped me understand myself and my family more clearly. All the McGoldricks from the Glen now live in my soul, as do the Cahalanes from Cork, whom I have visited whenever I could since I found them in 1975.

I majored in Russian in college and went on for a master's degree in Russian studies (my theses were on Dostoevsky and Pushkin) before switching to social work (my thesis was on children's use of humor in therapy) and falling in love with family therapy. My areas of special interest have included culture, class, gender, race, marriage, the life cycle, schizophrenia, remarried families, sisters, intermarriage, family therapy with one person, and the impact of loss on families. My professional books have included: *The Changing Family Life Cycle, Ethnicity and Family Therapy, Women in Families, Living beyond Loss,* and *Genograms in Family Assessment.* For many years I taught at the Robert Wood Johnson Medical School, before becoming the director of the Family Institute of New Jersey, in Metuchen, founded in 1991.

The specific idea for this book evolved from work on the book *Genograms in Family Assessment,* in which genograms of famous families were used as case examples and proved to be very successful in conveying systems ideas in a way that was easy to understand. It seemed that those ideas should be translated into a book for everyone—and ten years later the book has reached completion!

To go home may be impossible, but it is often a driving necessity, or at least a compelling dream. . . . Home is a concept, not a place, it is a state of mind where self-definition starts; it is origins—the mix of time and place and smell and weather wherein one first realizes one is an original. . . . Home . . . remains in the mind as a place where reunion, if it were ever to occur, would happen. . . . It is about restoration of the right relations among things—and going home is where that restoration occurs, because that is where it matters most.

—A. Bartlett Giamatti, *Take Time for Paradise*

You Can Go Home Again

WHY GO HOME AGAIN?

This book is about exploring our most important connections in life, the ties to our family, those people who gave us our first concept of "home." The more we know about our families, the more we can know about ourselves, and the more freedom we have to determine how we want to live. Even the worst and most painful family experiences—alcoholism, sexual abuse, suicide—are part of our accumulated identity. In fact, understanding what led to those behaviors can help us understand the dark side of ourselves and to relate more fully to others.

There is a saying, "Those who cannot remember the past are condemned to repeat it." By learning about your family and its history and getting to know—over several generations—what made family members tick, how they related, and where they got stuck, you can consider your own role, not simply as victim or reactor to your experiences but as an active player in interactions that repeat themselves. Learning about your family heritage can free you to change your future.

The notion of "family" is deeply tied to the sense of who we are in the world. We resemble other members of our family. Their quirks and gestures are similar to ours. They have been there (or we believe they *should* have been there) at all the important occasions of our lives: births, marriages, graduations, illnesses, deaths. Moreover, we feel very deeply that if our families cannot acknowledge us, love us, and support us, no one else will. No matter how old we are, no matter how distant emotionally or physically, we seem unable to get away from the importance of family. These relationships are our most important in life, yet how often we fail to connect with family members; we cannot find the door that opens up communication. Some may say that it does not matter if we never loved parents or siblings, or they us, but it does matter. No matter how far we travel in miles or achievements, our family belongs to us and we belong to it. In fact, in sometimes eerie ways, our experiences in our first families are repeated with our marriage partners and children and, in many cases today, with our subsequent "blended" families.

Family will inevitably come back to haunt us—in our relationships with our spouses, our children, our friends and even at work. Beneath each family's particular idiosyncrasies there lie patterns that cut across cultural and time differences. And though the specifics of family structure and roles are changing dramatically, the basic ways that families relate are universal.

More than a hundred years ago Abraham Lincoln, who did so much to create the "right relations among things," refused to be in contact with his dying father, whom he had not visited in twenty years, saying: "If we could meet now, it is doubtful whether it would not be more painful than pleasant."[1] Lincoln's frank hopelessness about changing his relationship with his father, who seems to have been abusive to him in childhood, is familiar to many adults today. In spite of Lincoln's brilliance and clarity on so many issues affecting our nation as a whole, his pessimism about his father led him to miss the possibility that in that final encounter between them something different might have happened. It is little different today, when many outwardly successful people seem incapable of relating to members of their own families, unable to look into their fathers' hearts so they do not die as strangers. Pat Conroy describes the power of family connections in all their complexity in the meeting between the narrator's wounded sister and their abusive father in *The Prince of Tides:* "There was something I . . . felt as they ran to each other . . . in the deepest part of me, an untouched place that trembled with something instinctual and rooted in the provenance of the species. . . . It was not [my sister's] tears or my father's tears that caused this resonance, this fierce interior music of blood and wildness and identity. It was the beauty and fear of kinship, the ineffable ties of family, that sounded a blazing terror and an awestruck love inside of me"[2]

What is it that makes approaching our families so hard for us? Why are we obsessed with how we are doing with our marriages and our children, while we tend to ignore our parents and our brothers and sisters? Why is it that so many people seem locked into boring or painful routines with their families or to be running away from home?

Most people recognize the emotional price they pay for maintaining a "nonrelationship" with important family members. Not to be in contact with your parents is an intense experience because deep down you cannot help longing for something more gratifying. The same is true of siblings. If two sisters do not speak for forty years, each experiences a profound loss. They may resemble each other, have the same voices and mannerisms, and have a shared history which belongs only to them. Anyone who happens to suggest that they both appear at the same family event will realize the intensity of feeling behind their apparent lack of connection.

Throughout this book famous people and their families are presented, often with their genograms (a kind of family tree) to illustrate family patterns. The particular families were chosen because of the patterns they illustrated and because biographical material was available over several generations. Many of the stories used here are incomplete, mainly because I was showing only certain facets of the family to illustrate my example. In truth, remarkably few biographers recognize the relevance of family context for their subjects, and it was difficult to find enough "famous families" in which this material was developed. I regret if there are inaccuracies in my information, but as with all family histories, we are always dealing with incomplete and often inaccurate information and must do the best we can with what we have.

While each family is unique in its particular history, all families are alike in their underlying patterns. Famous families may, because they are in the spotlight, have certain responses to their notoriety, but all families have basic ways they deal with love, pain, and conflict; make sense of life and death; cross time, class, and cultural barriers. All families must find ways of dealing with loss and of integrating new members. Thus famous families are, in terms of emotional process, as "ordinary" or "unique" as any other.

Many people would prefer to downplay family history. Sigmund Freud, who has probably influenced our thinking about human behavior more than anyone else, focused almost exclusively on the importance of childhood fantasies about parents, ignoring the realities of parents' lives, the role of siblings, and the importance of the extended family. Were there secrets in the Freud family that he dared not talk about? Recent research suggests that there were, but it is interesting that so many of Freud's biographers have gone along with his blind spot about exploring the family. One would assume, for example, that biographers of Freud would be interested in his mother, who lived to be ninety-five years of age, but little attention has been paid to her role in their family. We know nothing of her relationships with her parents, her siblings, her early life. Why not? Did Freud never ask her? As might be expected, Freud's theories seem to have been shaped by his own personal family history, in which there was much he wanted to ignore or forget. He wrote about himself that he felt like the heir of "all the passions of our ancestors, when they defended their temple,"[3] and he did his best to be sure that his family history would be told the way he intended—with the stories he could not handle erased. Embarrassed, as so many are, by the mental illness and criminal acts of various family members, he destroyed many personal and family records.

Unfortunately it is not possible to destroy our history. It lives on inside us, probably the more powerful for our attempts to bury it. We and our families are likely to pay a high price in the present for trying to block out the past. Attempts to cover up family history tend to fester, influencing others born long after the original painful experiences and relationships. Freud's biographers have had to struggle to uncover the intriguing private mysteries he left behind. We too will have to search for underlying patterns that often make our family histories so full of mystery, and we may need to use indirect methods to piece the puzzle together.

Fortunately in recent years there has been more interest in the extended family. I myself was profoundly influenced by Alex Haley's search for his family roots. Indeed, the impact of Haley's *Roots* has been immense. Haley, through remarkable persistence, was able to trace his African American family back to its African connections. His powerful description of his search alerted the entire nation to the value of understanding family origins. In part through Haley's endeavor, genealogy has become one of the most popular avocations in America.

From a family systems point of view, all family members are equally important: the renegades, the black sheep, the villains, and the heroes. We can learn as much from the "sinners," the skinflints,

Presidential nominee Bill Clinton and his brother, Roger, July 1992, at the Democratic National Convention. We can learn as much from the less illustrious members of our families as from the superachievers.
Reuters/Bettmann

and the hypochondriacs as we can from the saints, the martyrs, and the Horatio Algers. Those who have had problems with alcohol or drugs must be viewed in relation to their illustrious brothers who became presidents, as in the case of George Washington, John Quincy Adams, Theodore Roosevelt, Jimmy Carter, Bill Clinton, and others. Sometimes the ne'er-do-wells make the heroes look more heroic. In our own families the failures can provide lessons about the cracks in our families' relationship systems. We need to know about everyone, because without the whole it is impossible to understand the individual parts. Those who have not had a voice because they are poor or because they are women or for whatever reason may be equally important in a family's psychological reality, even if they lack visibility within or outside the family.

Problems in our families of origin are often repeated in the families we create ourselves, however much we may wish it were not so. Even people of remarkable abilities in other areas can be blinded to new ways of perceiving their families and may lose all objectivity when they return to their childhood homes. It is especially difficult to see how our own thinking and behavior can perpetuate problems that already have a long history.

For example, Queen Victoria's relationships to her husband and children were set up in her own childhood experiences. Her adoring father died when she was only eight months old, and she was raised as an only child. She slept with her mother every night until she was eighteen, sharing everything with her. Victoria was almost completely isolated from other close relationships, since her German mother had emigrated alone to England to marry, and the British relatives felt little connection to the mother after the death of her husband.

As Victoria matured, she began to feel smothered by the demands of her ostracized mother. When at eighteen she acceded to the throne, she turned her back on her mother. The earlier intense bond was replaced almost immediately with a passionate and turbulent relationship with her first cousin and husband, Prince Albert.

Victoria was forty-two when her mother died. The death sent the queen into paroxysms of grief, largely caused by guilt and remorse over their estrangement. As she sorted her mother's papers, her emotions gave way entirely; she saw that her mother had saved every scrap of Victoria's childhood memorabilia. Realizing too late how deeply her mother had loved her, she felt intense regret. In a typical response to such pain, she now blamed outsiders, especially her governess and her mother's advisor, for the cutoff she had effected herself: "Her love for me. It is too touching: I have found little books with the accounts of my babyhood, and they show such unbounded tenderness! I am wretched to think how for a time two people estranged us. . . . To miss a Mother's friendship, not to be able to have her to confide in when a girl most needs it . . . drives me wild now."[4]

Victoria, though a woman in middle age, described herself here as a "girl," elsewhere calling herself a "poor orphan child," who felt as if she were no longer cared for after her mother's death. She seemed, as one observer noted: "determined to cherish her grief and not be consoled."[5] For weeks she took all her meals alone, considering her children "a disturbance" and leaving all the business of government to her husband, who was already seriously ill.

The death of Albert a few months afterward overwhelmed Victoria completely. Since she had made Albert the centerpiece of her life, every other relationship had become secondary. She did not attend his funeral but for years slept with his nightshirt in her arms. She made his room into a "sacred room" to be kept exactly as it had been when he was alive. Every day for the rest of her long life she had his linens changed, his clothes laid out afresh, and water prepared for his shaving. To every bed in which Victoria slept she attached a photograph of Albert as he lay dead. And for the next forty years she wore mourning dress in the style of the year he died. Years before Victoria had written, "How one loves to cling to grief,"[6] and now she certainly did. She developed an obsession with cataloging everything, so that nothing would be changed. She surrounded herself with mementos of the past and gave orders that nothing would ever be thrown away. There were to be no further changes or losses, and as long as she lived, these orders were obeyed.[7]

Victoria's reactions, however constricted and rigid they may appear to us, are understandable human reactions to distress. Losses may make us feel as if time had stopped. Families may close down, attempting to control those aspects of their world over which they still have some power, since in the one area that really matters—human relationships—they have lost a sense of control.

Queen Victoria was a great and remarkable woman, whose personality dominated the nineteenth century and whose influence has in many ways continued through the twentieth. Ruler of Great Britain for two-thirds of a century, she wrote more than any monarch in history. She was by all accounts a woman of many paradoxes—difficult, demanding, and capricious but also gentle, passionate, humble, and scrupulously honest. On the other hand, she suffered, as many of us suffer, from the deep-seated effects of family problems. In fact, the problems of her isolated childhood seemed to have limited her relationships with her own children, with whom she said she never felt at ease. She once wrote to a close friend: "I grew up quite alone, always accustomed to the society of adults and never with younger people."[8]

One can only speculate, with the benefit of our current psychological wisdom, how Victoria's children must have viewed their childhoods. We know that Victoria refused to make any accommodation to her oldest son's need to learn the experience of ruling, treating him like a child until her last breath, when he was sixty. Most people avoid confronting family issues because they can't see a way to change the relationships they find so frustrating. The frustration leads them, as it did Queen Victoria, to seek new relationships in which they attempt to make up for whatever has gone wrong earlier. And if these new relationships don't bring fulfillment, the general bitterness and pain will most likely increase. In fact, running away from home (emotionally or physically) typically traps people in the past; it does not resolve current problems with children and spouses or eliminate lingering regrets about being a virtual stranger to their original families.

Perhaps the most famous runaway in American history was Benjamin Franklin, who in 1724 at the age of seventeen left his family in Boston and moved to Philadelphia, telling no one of his whereabouts. He was bitter about family conflicts, especially with an older brother, James, to whom he had been apprenticed as a printer at age twelve. This brother had beaten and humiliated him whenever he did not toe the line. Franklin could not stand his situation or, apparently, the lack of his parents' support.

Eventually a brother-in-law tracked Franklin down in Philadelphia and persuaded him to contact his family again. He returned to Boston to do so and, more important, to ask for some money. He was unsuccessful on both counts and remained estranged. Although his parents lived on for more than twenty-five years, Franklin rarely communicated with them and appears never to have repaired his relationships with them in any but a superficial way. In all his prodigious writings he hardly mentions them. In the next generation Franklin had an illegitimate son, William, to whom he became very attached and who became his companion and collaborator for many years until that relationship, too, ended in a bitter split.

Even when you try to do the opposite of what your parents did, a repeat of the same pattern may be created. In an almost uncanny way, Franklin's son, William, also had problematic family relation-

The famous kite experiment, 1752. Benjamin Franklin and his son, William. Franklin later wrote: "Nothing has ever hurt me so much and affected me with such keen sensibilities as to find myself deserted in my old age by my only son." The Bettmann Archive

ships. Like his father, he had a son out of wedlock and tried to fashion his son into a companion. But this father and son also ended bitterly estranged. Franklin's grandson then fathered two children out of wedlock, from whom he, too, became estranged. A further multigenerational coincidence of patterns occurred: Franklin doted on his grandchild after turning away his son, and William doted on *his* grandchild to the extent of pretending she was his own child.

Whatever has happened in your family shapes you. Events that occurred long before your birth, never mentioned in your family during your lifetime, may influence you in powerful, though hidden, ways. Take, for example, a child who dies before another's birth, for whom the next child becomes a replacement. If the "replacement" child tries to leave home as a young adult, the entire family may go into crisis. Yet no one links the upheaval to the loss that occurred years earlier.

Every fact of your family's biography is part of the many-layered pattern that becomes your identity. If your aunt commits suicide, for example, it affects most immediately her husband and children (your uncle and cousins), who are left with a legacy of pain, anger, guilt, and social stigma. However, it also affects her parents (your grandparents), who will forever wonder where they went wrong. It will affect her siblings (including your parents), who will share the most intense family pain, wondering what they might have done differently to keep her from that act. But those are only the obvious people affected. Your aunt's suicide will also affect her nieces and nephews (you, your siblings, and your cousins), who will have to wonder whether your parents might ever, like their sister/sister-in-law, decide on such a course of action. And it will affect your aunt's grandchildren, who will be influenced by their parents' pain over the experience as well as by their own fears about the meaning of their grandmother's death. And your own children, who will have similar doubts about whether suicide runs in your family and how it might again come into their lives. In addition, each family member will have to respond to the reactions of the others. Inevitably the impact of such an experience will ripple throughout the whole family and for a long time to come.

To understand your family patterns, you need to develop a perspective on this shared multigenerational evolution of the family life cycle. The "family" comprises the entire emotional system of at least three and increasingly four generations, who move through life together, even though they often live in different places. As a family we share a common past and an anticipated future. The patterns of the current family life cycle are changing dramatically, so that there is less continuity than ever before between the demands on current families and the patterns of past generations. Thus it is easy to lose all sense of connection with what has come before in your family, and this can be a serious loss. We have the technology in tape, film, photography, and video for transmission of the culture from one generation to the other, yet current families often fail to share the group stories that have long been a primary wellspring of culture and personal identity.

We are living a great deal longer than human beings ever lived before, so we have much more potential for connecting with previous generations. At the same time, as a culture we have become so mobile that we suffer from disconnection. Americans move on the average once every four years. And the divorce rate is approaching 50 percent, so that the separations among family members are even more serious.

Our image of "the family" with a working father, a homemaker mother, and several children now describes less than 7 percent of the households in the United States. While women of some ethnic backgrounds have always worked outside the home, increasingly women of all backgrounds are employed regularly throughout their adult lives. We thus require very different patterns of caretaking for children and for other family members—the elderly, for instance— who were traditionally taken care of by women in the home.

From a life cycle perspective it is important to track family patterns over time, noting especially those transitions at which families tend to be more vulnerable because of the necessary readjustments in relationships. A life cycle orientation frames problems within the course that families have moved along in their past, the tasks they are presently trying to master, and the future toward which they are moving. Any family is more than the sum of its parts. The individual life cycle, from birth to death, takes place within the family life cycle. Problems are most likely to appear when there is an interruption or dislocation in the family life cycle, whether because an untimely death, a chronic illness, a divorce, or a migration forces family members to separate or because the family is unable to launch a child or tolerate the entry of a new in-law or grandchild.

It makes sense to consider yourself within the entire three- or four-generational family as it moves through time. Relationships with your parents, brothers and sisters, children, and grandparents go through stages as you move along the family life cycle, just as parent-child and couple relationships do.

Issues that are not resolved at one point in the life cycle tend to linger for resolution at the next phase, even though some players in the drama may have been replaced. We also tend to evaluate our experiences differently at different points in the life cycle, depending on what else is happening in our lives.

Usually people take on certain roles in families: hero, villain, joke-ster, victim. These characterizations reinforce basic family messages by indicating who the "good guys" and "bad guys" are. As you become aware of your family's stories and the messages embedded in them, you can evaluate whether you want to maintain these "labels" or not. It is not unusual to feel acute embarrassment, shame, or even despair about certain details of family history. People worry that negative traits are inherited or that they are doomed to repeat family mistakes. Family skeletons may remain in the closet because some people don't want to know the truth and because others don't want to tell. Avoid-ance of painful memories distorts family relationships, causing more problems than the original behavior itself. When families keep secrets, their relationships become dishonest and insecure.

At times the coincidence of events in families, even over several generations, may seem mystical. How does it happen that patterns repeat without the participants' knowledge of the earlier experience? In one family a thirteen-year-old daughter ran away from home and was killed while hitchhiking. The parents kept her ashes on the man-tel but never spoke of the event. They moved to a different city and conceived another daughter, who also ran away when she was thir-teen. Fortunately the parents were able to find this daughter and at that point opened up the discussion of family relationships for the first time. The secret of the dead sister was revealed, and this earlier loss was finally dealt with by the parents. It turned out that the mother had had a twin sister who had coincidentally died at age thir-teen, a loss she had found too painful to speak about, even to her husband. While speculation about the precise method by which fami-lies transmit such secrets might be complex, the point is that much can be learned from the experience of previous generations. If you really think about how powerfully your family has influenced your life, it is easy to see that the more you can learn about them, the more perspective you will gain on the present.

Failing to connect with your family leaves you alone in important ways that lovers, children, friends, and work cannot replace. If you are estranged from your family, there remains deep within you a bur-ied part of your spirit. Your ghosts can haunt you: voices in your head, sounding out with disapproval, threats of further abandonment, and loss of your self. These ghosts can stand between you and all that you cherish in life, or they can taint an otherwise productive and satisfying life with sadness. By remaining unaware of family ghosts, a family can be locked forever into these formative experiences, unable to move beyond them.

Our culture tends to focus on the individual or at most on couples and children, downplaying the importance of extended families, though their role is enormous in shaping our lives; the idea of "moving on" whenever problems arise has been a time-honored concept with us. If you don't get along with your parents or if they don't like your choice of mate or way of life, just move to California and see the family once or twice a year. After all, anyone can get through family visits if they are infrequent. This book's aim is to show another way, to help you understand that at the deepest level we are a part of all that we have been and a part of all that our families have been.

Becoming a "researcher" on your family is the best way to start changing your experience of it as frustrating, boring, tense, or painful. This book will help you undertake a project—a lifelong project—to understand your family in a new way. This involves learning or relearning the family stories, so that you can judge the so-called villains and victims for yourself. You'll start by examining the basic facts about your family: the details of births, deaths, relationships, moves, weddings, lawsuits, and wills—the nitty-gritty of life. The charged emotional experiences of your family's history are hidden in these events. By collecting the material that forms your family tree and understanding the concept of what family therapists call a genogram, you can survey several generations of your family. As you consider further details about relationships and events, a chronology develops. Mapping your family in this way can be the start of a fascinating and profoundly rewarding study.

YOUR FAMILY TREE

The Past as Prologue

We ourselves are the embodied continuance
Of those who did not live into our time.
And others will be and are our immortality on earth.
—Jorge Luis Borges

C arl Van Doren once said of Benjamin Franklin that he was less a single personality than a committee, "a harmonious human multitude."[1] Probably all of us are less single personalities than committees. We play different roles in different relationships, and we are also perceived differently by others, depending on the context of their relationships to us. The project of revising the part you play in your family begins with an exploration of the time-honored opinions you have held about the "good guys" and the "bad guys" in your family. Each person in a family typically views his or her perspective as the correct, just, and objective one, yet as we know, every story is like *Rashomon*, made up of as many points of view as there are participants.

The comments of Benjamin Franklin's supporters and critics in their various biographies provide intriguing examples. The biographer Catherine Drinker Bowen concluded that Franklin was the best-integrated man she had ever studied: "I cannot bear to have done with this admirable, beguiling character, diversified brilliance balanced by talent for happiness, directed by his will to self improvement and tempered at all times by the discipline of his passions."[2] D. H. Lawrence held the opposite opinion: "The soul of man is a dark vast forest, with wild life in it. Think of Benjamin fencing it off! . . . He made himself a list of virtues, which he trotted inside like a grey nag in a paddock. . . . Middle sized, sturdy, snuff-colored Doctor Franklin . . . I do not like him. . . . I just utter a long loud curse against Benjamin and the American corral. . . . He tries to take away my wholeness and my dark forest, my freedom."[3] Mark Twain joked about the great man's accomplishments: "[Franklin,] full of animosity toward boys, [had] a malevolence which is without parallel in history, he would work all day and then sit up nights and let on to be studying algebra by the light of a smoldering fire, so that all other boys might have to do that also or else have Benjamin Franklin thrown up to them. Not satisfied with these proceedings, he had a fashion of living wholly on bread and water, and studying astronomy at mealtime—a thing which has brought affliction to millions of boys since, whose fathers had read Franklin's pernicious biography."[4] Herman Melville saw Franklin as "everything but a poet, full of platitudes, obtrusive advice and mock friendliness, possessed of a bookkeeper's mind."[5] And William Cobbett called him "a crafty and lecherous old hypocrite . . . whose very statue seems to gloat on the wenches as they walk the State House yard."[6]

Although we have no written comments from Franklin's own relatives, we can assume that their perspectives on him and one another would be as diverse as those of the biographers and commentators presented here. Where we stand in the family has everything to do with our perspective. Each family member has a different relationship with parents, siblings, spouses, children, grandparents, uncles, and so on. Each individual relationship flavors that person's opinions and interpretation of the actions and choices of everyone else. Our behavior in any family situation depends on the relationship we have with the others involved. Our view of our family depends on our position in it.

While the contradictory impression one gets of Benjamin Franklin is related to the particular position and belief of each observer, each view also reflects Franklin in different relationships. His multifaceted personality seems rooted in the special position he had in his family. Early on his father, Josiah, proclaimed Ben to be the most special of all his children. He vowed that this, his tenth son, would be the "tithe of his loins"—his offering to God in return for all the blessings the family had received since coming to America. He would see to it that

Benjamin studied at Harvard and became a minister. Yet later he reneged on this promise, not even allowing him a minimum education, although Ben's gifts as a scholar were evident from the start. Josiah withheld so much of what he had promised to give that we are forced to suspect a deep-rooted ambivalence in his attitude toward this son.

So the question is why. Who was Benjamin Franklin to his family? Whose shoes was he supposed to fill? Was his life course a reflection of roles and patterns laid out by the generations that preceded him?

THE GENOGRAM

To examine these questions requires us to look at Ben Franklin's life from various perspectives. Since the patterns of family history are enormously complex, family therapists have developed a simple tool—the kind of annotated family tree called a genogram—as an aid in learning about families. It is the unusual family that has fewer than fifty family members. A genogram, by helping us keep track of the basic facts of an entire family's history, is important not only for reminding us about what we know, but for alerting us to what we don't know. The main symbols employed in a genogram appear on the following pages (Reading a Genogram).

The genogram maps out the basic biological and legal structure of the family: who was married to whom, the names of their children, and so on. Just as important, it can show key facts about individuals and the relationships of family members. For example, in the most sophisticated genogram one can note the highest school grade completed, a serious childhood illness, or an overly close or distant relationship. The facts symbolized on the genogram offer clues to the family's secrets and mythology since families tend to obscure what is painful or embarrassing in their history.

A genogram consists of three types of family information: (1) the basic facts, such as who is in the family, the dates of their births, marriages, moves, illnesses, deaths; (2) information regarding the primary characteristics and level of functioning of different family members, such as education, occupation, psychological and physical health, outstanding attributes, talents, successes and failures; and (3) relationship patterns in the family—closeness, conflict, or cutoff. Once the primary family information is indicated on the genogram, it

Reading a Genogram

Males are drawn as squares, females as circles:

male = ☐   female = ○

Dates of birth and death are written above the person's
symbol. Age is shown within the square or circle.
Death is indicated by an X through the symbol.
Approximate dates are shown with a ? or a ~ (~1898 or ? 1989).

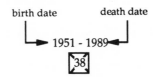

Couples are shown
by a line connecting
their symbols as
follows, with the
relevant dates
written on the line:

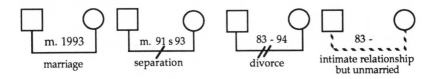

Children are shown left
to right, oldest to youngest:

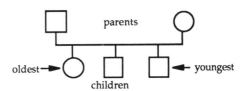

Here is an example of some of the things you can show:

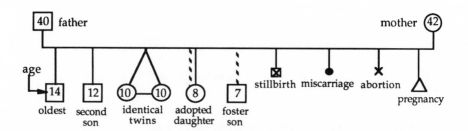

In addition to lines showing kinship, a second set of lines can show emotional relationships between people:

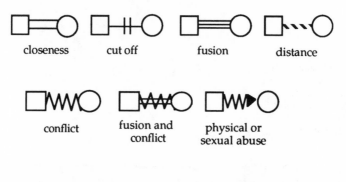

On an actual genogram the relationship lines might look like this:

A serious mental or physical problem is shown by filling in left side of square or circle:

Drug or alcohol problems are shown by filling in the bottom half of the square or circle:

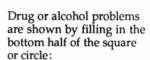

is possible to examine the "map" from the multiple perspectives of all family members. One genogram might emphasize the relationship patterns in a family, another might highlight the artistic patterns, another the patterns of illness, and so forth. A genogram is generally drawn from the point of view of a key person or the nuclear family, going back in time at least two generations and forward to the children and grandchildren of the key person or people. Other genograms may be drawn to show in detail other branches of the family or other aspects of their functioning and relationship.

Many predictable patterns of family conflict and alliance can be mapped on a genogram. Studying these patterns helps you see the automatic responses people often have to family events even when they think they are being objective. For instance, repeated gossip between a mother and her daughters about the "superficial, materialistic, and selfish" daughter-in-law may seem an objective response to the latter's clearly observed personality traits. Only when you realize that the "scapegoating" of the daughter-in-law has been a theme in your family for three generations can you step back and rethink the relationships. Perhaps your reaction is based more on the family view of your brother as the "family hero"; no woman he chooses will be good enough, especially if you think she is stealing him away. Furthermore, your brother "the hero" may be the counterpart to another brother who is "the loser"—one playing out the family dreams and aspirations, the other the family fears. So often when family members become polarized around an issue, it is not the issue itself but the emotional alliances in the family that determine who takes which side.

THE INDIVIDUAL AND THE FAMILY

As we look at Benjamin Franklin's genogram *(Genogram 2.1)*, it is necessary to consider three specific aspects beyond his individual characteristics: (1) his sibling position; (2) his name in relation to others in the family; and (3) the timing of his birth in the family history.

With this in mind, we can begin to make some sense of his special position in his family. Franklin was "the youngest son of a youngest son for five generations back." He knew that fact, but apparently not its family implications; undoubtedly his father identified with him in a special way. We all tend to identify with a child who is in our sibling

The Franklin Family
Genogram 2.1

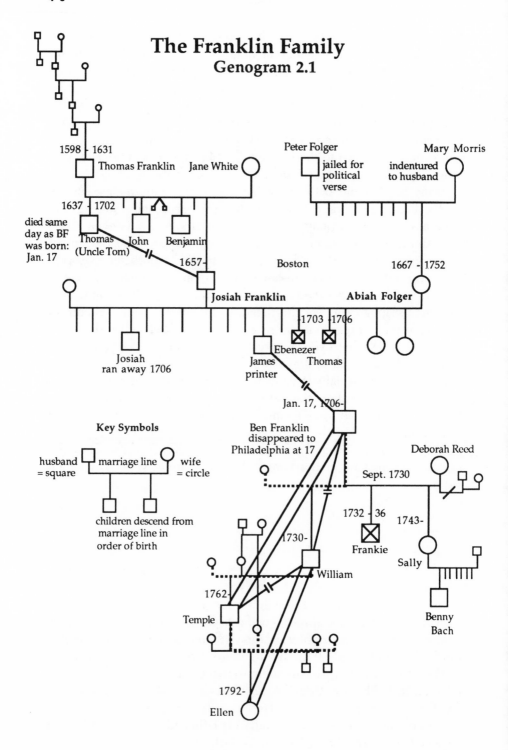

1598 - 1631
Thomas Franklin   Jane White

Peter Folger   jailed for political verse   indentured to husband   Mary Morris

1637 - 1702
died same day as BF was born: Jan. 17
Thomas (Uncle Tom)   John   Benjamin

1657-
Boston

Josiah Franklin   Abiah Folger   1667 - 1752

1703 - 1706

Josiah ran away 1706

James printer   Ebenezer   Thomas

Key Symbols

Jan. 17, 1706-

Ben Franklin disappeared to Philadelphia at 17

Deborah Reed

husband = square   marriage line   wife = circle

Sept. 1730

children descend from marriage line in order of birth

1730-

1732 - 36
Frankie

1743-
Sally

William

1762-

Temple

Benny Bach

1792-

Ellen

position, just as we identify with the child who most resembles us physically. If this pattern is repeated for many generations, there is a special legacy—an even greater intensity about our wish for this child to fit our image of him or her. Josiah's decision that Benjamin would be "the tithe of his loins" seems clearer now.

Examining the timing of his birth, we see that Franklin was also a "replacement child" for no fewer than three other sons who were lost around the time of his birth. The first, Ebenezer, had drowned unattended in the bath at age two. The next son, Thomas, named for the paternal grandfather, died a few months after Benjamin was born. During the same period Ben's older brother Josiah, the father's namesake, ran away to sea at age twenty-one—to return only once briefly nine years later before disappearing forever. Very likely the Franklins blamed themselves for these losses, especially for the accidental death of Ebenezer. They probably hoped that their last son, Benjamin, would accomplish enough for four sons (as he did!). Yet they may also have feared becoming too attached because of their previous losses.

The fact that Franklin's birth was near in time to the death of two baby brothers would have added to his special place in the family. A child's death has a tremendous effect on the entire family, often for generations afterward. Families frequently misremember miscarriages, stillbirths, and childhood deaths because of the trauma involved. Children born later may not even be told about the dead child.

We also know from Franklin's autobiography that he dreamed of following his lost brother, Josiah, Jr., to sea. Did the family convey to him an expectation that he should replace this brother? Had there been conflicts with him that led to his leaving the family? Were Josiah's conflicts with his parents part of the legacy that Ben inherited once the brother was gone? We cannot be sure, but we know that Franklin remembered all his life the last time the family was together during his brother Josiah's brief return. Josiah Jr.'s loss apparently made a deep impression on all of them.

Further exploration of the timing of Franklin's birth shows that he was born four years to the day after the death of his father's oldest brother, Tom. Anniversary dates are generally important in families, at times creating almost mystical connections between events or people. In Franklin's autobiography, written to his son, he mentions the resemblance between his uncle Tom and himself: "[Tom] died in 1702, on the 6th of January (old calendar), four years to the day before

I was born. The recital which some elderly persons made to us of his character, I remember, struck you as something extraordinary, from its similarity to what you knew of me. 'Had he died,' said you, 'four years later, on the same day, one might have supposed a transmigration.' "

This Uncle Tom—whose death without heir ended five generations of Franklins in their home community of Ecton, England—was a very learned man, an ingenious inventor, trained as a smith, but qualified also as a lawyer. He became an important man in his community and "the chief mover of all public-spirited enterprises" for his county. Indeed, this does sound remarkably like Benjamin, founder of one of the first newspapers in America, the first public library, the first volunteer fire company, the first hospital, the postal service, and one of the first universities (University of Pennsylvania). What is more, he was president of the Pennsylvania Society for the Abolition of Slavery, ambassador to Britain and France, and, of course, a major force in the fashioning of our Declaration of Independence and Constitution.

With further investigation we discover that Franklin's identification with his uncle Tom probably elicited mixed feelings in his father. Just as there was a bitter split in Ben Franklin's generation involving himself, his brother, and his parents, there had been a bitter split over religious differences in his father's generation. Ben's father, his brothers, John and Benjamin (Franklin's godfather and namesake), and their father became estranged from this oldest brother, Tom (Franklin's uncle), who kept the family homestead while they were forced to move away. The family was never united again.

Dates may have other idiosyncratic meaning for a family and are worth inquiry. For example, in the Franklin family the fact that Franklin's birth took place on a Sunday created a problem. According to the beliefs of the times, this implied that the parents had had sex on Sunday and were, therefore, sinners, while Franklin was a child of the devil—not a small consideration for Franklin's staunchly religious father, who was "the keeper of the morals" of their church community! The family dealt with this "sin" by maintaining strict secrecy about the exact date of his birth. A birth that takes place on Friday the thirteenth or on the same day as an important family member leaves, dies, or has some other significant experience may also gain special meaning for the family.

Yet another possibly controversial decision arising at the birth of a child is the choice of a name. Shakespeare asked, "What's in a name?"

From a family systems perspective, the answer is: A lot! Names in a family can tell you a great deal about the role that different children were meant to play, whom they were to be like. Some cultures have prescribed rules for naming. In Greek culture children are named for particular grandparents, depending on their birth order. In the Jewish tradition children are generally named for the dead, not the living. When families do not follow the typical patterns of their culture, one needs to ask why. John Quincy Adams, for example, changed a four-generational family pattern of naming the oldest son John by naming his oldest son for George Washington, who was not a favorite of Quincy Adams's father, John. Thus he apparently compounded in his son's name family conflicts about the expected or desired role of the eldest son.

In the Freud family Sigmund was named for his paternal grandfather, a rabbi who died shortly before his birth, and he grew up to believe that there was much in a name—"perhaps even a piece of the soul." He, the "golden Sigi," as he was called by his mother, was given the honor of naming his younger brother; he chose Alexander, after his hero, Alexander the Great. And in the next generation he alone named all six of his children, including his four daughters, for his male heroes, teachers, or friends or for their female relatives. In other words, Freud's power to name the names in his family continued in his adult life, reflecting how his position as his mother's golden son lasted through his life. We do not know why his younger brother Julius, who died in infancy was named for an uncle who was still alive (though probably dying at the time) since this was against the Jewish custom of the era. Perhaps it reflected an emotional process in the family that was stronger than the cultural rule.

The name chosen for a child may tell a lot about a family's "program" or dreams for a child. In Franklin's case he himself thought it significant that he was named for his father's favorite brother, Benjamin, who was also Franklin's godfather. This uncle, like so many others in the Franklin family, was an ingenious man, who lived with Franklin's family for several years while Ben was growing up. But what did the connection between these two Benjamins mean to the family? And what did it mean that this second father figure, who had lost his wife and nine of his ten children, moved into their home? Apparently a very great deal, as we shall see. Josiah soon became locked in conflict with this brother, Benjamin, over Ben's future and not only retracted his promises about Ben's education but repeatedly stood in the way of his son's advancement.

THINKING ABOUT FAMILY RELATIONSHIPS

When you see a pattern in which insiders move out (such as Ben's brother Josiah running away to sea or Ben disappearing at seventeen) or outsiders moving into the family (Uncle Ben coming to live with the family), a natural inquiry arises about conflicts and alliances that may have divided the family's loyalties. With the Franklins there is a repeated pattern of intense closeness, conflict, distance, and cutoff with attempts at closeness seeming to complement the cutoffs, all this leading to further predictable cutoffs. For example, it is predictable that as the estrangement developed between Ben and his son William, Ben reached for closeness with William's son, Temple; tension then developed between Temple and his father, William. This was repeated in the relationship between William, his son, Temple, and his granddaughter Ellen *(Figure 2.1)*.

The central triangle in the Franklin family while Ben was growing up involved Ben, his father, Josiah, and his uncle Benjamin, who had come from England to live with the family when young Ben was 6 *(Genogram 2.2)*. This uncle had lost all his family but one child. He stayed with the Franklin family for the next four years, during which time he and Josiah began a long tug-of-war for the boy's allegiance.

The two brothers had not seen each other for thirty years. They were opposites in personality. Josiah was pragmatic, business-

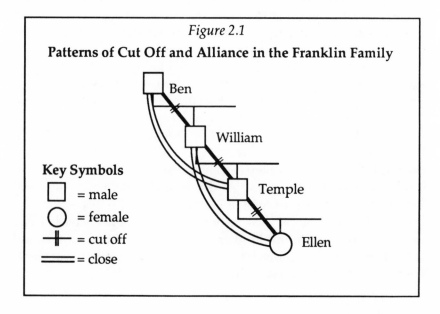

Figure 2.1

Patterns of Cut Off and Alliance in the Franklin Family

Ben

William

Temple

Ellen

Key Symbols

☐ = male

○ = female

╫ = cut off

═ = close

Triangle in Young Ben Franklin's Family
Genogram 2.2

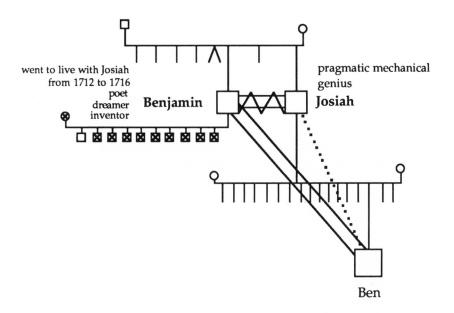

went to live with Josiah
from 1712 to 1716
poet
dreamer
inventor

Benjamin

pragmatic mechanical
genius

Josiah

Ben

minded, a mechanical genius, but a fanatical Puritan. Uncle Benjamin was a bit fantastic in personality, a freethinker, a great talker, a dreamer, and a poet, given to endless philosophizing, reading, and perpetual rhyming. He was also an inventor, but always hard up for money, while he concentrated on his poetry. As Uncle Benjamin began to inspire his young nephew in the direction of humorous, iconoclastic writing, Josiah became more and more hostile toward both of them. As Franklin later wrote, "Our father . . . used to say nothing was more common than for those who loved one another at a distance to find many causes of dislike when they came together. I saw proof of it in the disgusts between him and his brother Benjamin."[7]

The more Uncle Benjamin agreed that young Ben should get the best education possible and go into the ministry, the less enthusiasm Josiah had for his old promise, and finally, although Franklin was a brilliant student, Josiah withdrew him from school and humiliated him by insisting he take a trade. Yet like uncle, like nephew: The more his father resisted his education, the more Ben himself loved learning. Although his father terminated Ben's formal schooling by the time he was eight, he eventually received honorary degrees not only from Harvard but also from Yale, St. Andrews, and Oxford. Perhaps in the end Josiah feared being outstripped by this replica of his own brother more than he wished his favorite son to be "the tithe of his loins."

QUESTIONS AND STORIES: KEYS TO UNDERSTANDING

To get to know your family in a different way, you need to become an expert at asking questions. It's strange how often we do not ask the right questions. Some questions occur to us, but we don't ask them because we sense they would make others upset; we may be wrong in these perceptions, but we may be right, too. Other questions never even come to mind because unspoken family rules forbid our broaching them. Family wisdom may have it that "Uncle Charlie isn't worth talking to because he's a pompous fool who never did a good day's work in his life" or that "Cousin Betty is an inveterate liar and doesn't remember anything about the family anyway." In all families there are rules, assumptions, and stories that members are expected to take at face value. It often takes close scrutiny to divest ourselves of the assumptions we make about close relationships. You may have been told that Aunt Charlotte "can't handle stress, so don't discuss anything important with her." She is never asked to help out when problems arise, and no one ever thinks of asking her opinion. You may need to wonder *who* decided Charlotte couldn't handle stress and on what basis. It would be best to question each assumption you have about your family, to ask yourself who came to each conclusion and how.

Questions about the facts of birth and death in a family—who, when, where, how?—may uncover emotionally charged events such as suicide, alcoholism, pregnancies outside marriage, stillbirths, miscarriages, abortions. You may have forgotten that your grandfather had a twin whose death at age ten left a legacy that is still affecting the family two generations later. You may not have noted that your parents' separation occurred the same year as Grandma's heart attack. And the family may not mention, unless you dig for the facts, that Grandma was actually married once before. The excuse you heard was that it didn't really count because it "never took"; her first husband was a scoundrel and left her after two months.

Once you are aware what questions you might want to ask your own family, you need to figure out how and when to approach different family members for possible answers. This is a complex issue to be discussed in greater depth later. The important thing is to develop a questioning attitude and a healthy skepticism, never to be too sure that anyone's point of view is the "truth." With the concept of a genogram as guideline, you can begin to explore how each family member would have experienced the relationships and events of your family's history.

You become like Lieutenant Columbo, looking to make connections: between important dates, between the kinds of relationship patterns your grandparents displayed and those played out by your parents, between the way you are and the way they were at your age. There may be intense anxiety around weddings, stemming from the fact that your grandfather died three days before your mother's wedding. Your father may have feared ending up a failure like his father. Or your mother and her sisters may be anxious that they will be deserted as their grandmother was with five small children. Unacknowledged, such information may wreak havoc by generating unexplained anxiety throughout the family. Known, such information can create understanding and strengthen bonds.

From this perspective, information is power; you try to learn whatever you can wherever you can because you never know when a certain piece of information will help you make a connection. Any detail may turn out to be significant. If you want to understand your mother as more than the "Dragon Lady," whose domineering intrusiveness overwhelms you even at the age of forty, you will need to get a picture of her as a daughter, a niece, a sister, a friend, a coworker, a granddaughter, a lover, and a cousin. Furthermore, learning more about *her* mother in each of those roles will give you clues to *your* mother. For this reason it is worth asking each relative for the facts as well as the myths and stories heard in childhood. It is also useful to ask family members about the reactions of others to a given family experience. For example, "Mom, how did your father react when his father stopped talking to him? How did Uncle Al take it? And what about Aunt Martha? Who was actually there when the fight occurred? What did they do after that about holidays and family get-togethers?"

Respect for the family's resistance to change is crucial to this project. As the researcher you must have respect for your family's reluctance to expose secrets or change the way they relate, however harmful these ways may have been. Families often believe, as the saying goes, "The devil you know is better than the devil you don't know." There is a great security in what is familiar. Change is stressful because of the uncertainty it brings. The fear is "If I mention my father's suicide, things might get worse." It is best to proceed gently and respectfully in opening things up.

An important assumption behind all family questioning is that human beings are always doing the best they can, given the limitations of their particular perspectives. Typically we think of ourselves as the reactors in the family drama, while we see our parents as the actors who determined our fate. You need to shift this perspective to realize that we are all actors and reactors. The father who abused his child was probably himself abused in his childhood; statistics tell us that abuse tends to beget abuse. The past does not justify current behavior, of course; it only provides insight into its curse. This is a complex concept and a bit paradoxical. At the same time that you take responsibility for your own behavior, you need to develop empathy for the "programmed" behavior of others. Understanding how you have been "programmed" allows you the chance to eliminate behaviors of your own that adversely affect your relationships. You may have decided, for example, that your father never "gives" anything. It may take some thinking to realize that in your frustration you have stopped asking or expecting him to "give" and that this behavior perpetuates his distance.

Before asking questions, be sure of your intentions. If the goal is self-justification or to prove others in the family wrong, they will sense it immediately. Questions like "If your father was so abusive, how come you didn't tell someone or get out of there?" will probably elicit a defensive response. If you imply that your parents should have "known" your feelings and owe you their approval, you are likely to get a defensive and angry reaction. But if you express a genuine and noncombative interest in what happened, family members might actually welcome the opportunity to tell you their versions of a story.

The ability to maintain your sense of yourself without becoming defensive, regardless of how others perceive you, is essential to this process. It requires coming to the point where you are the sole judge of your own worth and do not depend on the approval of others. This means that you do not "need" others to feel "worthwhile" *and* can judge the rightness of your own values and behavior for yourself, whatever misperceptions of you might exist.

At the same time, don't begin asking questions unless you are prepared to handle the answers. That is, if you ask your mother about her overall experience with you as a child, be ready to hear how frustrating she may have found you without launching into a tirade about all *her* motherly inadequacies. Becoming defensive or attacking in reaction to a family member's response to your questions will never produce anything fruitful. The goal is to assess whatever information you receive for yourself on the basis of your own considered belief about the issue. (Remember that all reactions, however hostile or rejecting, are also "information.") You must be prepared to hear negative feelings and observations: that your beloved father was perceived by his brothers as a patsy or as a Shylock in business or that the family views you as arrogant, spoiled, selfish, or succeeding by luck. You will then need to consider whether there is any truth in what has been said and, if not, how they came to this perception. How has this perception affected the behavior of each family member?

The stories people tell about themselves and their family histories must be listened to carefully—both for what they tell and for what they omit. Again, we have a remarkable source in Benjamin Franklin's autobiography. The first part of the autobiography was written in 1771 and addressed, "Dear Son," to William, who was then governor of New Jersey. The moral imperative of his cautionary tale is clear: to inspire the son with the story of the father's frugal, industrious rise from poverty and obscurity to affluence and reputation: "Having emerged from the poverty and obscurity in which I was born and bred, to a state of affluence and some degree of reputation in the world, and having gone so far through life with a considerable share of felicity, the conducing means I made use of . . . may . . . therefore be fit to be imitated."[8] Franklin admits many of his youthful follies or "errata," as he refers to them, directly, including mistreating his future wife by leaving her, failing to write after promising to marry her, and attempting to seduce his best friend's girl friend. On the other hand, he passes over the biggest secret in his personal history: the secret of who William's mother was and exactly when he was born, leaving the impression that one of the rules in the Franklin family was not to mention that subject.

Franklin's wife, Deborah, apparently raised William from infancy. However, she and Franklin were never formally married in a church, and they maintained some secrecy about their marriage, though its date, September 30, 1730, is given in the autobiography. Their silence about their marriage resulted, it appears, from Deborah's having been married already to a man who had disappeared but who might still be alive. However, this does not explain the secrecy about

William's birth, which was a matter of concern to him in adult life, when rumors that he was illegitimate began to influence him politically. Because there was such an obvious need for clarification, Benjamin's silence on the matter is all the more surprising.

The family tradition of secrecy continued in the next generation with initial secrecy about William's marriage, which Franklin seems to have made a point of missing, as well as about the birth and parentage of William's son, Temple. The story was apparently put out that Temple was the son of a "poor relation." He was often sent greetings by family and friends in their correspondence, but Deborah never once mentioned him in her letters. Perhaps this reflected her resentment of the second generation's fathering a child out of wedlock, but more likely she was never informed about Temple, since Franklin makes not the slightest allusion to him in any of his letters to her, though he continuously gossips about all other members of the family. Years later a family friend referred with amusement to the game the whole family played in pretending they had not guessed the nature of Temple's relationship to the family.[9]

Again in the fourth generation there was secrecy regarding Temple's illegitimate children, and after the cutoff between William and Temple, William even tried to make people believe that Temple's daughter Ellen was his own child.

The repetition of illegitimacy for three generations in the Franklin family seems almost uncanny. What was the connection between the generations in repeating this so-called secret? A pattern of secrecy in a family tends to breed more secrecy and distortion. It teaches family members that the truth cannot be handled and that some experiences can never be integrated.

Several of Franklin's biographers commented on the conspicuous omissions in Franklin's writing. Esmond Wright said: "Here is a man who talks to us apparently so frankly about himself while increasingly obscuring himself behind the public images, that at intervals we do not know what is fact and what is fiction."[10] Claude-Anne Lopez and Eugenia Herbert, who wrote about the "private" Franklin, comment: "His present family is practically nonexistent in the Autobiography: his daughter not mentioned a single time, his son alluded to quite casually, his wife brought into the picture mainly in the days when they were not yet married—and then not as a personality but as the illustration of a wrong set to right. The focus is exclusively on himself, or rather on a portion of himself. No soul-searching here." If the son, William, knew about the negative relationship Franklin had with his own father, he may have resented his father's presentation of the family stories in such a positive light, especially when Franklin was pressuring him to conform to his political views.

Franklin's autobiography reflects his complex ambivalence toward his own father, which he never really worked out. He says his father, who had a very strong constitution, was ingenious: "Could draw prettily and was skilled a little in music. . . . But his great excellence lay in a sound judgment in prudential matters both in private and public affairs." However, in each reference to his father that follows we cannot help seeing the implied criticism behind the compliment. He says, for example, that his father focused so much on having educational conversation at mealtime that he taught him to have a perfect inattention to food and a total indifference to what meals were placed before him. Franklin says this lesson served him well in traveling because he was never bothered by the lack of suitable food. In fact, we know that Franklin was, if anything, an epicure who cared a great deal about what he ate. Clearly he thought there was something missing in his father's rigorous inattention to good dining, which makes his remark seem ironic.

Franklin goes on to describe how his father withdrew him from school because he had decided that "he could not well afford" college education and that those who were educated ended up making only a "mean living." It seems unlikely that Franklin himself accepted these excuses since he already showed such intellectual gifts. Scholarships were available at the time, and ministers, one of whom he was to have become, certainly did make fair livings. We can also sense the covert resentment toward his father's squashing his poetic writing. He says that at about age thirteen he began writing poetry, some of which sold "wonderfully." He adds: "But my father discouraged me, by ridiculing my performances and telling me verse-makers were generally beggars; so I escaped being a poet, most probably a very bad one." Again, his tone about his father's criticism seems ironic. As we know, he went on to prove his father wrong, and we have all been absorbing Poor Richard's witticisms for more than two hundred years.

When Franklin wrote his autobiography, he was already at the point of disapproving of William's direction in life, although they were still close. Franklin was trying to tell William to listen to him, emphasizing the value of accepting the wisdom of the father, which he himself had rarely done. Over and over again in Franklin's version of his family story he suggests that while he often did not agree with his father, his father tended to be right. Yet Franklin related the story of his adult life as if the family he came from had not mattered at all. He seems to be reflecting his disappointment in his own family experience and may have been passing along an ambivalent message about the value of family life that played itself out in three generations of parent-child cutoffs.

The facts we know about Benjamin Franklin and the details on his genogram lead to interesting inquiries about him and his family: Why did he believe he could not survive within the confines of his family? Did he feel forced to escape the pressure of their dreams, ambitions, and fears about his performance? Were he and his older brother James replaying a multigenerational family drama in which the younger brother excels, is forced into submission, and is finally exiled?

For a more complete understanding of Franklin and his family, it would be essential to ask questions about other members of the family. Whom were the other brothers named for? Did anyone else's birth coincide with family losses or important family anniversaries? Were there losses in the parental families that constricted the parents' functioning and pressured them into molding an infant into the role of replacement child?

To understand the family that Franklin himself created, we would have to ask many other questions. In choosing to marry a simple woman with little education, was Franklin repeating the experience not only of his parents but also of his maternal grandparents? His maternal grandfather was a poet, an author, and a remarkable public figure who married his servant. In later years Franklin himself lived more closely with the families of others than with his own. Was this a departure from the Franklin traditional pattern, or was there a history of developing such intense connections outside the family?

If we look at Franklin from a family systems perspective, his personal accomplishments and idiosyncrasies take on a different meaning. To begin with, he was gifted genetically with a remarkable intellect, physical constitution, and temperament. In addition to this inheritance, he seems to have taken on many of the best qualities of members of his family: He was a mechanical genius like his father, a writer and an iconoclast, a poet, a philosopher, an inventor, a statesman, a diplomat, a humorist, and a freethinker like his uncles and grandfathers. Perhaps these personal characteristics derived from a special identification with so many family members: his father by birth order, his uncle Tom by date of birth, his paternal grandfather because this grandfather's namesake (Benjamin's brother Thomas) died just after Franklin's birth, his uncle Benjamin by baptism, by name, and by this uncle's move into the Franklin home after the loss of his own family.

All too often people are not aware of the traits—whether positive or negative—they have absorbed from their families. You may feel contempt for your family's pretentiousness and be unaware that you have absorbed some of the same mannerisms. Awareness of the trait could easily lead to its amelioration. Similarly, a positive awareness of connectedness to family can give you a sense of belonging and a feeling of continuity that will strengthen your own sense of identity.

Gender is, of course, another major factor in establishing identity. You need to ask what the rules have been for men and women in your family and to what extent they conform to the society of the time. Cultural groups also differ in the specific rules defining gender arrangements. For example, Irish women have a long tradition of independence and even of being warriors and rulers that may be very different from some Asian cultures where women traditionally had no status apart from marriage and childbearing.

The gender role constrictions on both men and women in families have played a powerful role over the centuries. This will be a fascinating area to explore. One of the most interesting things to look at is how members of your family responded to these constrictions. Did they sometimes break out of the stringent gender roles of their times? If so, how was this received by others inside and outside the family. I like to encourage people to explore especially those family members who did not completely conform to the gender norms of the society: the women who were assertive and daring, who did things on their own and were not cowed, and the men who were sweet and nurturing, who did not play "the good provider" role for whatever reason. You will learn a lot about yourself and your family by exploring this dimension.

In some ways, of course, family patterns of gender may not have changed all that much despite recent dramatic changes for women. The content of what gets said about women may change, yet overall family attitudes toward them may remain remarkably constant. Perhaps your grandmother was viewed as a saint because she cooked, cleaned, and took care of everyone, but still she was " a bit daffy." And now, perhaps in this generation, your mother is talked about as "a remarkable woman," very successful in her computer business, able to handle a hundred things at once, but "She's quite flaky, you know!" It is important to look beyond the family descriptions to the underlying patterns that repeat in spite of changed details.

In Franklin's case he had very little to say about his mother. Like so many others of our Founding Fathers who seem to have had problematic relationships with their mothers, he left almost no informa-

Maya Angelou's Family
Genogram 2.3

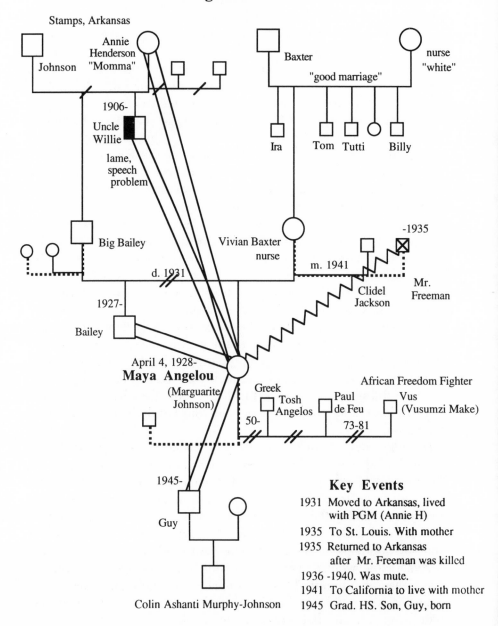

Stamps, Arkansas

Johnson | Annie Henderson "Momma"

Baxter | "good marriage" | nurse "white"

1906-
Uncle Willie
lame, speech problem

Ira | Tom | Tutti | Billy

Big Bailey | Vivian Baxter nurse | m. 1941 | -1935

d. 1931 | Clidel Jackson | Mr. Freeman

1927-
Bailey

April 4, 1928-
Maya Angelou
(Marguarite Johnson)

Greek | African Freedom Fighter

50- | Tosh Angelos | Paul de Feu | Vus (Vusumzi Make)

73-81

1945-

Guy

Key Events
1931 Moved to Arkansas, lived with PGM (Annie H)
1935 To St. Louis. With mother
1935 Returned to Arkansas after Mr. Freeman was killed
1936 -1940. Was mute.
1941 To California to live with mother
1945 Grad. HS. Son, Guy, born

Colin Ashanti Murphy-Johnson

tion about his mother, in spite of voluminous correspondence on many other subjects. Jefferson, Lincoln, and Washington as well said almost nothing about their mothers, and John Adams was not very positive about his. Perhaps some of the dedication these men had to the concept of a nation was compensation for a perception of their families as unprotective or unfulfilling.

To understand your family, you need also to go beyond society's conventional views of family as limited to your biological family of parents, siblings, and children. Most of us have had an informal family system which was also crucial in our formative development. I myself had a caretaker, who played a central role in my family life, and a grand-aunt, Mamie, my grandfather's unmarried sister, who was like Santa Claus to us and to many others for three generations of our family. There were also friends of our family who were informal godparents, aunts, uncles, and grandparents. The parents of several of my friends played an important role in my childhood, as well as provided another home base for me, just as my family provided a home base for others. Your family, of course, includes anyone who belongs to you, whether biologically linked or not, and this includes anyone who was part of your family as you grew up: caretakers, teachers, ministers, friends, neighbors—whoever played a role in your becoming who you are. These people are often unsung heroes and "sheroes" of our families. Maya Angelou (*Genogram 2.3*) has described often her uncle Willie, a lame and severely disabled man, who had a powerful influence on her education and values, teaching her the multiplication tables so well that she can still say them in the middle of the night. Angelou discovered when she went home for Uncle Willie's funeral in her tiny hometown of Stamps, Arkansas, that he had had a profound mentoring impact on many others, not only his relatives. She wrote a poem about him which is a message to us all about listening to the unsung voices, who may be "present in the songs that our children sing," who have influenced us, whose lives did not make it to the history books, or even to greatness in our families, but whose private and personal influence was tremendous nonetheless. She says, in part:

> *Willie was a man without fame*
> *Hardly anybody knew his name.*
> *Crippled and limping, always walking lame,*
> *He said, "I keep on movin'*
> *Movin' just the same."*

Solitude was the climate in his head
Emptiness was the partner in his bed,
Pain echoed in the steps of his tread,
He said, "I keep on followin'
Where the leaders led."

I may cry and I will die,
But my spirit is the soul of every spring,
Watch for me and you will see
That I'm present in the songs that children sing.[11]

JOSTLING YOUR VIEW OF YOUR FAMILY

A good way to jostle rigid views of your own family is to go through
the exercise of telling family history from each person's point of view.
If negative feelings about a certain person overwhelm you, try to
expand your perspective to include how that person was seen by his
or her favorite relative or friend. If you think of your father as an
archvillain because of the awful way he treated you, it may help to
explore his early life and think about how his parents, siblings, and
grandparents viewed him as a little boy. It may help to imagine what
it would be like to take the opposite position: to think of your rigid,
domineering mother as a positive influence, perhaps because she
taught you about self-discipline and was a hard worker.

How might your mother's older sister have viewed her when she
was three and the sister was nine? How might she have felt when she
was five and her father deserted the family? How did her best friend
feel about her in high school? How did your father feel about her
when he was courting her? It may be especially helpful to think of
how she felt about her own mother and her childhood, as a way to
put the history of the women in your family in perspective.

In severely troubled families there is a tendency for some members to be the caretakers of others, whom they may unwittingly treat
in a patronizing way. Even in less troubled families, members are
often "protective" of one another in ways that constrict their relationships. Before you say, "Oh, I can't bring up that issue, my mother's
too old and feeble, and it would kill her to try to break through her
denial now," try to be very clear as to whose denial you are worried
about. Work on the assumption that all people do the best they can.

Given the benefit of a doubt, people often respond to a sincere request to learn about the family—even if they have spent a lifetime acting crazy, rejecting, hostile, intrusive, oblivious, or in other ways inept.

Even in-laws (so often viewed as crass, materialistic, haughty, dippy, or "lower class") can be astonishing sources of information about your family. Let's face it, they have spent years observing your family in action, and by now they are probably experts. Another good source is family friends or even former family friends. They, like in-laws, might tell the stories that everyone else avoids because they are not as bound as the insiders by rules about "family secrets."

Here are a few questions that may help you get started on your family journey:

■ How do family members think about one another? What characteristics are brought up? The loudmouth? The spendthrift? The soft touch? The dead hero? The all-knowing matriarch? What are the roles and labels in your family? Does someone play Goody Two-shoes and somebody else the Bad Seed? Is one the villain and another the hero? Is one weak, boring, slow, and another brilliant, domineering, and manipulative? Could you make a list of the different ways family members are described, noting especially the opposites in role or label?

■ Who was named for whom in your family, and why? Do names reveal the roles people have played? Who chose the names? Why were they chosen? If names seem to have no rhyme or reason, could there be hidden meanings? Was someone named for a mother's lost sweetheart? If members are named for the dead, have they taken on their characteristics? What were the naming patterns in your family, and can you see ways that they reflected the structure or influenced the psychological patterns of family members?

■ Were there coincidences between the births of family members and moves or migration? Illness or death? Changes in family finances? How did migrations influence children's family experience? How did financial changes influence the lives of children? How did illnesses and deaths influence them at different ages?

■ How much did your family conform to the gender stereotypes of their culture and era? Which family members did not conform to these expected gender roles, and how were they viewed by others? What can you learn about your family's flexibility (or inflexibility) from their history of allowable gender roles?

THREE

FAMILY STORIES, MYTHS, AND SECRETS

Storytelling is fundamental to the human search for meaning . . . each of us is involved in inventing a new kind of story.
—Mary Catherine Bateson, *Composing a Life*

Remember, what you are told is really threefold: Shaped by the teller, reshaped by the listener, and concealed from them both by the deadman of the tale.
—Vladimir Nabokov, *The Real Life of Sebastian Knight*

All history, including the histories of our families, is part of us, such that when we hear any secret revealed, a secret about a grandfather or an uncle, or a secret about the battle of Dresden in 1945, our lives are made suddenly clearer to us, as the unnatural heaviness of unspoken truth is dispersed. For perhaps we are like stones—our own history and the history of the world embedded in us.
—Susan Griffin, *A Chorus of Stones*

We are born not just into our family, but into our family's stories, which both nourish and sometimes cripple us. And when we die, the stories of our lives become part of our family's web of meaning.[1] Family stories tend to be told to remind members of the family's cherished beliefs. We sing of the heroes and even the villains whose daring the family admires. Taping or writing down the stories of older family members can bring a richness to our search for perspective on family that cannot be achieved in any other way.

The passage of time shears away some details and highlights others, yielding a subjective, edited overview of memories and stories that strive for a meaningful narrative. When a disjunctive experience is introduced that doesn't jibe with our family's or our culture's dominant story, we may be left challenged and bewildered. Everything that gets said in a family falls at the intersection of the said and the unsaid. Traumatic family experiences can create myths and superstitions about the dangers of the outside world that flow down the generations, influencing descendants who have no conscious awareness of the origins of the beliefs. Nor do they understand how family stories develop around the facts to reassure, to explain, or to limit the pain of certain family experiences. Family stories and myths are worth analyzing for the signals they contain about the family's covert values and rules. How do families transmit messages that seem to prescribe behavior for generations to come? Embedded here are the narratives through which they make sense of their lives, relationships, and behavior.

One family's stories may revolve around the courage of family members against great odds, another's about their humorous comeback after humiliation. In families characterized by pessimism, stories may carry a message that "you never win." Usually people have stereotyped roles in family stories, such as the hero, the villain, the jokester, the victim, roles that, by identifying the "good guys" and "bad guys," reveal the values in your family. By becoming aware of family messages, you can decide for yourself whether or not you want to maintain these roles and beliefs.

Family myths are transmitted both explicitly and—more often—implicitly, and this increases their power to influence the next generation. Since these beliefs are generally accepted as reality, you may need to be exposed to values different from those of your family before you question or become fully aware of your family's rules. Families communicate in any number of subtle verbal and nonverbal ways. All families develop private jokes, routines, and references which are transmitted from one generation to another. My mother used to say, "Never trust a short woman," she being five feet eight, while her mother-in-law was about four feet six. Other messages, such as putting a plate under the orange juice when we wanted to impress certain guests, conveyed important class messages about where our parents thought we stood in relation to others. Other rules about never mentioning a person's color or cultural background conveyed messages about our place in the social setup. Children learn early what can and cannot be discussed.

Children may, in addition, be bound into a special role to maintain a family myth or carry out missions left incomplete by a death, or they may be constrained by parental fear of repeating a painful past drama. Whether critical family experiences lead parents to compensate by neglecting or overfocusing on a child, the legacy can become a burden for the next generation.

THE BRONTË FAMILY

The Brontë family *(Genogram 3.1)* seems to have developed the belief that leaving home was dangerous, and in the end no one could leave at all. Their belief must have developed in part through the family's early experiences of illness and death, when members did try to leave, but probably the myth itself influenced later occurrences of illness when family members left. Charlotte, the oldest to survive to adulthood, once wrote an epitaph for one of her heroines which might apply directly to her family: "The orb of our life is not to be so rounded; for you the crescent-phase must suffice."[2]

We don't have much information about the earlier generations of this extraordinary family, which produced two of the greatest novelists the world has known: Emily Brontë, the author of *Wuthering Heights*, and Charlotte Brontë, the author of *Jane Eyre*. We may suspect that there was a legacy of emotional conflicts in the family of the Brontë father, Patrick, since his father, Hugh Brontë, and grandfather, Welsh Brunty, were both apparently adopted and then mistreated in their adoptive families in a story extremely reminiscent of *Wuthering Heights*. The Brontë mother, Maria Branwell Brontë, came from a family in which four children died in infancy or childhood, including the three closest to her in age. Patrick and Maria were married in a double wedding with Maria's first cousin and Patrick's best friend and on the same day Maria's younger sister Charlotte married another cousin of theirs, Joseph Branwell, in a different town. If we take a systemic view of the "coincidence" of events, concurrent events in a family often represent more than random happenings. The fact that four members of the same family were married on the same day may suggest some fusion in the Brontë family, which often results from loss. And indeed, the family had suffered a series of pivotal losses just before. Maria's father Thomas Branwell, had died in 1808 and her mother in 1809. The family business had then been taken over by Thomas's older brother, Richard, and Richard's son, Thomas, who died tragically in December 1811; his father died the following year, 1812. This final death precipitated the breakup of the family. Richard's other son, Joseph, married Charlotte, Maria's youngest sister, and Maria married Patrick Brontë, while her cousin Jane (daughter of Richard's only sister) married Patrick's best friend.

There followed in the family of Patrick and Maria Brontë a series of tragic losses which seem to have deeply influenced the future behavior of family members, limiting their ability to leave and turning them inward on themselves and one another. Patrick came to see

The Bronte Family
Genogram 3.1

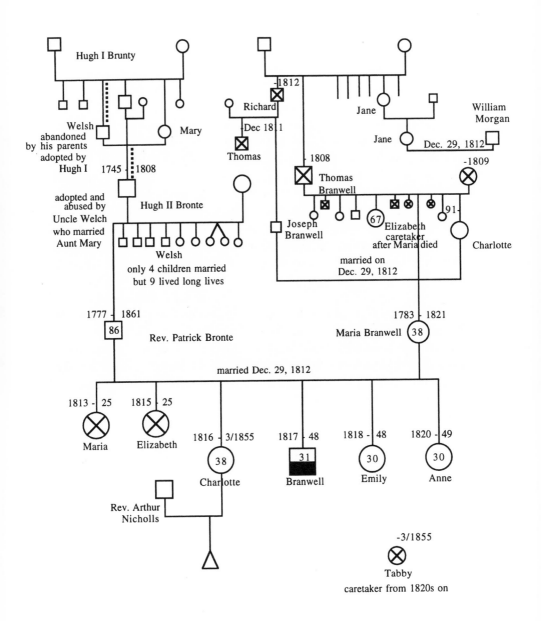

himself as "a stranger in a strange land" and seems to have conveyed
to his children this sense of alienation and need to protect themselves
from the outside world. The six children were born in short succes-
sion, and soon after the birth of the last, their mother apparently
developed a serious blood disorder which finally took her life. During
the last period of Maria's illness, all six children developed scarlet
fever, which must have intensified the family tragedy. Maria died an
excruciatingly painful death a year later. Her eldest daughter was
only nine, and the youngest not yet two. Patrick seems to have found
his children's presence a painful reminder of his wife rather than a
comfort: "Oppressive grief sometimes lay heavy on me . . . when I
missed her at every corner, and when her memory was hourly
revived by the innocent, yet distressing prattle of my children."

Patrick withdrew into himself and began dining alone, as he continued to do for the rest of his life. His daughter Charlotte later said:
"He did not like children . . . and the noise made him shut himself
up and want no companionship—nay, to be positively annoyed by it."
After Maria's death, nothing in the Brontë home was changed—no
furniture was moved, added, or eliminated—and very few people visited. Such rigidity is a common response in families that have been
beset by trauma.

The mother's unmarried sister, Elizabeth, moved in and remained
there for the rest of her life. Four years later a family caretaker,
Tabby, was added. She also stayed for the rest of her life, dying
within a few weeks of the death of the last surviving Brontë child,
Charlotte. Throughout their childhood the six children were left very
much on their own, and while the externals in their lives remained
constricted, they developed a most extraordinary inner life of imagination and fantasy.

When the eldest daughter was twelve, she and her sisters were
sent to a local boarding school for ministers' children, but unfortunately further tragedy followed this attempt to expand the family's
horizons. The two oldest sisters developed tuberculosis at the school
and died within a few months. The death of the eldest, Maria, named
for her mother, was especially tragic because the school authorities
were extremely abusive to the dying child in her last days. The other
sisters had to observe the tormenting of their favorite sister, who had
for so long been their mother's replacement. The morbidity of it all
must have been exaggerated by the fact that the cemetery where
mother and sisters lay buried surrounded the family house on two
sides, and there could be no getting away from the eerie sense of
death in those gravestones. Probably the stories about children mis-

treated in school situations and misunderstood by parent substitutes in the writings of Charlotte and Emily Brontë reflect attempts to work through their painful memories of these childhood experiences.

Such early losses must have reinforced the developing Brontë "story" or belief that life in the outside world was dangerous. The children were withdrawn from school, and from then on, when any of the remaining four children tried to leave home, they were forced to return whether because they became ill away from home or because someone at home became ill or needy. The only son, Branwell, on whom the greatest hopes were placed, was accepted at the Royal College of Art in London and left home to attend, but he never actually signed in and returned home soon afterward addicted to drugs and alcohol. Thereafter he periodically left home for jobs which he never managed to keep. The real deterioration of Branwell coincided in reciprocal fashion with his three sisters' initial publishing success, which they accomplished under male pseudonyms, telling neither their father nor their brother what they were doing. Eventually they told their father, who scarcely reacted, but they never told Branwell. As Charlotte said, "My unhappy brother . . . was not aware that . . . [we] had published a line. We could not tell him of our efforts for fear of causing him too deep a pang of remorse for his own time misspent and talents misapplied. Now he will never know. I cannot dwell longer on the subject at present—it is too painful." By the time Branwell died three years later, the sisters were renowned under their own names. Of the three surviving sisters, Charlotte was the most successful at leaving home, managing at one point to stay away at a school for two years, and she was the only one able to develop friendships outside the family. She too, however, always returned home.

As is the case with many families, there was something eccentric as well as extraordinary about the Brontës. Patrick Brontë rarely spent time with his family, though he could not tolerate their leaving him. The children, deprived of outside stimulation, created the most amazing fantasy world of shared stories, invented and written jointly, in minuscule, almost indecipherable handwriting and put together in about eight hundred tiny manuscript books, about four hundred of which survive. It is almost as if they were fusing in the private world of their imaginations; their minds roamed free in fantasy, creating historical sagas with imaginary characters as well as historical personages they had heard about. As Charlotte later wrote, they "wove a web in childhood." As an adult she feared their childhood dreams "withered the sod."

A 1825 painting of the Brontë sisters—Anne, Emily, and Charlotte—by their brother, Branwell, who, perhaps significantly, removed himself from the center of the group portrait.
National Portrait Gallery, London

Three of the eight hundred manuscripts (less than two inches high) written jointly by the Brontës in childhood.
The Brontë Parsonage Museum

Haworth Parsonage, the Brontë family home. The adjacent cemetery must have been a constant reminder of their many losses.
The Brontë Parsonage Museum

Charlotte in her youth looked somehow like a little old woman but described herself as "undeveloped" even when she was a woman in her mid-thirties; on the other hand, she wore children's chemises all her life. Her fantasy world remained her "secret joy," and when forced to work as a teacher, she found it difficult to stay at her task, longing for her fantasy life, on which she had become extremely dependent and which she used as an escape from her mundane existence: "I carefully avoid any appearance of preoccupation and eccentricity which might lead those I live amongst to suspect the nature of my pursuits." Whenever she was away, Charlotte tended to have an "indefinite fear" about those at home, a legacy, as her biographer Rebecca Frazer calls it, "of her overcast youth," worrying unceasingly about her father, as he himself always exaggerated fears about his health. When she was away, she experienced a variety of symptoms from a hysterical form of blindness to chronic and severe headaches, anxiety, and depression, though she was the one most able to leave home. She wrote: "At home . . . I talk with ease and am never shy— never weighed down by that miserable 'mauvaise honte' which torments and constrains me elsewhere." A friend warned her that staying home would "ruin her" but gave up when she saw Charlotte's response, though she could never "think without gloomy anger of Charlotte's sacrifices to the selfish old man." Charlotte herself wrote of her life: "I feel as if we were all buried here—I longed to travel— to work, to live a life of action but saw these as my fruitless wishes." And to another friend she wrote: "Whenever I consult my Conscience it affirms that I am doing right in staying at home—and bitter are its upbraidings when I yield to an eager desire for release."

The other siblings were even more unable to leave the family. Emily, after a few unsuccessful forays, gave up completely. She became ill at the time of Branwell's funeral and never left the house again. She died three months later. Anne became ill at this time as well and died five months after Emily, leaving only Charlotte of the six siblings. Charlotte feared that the shadow of her brother's and sisters' "last days must now, I think, linger forever." Her description of her reactions at the time are an excellent expression of ways the legacy of trauma can shut a family down, locking them into myth, secrecy, and avoidance of any experience that reminds them of what they cannot bear to face: "I must not look forwards, nor must I look backwards. Too often I feel like one crossing an abyss on a narrow plank—a glance round might quite unnerve." She buried herself in her work, clinging to her faculty of imagination to save her from sinking.

Several years later a most persistent suitor, her father's curate, Arthur Nichols, persuaded her to marry. Her father went into a rage and fired him; a year later, unable to put up with Nichols's replacement, Patrick Brontë relented and agreed that Nichols could marry Charlotte if they would both agree never to leave him. They agreed. Charlotte was not really in love with Nichols, as we know from her letters to her two close friends, but shortly after the marriage she accompanied her husband to his home in Ireland and there began to regard him in a different light. She saw his humor and found him more interesting in the context of his family. She began to fall in love with him. She became pregnant. She returned from her honeymoon, however, out of anxiety about her father's health, which soon improved. Hers, however, began to deteriorate, and she died shortly after, losing the baby as well.

The cause of Charlotte's death is unclear. Many have speculated on the possible psychological component. Her beloved caretaker, Tabby, had died just before her. At the time of Charlotte's death she was thirty-eight, the same age her mother had been at death. The pattern of early death in the Brontë family seems uncanny. Only Patrick lived on, dying at the ripe age of eighty-six.

Thus came the end of a most creative family. One might almost believe they were "doomed" psychologically by the stories they had created in response to their many losses.

THE ADAMS FAMILY

The Adams family story *(Genogram 3.2)* was one of spectacular highs and lows—amazing successes and abysmal failures. Charles Francis Adams, the most successful member of the third generation, observed: "The history of my family is not a pleasant one to remember. It is one of great triumphs in the world but of deep groans within, one of extraordinary brilliancy and deep corroding mortification."[3] The public accomplishments of many members of the Adams family are astonishing, as are the catastrophic failures of others. As their biographer Paul Nagel has pointed out, "No Adams, success or failure, made a comfortable accommodation to life."

Across four generations in this family there were two American presidents, a famous diplomat, accomplished essayists, historians, and wealthy businessmen. Also in the same family there were illiterates, alcoholics and ne'er-do-wells, failed marriages, and suicides. It was as if in the Adams family you either did very well or very poorly. In fact, even the most successful family members were often depressed, full of self-doubt, and rarely satisfied with their efforts.

The Adams family had a sense of being different from the common crowd. This is not surprising considering that no other family has produced two American presidents. They saw themselves as having a unique independence of mind and devotion to public service and as being free of the impulses of greed and political ambition. Along with this sense of specialness and expectation of greatness came self-criticism. They were hard in their demands of others but even harder on themselves and held themselves to impossible standards.

John Adams, the second president, was his own greatest critic, extremely sensitive to the criticism of others, full of self-doubt and questioning of his own motives. He was equally quick to criticize his children in the hope that they might avoid succumbing to what he saw as their inherently weak nature. As Abigail once said to her husband, "Sometimes, you know, I think you too severe. You do not make so many allowances as Human Nature requires." John's letters to Abigail are marked by the self-criticism that continued to characterize the Adams family. Despite his extreme diligence as a lawyer and patriot, he repeatedly castigated himself as a lazy wastrel. The family intolerance for human frailty was met by their pessimistic view of human nature that led them to expect it.

John Adams, like his father a deacon, believed in dedication to family, self-reliance, and service to others. The father of his wife, Abigail Smith, was an independent-minded minister, who resisted the religious hysteria of his day. Both families were steeped in a Puritanism that emphasized original sin and human fallibility. Like many families living in times of great change, the Adamses developed a strong sense of family identity that brought the parents and children together in common cause against adversity. As the family grew in eminence, they developed a sense of mission as the moral conscience of the nation.

John, as he became more involved in politics, spent more and more time away from his New England home, leaving Abigail to run the farm and rear the children. She had nurtured the hope that out of the American Revolution would come greater equality for women and recognition of their rights. She was to be sorely disappointed, as even her husband did not take her cause seriously. To justify her deprivations and disappointment, she tried to identify completely with the goals and ideals of her husband. Abigail commiserated with

The Adams Family
Genogram 3.2

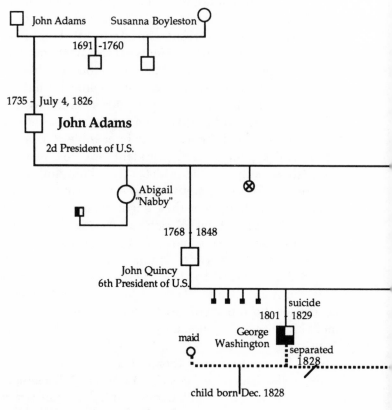

Key Genogram Symbols

◼ = alcohol or drug abuse

◨ = psychological or physical illness

◪ = physical/psychological and / or drug problems

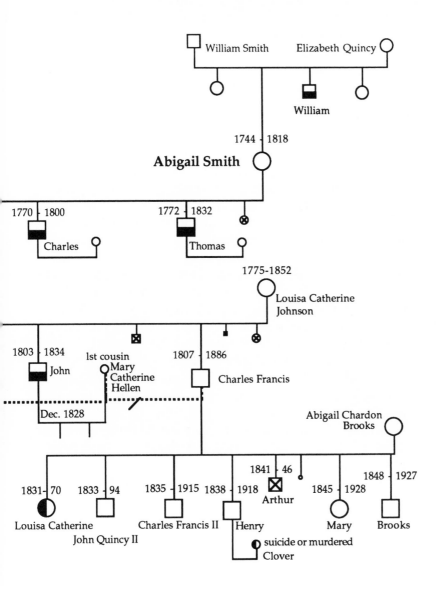

John that his efforts and sacrifices for his country were never sufficiently appreciated, that he alone was not stooping to partisan politics
and knew what was best for those he governed. For her part, Abigail
focused on the children. His project was to start a nation, and hers to
produce a new generation that would lead that nation. John too was
interested in raising the children correctly, but he often had to be
satisfied with giving advice and admonitions by mail.

Abigail, like her husband, was demanding of her children. Perhaps
because her brother's dissipation had devastated her family of origin,
she was obsessed with her children's good behavior and achievement.
She pondered the sins of her brother, knowing that despite the most
earnest parental efforts, vice and viciousness could take early root
and, as she put it, "tho often crop'd, will spring again." As she once
told her eldest son, John Quincy, when he was only ten, "I had much
rather you should have found your Grave in the ocean you have
crossed, or any untimely death crop you in your infant years than see
you an immoral profligate or a Graceless child."

As much as they tried to get their children on the right track, however, John and Abigail Adam's entire lives were marred by problems
with their children. They never realized that their anxiety, high standards, harsh criticism, pessimistic expectations, and the suffocating
togetherness of the family might contribute to their children's difficulties. To a considerable extent their worst fears were fulfilled. Their
oldest daughter, Abigail ("Nabby"), partly in response to her parents'
intrusions, ended up marrying an uncaring, irresponsible husband,
who eventually went to prison for fraud and debt. Two of the sons,
Charles and Thomas, were alcoholic, became cut off from their parents and from the families they created and abandoned, and made
disasters of their lives.

The one exception seemed to be the eldest son, John Quincy. At
the age of fourteen he accompanied his father to Europe on a diplomatic mission. He returned to go to Harvard and eventually start a
law practice. At the age of twenty-seven, he was sent to his own diplomatic post in Holland and began a career in public service. Eventually he became the sixth president of the United States. John Quincy
shared not only his father's dedication as a statesman but also his
outlook on life and took it even farther in harshness and severity. The
expectations for him had been great. His father had said to him: "You
come into life with advantages which will disgrace you if your success
is mediocre. And if you do not rise to the head not only of your Profession, but of your country, it will be owing to your own Laziness,
Slovenliness, and Obstinacy." Unlike his brothers, John Quincy was

partly able to fulfill these expectations, but at great personal cost. Despite his achievements, his life was even more overshadowed by self-doubt and depression than his father's was. He never believed that he was living up to the standards handed down to him by his parents. Like his father, he was defeated after a single term as president and saw the world of politics as crass, devoid of ideals, and unappreciative of what the Adams family had done for the nation. It was not until years later, when he returned to Washington as a congressman and became the major spokesman for the antislavery movement, that he developed some sense of accomplishment.

John Quincy's marriage was a difficult one. His wife, Louisa Catherine Johnson, an extraordinarily capable woman, was a joyous and affection-craving spirit. She wondered in later life whether if she had been more mature, she might have recognized that her husband's "unnecessary harshness and severity of character" would make the marriage a perpetual trial. Not surprisingly, she had problems with the outlook of the Adams family that took itself so seriously and saw the world as such an evil place. Her father's bankruptcy at the time of her marriage humiliated her and left her painfully dependent on her critical and distant husband, who ignored her as he attended to his career or withdrew in bouts of depression. Often left alone, she became depressed herself. Her husband could not or would not respond to her emotional needs. She had four miscarriages before she had a child who survived. Many more losses followed. In all she bore ten children, only three of whom lived to adulthood.

John Quincy took up the family escutcheon of public service, family greatness, and intense anxiety about child rearing and passed it on to the next generation. He taught his children that much was expected of an Adams in the constant struggle against an unappreciative world. He once wrote to his son Charles Francis: "Your father and grandfather have fought their way through the world against hosts of adversaries, open and close, disguised and masked . . . and more than one or two perfidious friends. The world is and will continue to be prolific with such characters. Live in peace with them; never upbraid, never trust them. But—'don't give up the ship!' Fortify your mind against disappointments."[4] He also taught that the family must stay together and recognize its special place in history. However, long separations again had their impact on the next generation. Because of his diplomatic duties, John Quincy and Louisa spent many years abroad, leaving the older children behind to go to school. Their eldest, George Washington Adams, later felt that his parents' absence during those formative years left him unprepared for life.

George was the eldest grandson of John Adams, who was the eldest son of another John Adams. As if this weren't enough, George's birth followed four miscarriages, which must have intensified the expectations for the first surviving son. A lot was expected of this unfortunate young man, who was born just after his grandfather had just lost an election for a second term as president. Instead of being named John Adams, he was named for our first president, whom his grandfather had always viewed with great jealousy, believing that Washington owed his career to Adams.[5] Surely there must have been a family story around this naming.

Sadly, George Washington Adams was ill equipped to live up to the expectations of the Adams family. He once said he could not remember a day when he didn't think about becoming president. He spent few of his early years with his parents, who left him behind when his father became minister to Russia. His parents' letters from abroad exhorted him to live up to his legacy. He never could. Just before entering college at sixteen, he had a dream in which he was showing interest in a young woman when his father appeared, "his eyes fixed upon me."[6] Under his father's gaze George lost interest. He said he was always trying to escape that gaze.

Years earlier in 1816 his grandfather had written to him: "I fear that too many of my hopes are built upon you."[7] George, in fact, was unruly and difficult from childhood on. He did poorly at everything he tried. He blamed his parents' long absences during his childhood for his difficulties and lack of self-discipline, though he seemed relieved of the pressure of their presence when his father moved to Washington to become our sixth president. Left behind in Boston to handle family affairs, he made a mess of them and of his own life over the next four years. Finally, in 1828, his father was defeated for reelection. George's engagement to a flirtatious first cousin, Mary Catherine Hellen, was broken in February, when she married his younger brother, John. That must have been painful to endure. (She had also had a romance with the third brother, Charles Francis.) George then impregnated a maid, and she gave birth in December.

By the spring of 1829 his life was in shambles. His parents requested that he come to Washington to accompany them home to Boston. On the boat on the way to meet them, he became very disturbed, and in the middle of the night he jumped overboard and drowned, probably in anticipation of having to live again in the shadow of his father.

John Quincy's second son, John, also became an alcoholic failure and died from a mysterious disease at the age of thirty-one. As in the earlier generation, only one son, the third, Charles Francis, survived

A painting of George Washington Adams by Charles Bird King, 1827. The Adams family story was one of spectacular successes and equally spectacular failures. As one member put it, "The history of my family . . . is one of the great triumphs in the world, but of deep groans within. . . ."
U.S. Department of the Interior. National Park Service, Adams National Historic Site, Quincy, Massachusetts

to carry on the Adams world view. As a youngest son and probably freer of the family constraints, he was a very different man from his father. Charles Francis was also the only child to accompany his parents on their travels. Perhaps Louisa was better able to soften for him the negative aspects of the Adams family legacy. She later warned

Charles Francis: "Go on and do not suffer yourself to be intimidated or brow beaten as your brother was, but pursue your course steadily and respectably." Charles Francis was more relaxed, less self-critical, and better able to face differences with his father squarely without letting his father dominate him. He still had the strong sense of the Adams legacy and the family's special place in history. It was he who began editing the family papers, which were to demonstrate to the world the uniqueness of his parents and grandparents. At first he did not follow the same path to public duty but was content to manage the family finances and be a family man. He even used the pessimistic Adams views about the corruptibility of his countrymen as an argument against entering the dirty business of politics. He did eventually become a congressman at age fifty-six and even later ambassador to Great Britain (like his father and grandfather before him), where his remarkable diplomatic skill managed to keep Britain out of the Civil War. His success at this made him the most noted American diplomat of his time. Indeed, Charles Francis found considerable satisfaction in fulfilling the family tradition of public service. But perhaps luckily for him, when his name was submitted as a candidate for the presidency in 1872, he lost.

He married Abigail Chardon Brooks, the favorite daughter of a wealthy Boston businessman. Abby was not a strong personality in the mold of Abigail and Louisa. She depended on her husband for constant reassurance and allowed him to think for her in all areas except the social. She loved to entertain and successfully resisted the Adams tendency toward social isolation.

It was in the area of child rearing that Charles Francis departed most from the generations before him. Perhaps aware of the fate of his brothers and uncles, he was determined to be an easier, less demanding, and more available father. He considered parenthood the most serious of all his duties. Although he still focused on his children's development, he was determined to raise them differently. He spoke of his mission: "I hardly dare to look at my children with the hope that I can do for them what I ought in order to save them from the dangers which I barely escaped myself without shipwreck." He believed in offering sympathetic encouragement and nourishing independence, and recognized the limitations of parental influence. Most of all, he spent a good deal of time with his children when they were young.

Charles Francis partially succeeded in shifting the Adams legacy. Among the sons of the fourth generation, there were no great failures, early deaths, or alcoholism. The only early deaths were the women, although the eldest child and daughter, Louisa Catherine, thought to be the most brilliant of all the children, was difficult and resentful from an early age, believing she could have become president if she had been male. The family was indeed dismayed that this first child was a girl.[8] She rebelled against the family and attempted to escape the legacy by marrying and living in Europe, where she led a hedonistic, almost suicidal existence. She died in an accident at the age of thirty-nine. The other tragic woman of this generation was the wife of Henry Adams, Clover, a gifted photographer, who committed suicide at the age of forty-six, having apparently struggled much with the gender constraints of her time.

John Quincy II, the eldest son, felt acutely the burden of the family legacy. "John Adams," he said, was a "grievous heavy name to bear."[9] He felt overwhelmed by the expectations others had of him. "What can a man say when he is thus absolutely beaten over the head with ancestry?" His relationship with his father was never easy, dominated by the son's self-doubt and the father's encouragement, mixed with impatience. It might have been easier if others had left him alone, but because of his position, his family heaped counsel and then criticism on him. He burned his diary and his letters, believing "the less weight you carry the better." He wanted to be left alone (a dream shared by all the generations of the Adams family), but this could not be. In response to his father's continuous prodding, he replied: "I am afraid you, like most parents, overestimate your children. I am of no consequence here under heaven except to my home." John Quincy II blundered in the face of his father's pressure to become a family leader. He viewed himself as his father's errand boy: "I should be grateful once (but I know it is useless) if I might in any one thing be considered as an individual and not a Son or Grandson." As a consequence, John Quincy II retreated from responsibility, handing over even the management of the family finances to his younger brother, Charles Francis. He was put up to run for election several times, as state representative, as governor, and even once as vice president, but he enjoyed his candidacy only when he was sure he would not win. John Quincy II wanted to lose. He shrank from the unpleasant grind of politics, which would come with victory. He once confessed to his father: "Politics, except just at election time, had not much attraction for so lazy a devil as I am." Even in the personal arena John Quincy II's life was doomed to misery, for two of his beloved children died of diphtheria, an experience from which he never recovered. He became a sad, quiet, retiring figure, who carefully destroyed all his papers, as if to make sure that the legacy would stop with him.

The three younger sons of the fourth generation all became accomplished in their fields, though they, too, had their problems. Where

John Quincy II resolved to obliterate all traces of his life, Charles Francis, Jr., determined to leave a huge written record about himself (carefully edited, of course). He also determined from his earliest years to succeed in areas beyond the traditional Adams role of states-manship. He became a successful entrepreneur and the president of the Union Pacific Railroad, although he eventually lost it to Jay Gould. He said of his failure: "There being nothing more for me to do, I got up to go. . . . My ideas were right, but I did not hold to them. I was weak of will."[10] Here we see again the underside of the Adamses "success:" their lack of self-assurance, evident even for those who achieved greatness as Charles Francis, Jr., did. He was continu-ally disabled from digestive ills and, after losing much of the family fortune in 1893, cut off from his brothers and sister.

Henry Adams, the most famous of the fourth generation, was an eminent historian, and Brooks, also a historian, was one of America's earliest geopoliticians. There was still a sense of specialness and com-mitment to public service, but this fourth generation consisted more of thinkers than doers. Rather than enter politics, they wrote about it. These three sons were all philosophically interested in the family outlook they had inherited from the earlier generation. They edited the family papers and speculated on the fate of humankind. With them the traditional Adams ability to view the world with derision and pessimism was harsher than ever. Henry and Brooks wrote cyni-cal historical essays with emphasis on the poor prognosis for the social ailments of their times. They saw little hope in modern trends. Brooks was in everything argumentative and misanthropic, while Henry, in particular, felt he was being left behind by the industrial age.

A family historian, David Musto, has written a penetrating analysis of the patterns in the Adams family patterns:

> The middle generations of the Adams family had an unusual disparity in life-spans between the successful and the less successful. Not all the shorter lives can be attributed to failing the family's imperatives, but the contrast is sugges-tive. The successful: John, John Quincy, and Charles Francis Adams, lived an average of 80 years, while the remainder: Charles, Thomas Boylston, Nabby, George Washington, and John 2nd lived an average of 40 years. The fittest survived. The imperatives of excellence and achievement which developed in the Adams family during the first years of our national life were a burden as well as a spur to subsequent generations.

By the fourth generation there was no longer the unifying shared family outlook to keep the Adams family together. Rather, each of the

Adamses in this generation was strongly individualistic, brilliant, but often eccentric. Each strove to escape the Adams legacy. Each found his or her own way. On the other hand, there was little to keep the siblings together, and after the father died, each went his own way, and the estate was eventually divided. Ironically, Charles Francis's sympathetic encouragement of independence and individual development did not lead to stronger family ties, as he had wished. Perhaps the fear of the world was no longer there to keep the family together. In any case, the loss was not mourned by the children. As Brooks, the last member of the fourth generation, argued, "It is now full four generations since John Adams wrote the constitution of Massachusetts. It is time we perished. The world is tired of us."[11]

The high expectations of achievement in the Adams family did not apply to the daughters. Abigail Smith Adams (wife of the second president) and her sisters were given a certain latitude to distinguish themselves, perhaps because their only brother was a failure. In the next generation John Quincy Adams's older sister, Nabby, took considerable responsibility, particularly when her father and brother were in Europe, but in terms of achievement, she was expected only to marry well and be a good wife. Her husband, like her mother's brother, turned out to be a failure, and she ended up spending time in prison with him for debt. John Quincy's wife, Louisa, a very gifted woman, like her mother-in-law, Abigail, often lived a life of quiet desperation. In the third generation no daughters survived infancy. Charles Francis's wife, Abigail Chardon Brooks Adams, was a lighthearted, spontaneous, and sociable woman. After a few years of marriage into this demanding, self-critical family, however, and with the arrival of babies, public life, and other distresses, she found that "the poetry of life has fallen into prose."[12] However, through the tragedy of the early death of one of their sons, Arthur, Charles Francis fell into a collapse of depression and self-reproach for having punished the boy just before his fatal illness. In her husband's time of trouble, Abby's strength emerged, and over their many years together they evolved a strong closeness and ability to enrich each other.

FAMILY SECRETS

Agatha Christie's Miss Marple says, "[S]ecrets are like bindweed, with its roots that go down underground a long way." Indeed, family stories and myths are profoundly influenced by the secrets families keep. All families have secrets. They remind family members of their boundaries. At times it is the content of the secret itself that is powerful: a suicide, a pregnancy that occurs outside a marriage, or a sexual liaison. In other cases the boundary established by the secret gives it its power—for example, when family members distort their behavior to cover up alcoholism or drug addiction. A secret may be a source of power, binding together those who share it, though it may also create shame and guilt because of its rule of silence. Because they create covert bonds and splits in a family, secrets also have a mystifying power. Imagine, for example, the power of a parent's naming a child for a secret lover. The spouse may not know the meaning of the child's name. The child may grow up to feel a distance from siblings and the other parent that none of them understands. This could ripple down to that child's experience of being a parent to his or her own children. Winston Churchill's mother, Jenny Jerome, seems to have been named for her father's lover, Jenny Lind. Jenny Jerome named her younger son John Strange Spencer for her lover, John Strange Jocelyn. One can only guess at how the secrets in this family may have influenced family relationships under the surface.

Secrets usually reveal a family's vulnerabilities. The playwright A. R. Gurney has described the legacy of his great-grandfather's suicide, never mentioned in his lifetime: "My great-grandfather hung up his clothes one day and walked into the Niagara River and no one understood why. He was a distinguished man in Buffalo. My father could never mention it, and it affected the family well into the fourth generation as a dark and unexplainable gesture. It made my father and his father desperate to be accepted, to be conventional, and comfortable. It made them commit themselves to an ostensibly easy bourgeois world. They saw it so precariously, but the reason was never mentioned."[13]

Four generations later the patterns set in motion by this death were still operating. Gurney was forty-eight when he first learned of the suicide from his father-in-law, who was a genealogist. This was at the time when Gurney's own father died, and in an interesting continuation of the pattern, Gurney refuses to talk about *his* father's death. We may go for generations following patterns set up by the secrets in earlier generations.

Secrets are especially important in families, because of the potential trauma their revelation may cause for those not prepared for the knowledge. When Peter and Jane Fonda's mother committed suicide, the entire community colluded to keep the facts from them. (Reportedly Henry never discussed his wife's suicide with his chil-

Henry Fonda and his first wife, Frances Brokaw. The night of her suicide
Fonda went onstage, as usual, and a conspiracy of silence was created to
keep the truth from the children, Jane and Peter, shown with their father
(below). Museum of Modern Art

dren.) Jane read about the death in a movie magazine six months later, surely a horrendous way to learn such a secret; shortly afterward Henry Fonda remarried. While he was on his honeymoon, Peter Fonda "accidentally" shot himself in the stomach. One wonders whether the dreadful secret wasn't already showing its power.

Even in less troubled relationships family members are often protective of one another in ways that constrict their relationships. Some secrets exist to protect family members, as in this instance, or may evolve to protect an entire family from the shame of outsiders' disapproval. Some secrets are kept because of society's sanctions for certain behaviors, as has often been the case with sexual orientation. But society also plays into distortions and secrecy of various kinds that support the dominant values of the culture. For example, until very recently the media have generally participated in keeping the extramarital secrets of male politicians.

Secrecy is often maintained about money—whether to hide wealth or to hide poverty. Men often keep their finances secret from their wives, considering this "none of their business." Male power is thus protected, but such secrecy also reflects ways men are valued for their money. Women have their money secrets, too. They may hold back a certain amount of the household money in separate funds, or they may keep secret how much they spend for clothes or presents or how much they give to help friends or relatives, for fear of their husbands' disapproval. Money secrets obviously have different meanings in different families, but they may have different meanings for different family members as well. To understand secrets, it is important to assess who is protected or excluded by the secret.

Women are generally the confidantes for other women as well as for men. They keep secrets to protect men's vulnerabilities or to keep secret their alliances with other women, which might threaten the men in their lives. They may keep secrets to protect children from their fathers' rage. They may also keep secrets about their ages or looks, generally a response to the sense that they are valued primarily for appearance. Men's secrets pertain mostly to their main areas of vulnerability: financial problems, job problems, and perceived or real incompetencies. The culture generally tells men to be strong, all-knowing, and capable of *handling* anything, so they are pressed to keep secret those fears and attitudes that would give the opposite impression. Most of all, men keep their private selves secret from other men. In your own family pay attention to who kept which secrets from whom and how that has influenced relationships.

Secrets in families tend to beget other secrets. If your parents married because your mother was pregnant and this has become a family secret, the entire family history may end up being distorted to keep that one secret. The subject of family history may be completely avoided for fear that one question could lead to another and expose the secret. The family story then becomes imbued with an aura of unreality because of one secret that cannot be told. In exploring your family history, you need to be aware of a few indicators of deeply embedded family secrets: (1) The subject of the past is entirely avoided; (2) there is tension whenever a particular relative or period in the family history enters the conversation; (3) there is more emotion than would seem to justify the "facts" of a certain aspect of the family story. Generally, the greater the family anxiety is about disclosure, the more aspects of family life and history will require distortion to maintain the secret and the longer-lasting its power will be.

Maxine Hong Kingston's powerful autobiographical memoir starts out with her mother's revelation of a chilling and defining family story and the mythmaking around it to keep secret the shame of an aunt's pregnancy and death in China. Such horrifying cautionary tales were told to warn her about life. Hong Kingston goes on to describe the family secrets and the way they played out in the family down the generations. "Those in the emigrant generations . . . confused the gods by diverting their curses, misleading them with crooked streets and false names. They . . . try to confuse their offspring as well, who, I suppose threaten them in similar ways—always trying to get things straight, always trying to name the unspeakable. The Chinese I know hide their names . . . take new names when their lives change and guard their real names in silence." [14]

Perhaps no writer has shown more preoccupation with the multigenerational power of secrets than Nathaniel Hawthorne. His stories show an obsession with both anguished confession and concealment of potentially ruinous ancestral secrets, along with an eerie, mystifying multigenerational legacy of guilt for the misdeeds of those long dead. This is the overt theme of *The House of Seven Gables*, in which the ghosts of the participants in Salem witch trials who are responsible for ominous misdeeds overshadow the lives of people more than a hundred years later. *The Scarlet Letter* is also about the damage caused by sins kept secret and the mystification that develops in relationships that are governed by secrecy. As the narrator states, "It is singular . . . with what security two persons who choose to avoid a certain subject may approach its very verge without disturbing it." Hawthorne's friend Herman Melville believed there was a dark secret in Hawthorne's life that would, were it known, explain all the mysteries of his career. Others who knew Hawthorne had the same suspicion. Hawthorne's lawyer wrote: "I should fancy from your books you were burdened by secret sorrow; that you had some blue chamber in your soul into which you hardly dared enter yourself."[15] The theme of sibling incest seemed to concern Hawthorne from first to last. At his death he left two unfinished manuscripts on sibling incest. There was an early incest story, which he had published at his own expense and then tried to retract by destroying. He never mentioned this story again, nor was it included in his collections. Fifty years later his sister Ebe, who was also herself preoccupied with sibling incest, referred to this early story as a good example of her brother's special genius.

The story takes place in the early days of Salem. It involves a brother and sister who have lived in fervent affection and "lonely sufficiency to each other" since they alone of their family appear to have survived an Indian attack. The brother realizes that by the death of the parents, the sister becomes his. Hers was "the love which had been gathered to me from the many graves of our household." These events mirror the story of Hawthorne's family itself, in which the death of his seafaring father, when he was six, led his mother to become a recluse within their home. This left Nathaniel isolated with his sister Ebe, who greatly resembled him and to whom he was deeply attached. A younger sister was much different in looks and personality, and the family lived amid relatives who were "uncongenial," all elements included in this and other Hawthorne stories.

In his preface to *The Scarlet Letter* Hawthorne alludes to misdeeds in his family generations earlier. He says that his hometown of Salem possesses a mysterious hold over him and that the figure of his first ancestor has haunted him since childhood; he wonders if his ancestors ever repented the sins they committed, "which have been written up in various histories." He continues: "At all events, I . . . as their representative, hereby take shame upon myself for their sakes, and pray that any curse incurred by them . . . may be now and henceforth removed. . . . Such are the compliments bandied between my great-grandsires and myself across the gulf of time! . . . Strong traits of their nature have intertwined themselves with mine."

Hawthorne had isolated himself for years, studying the old records of the town of Salem, just like his narrator in *The Scarlet Letter*. Generally unknown until recently but apparently discovered by Hawthorne himself, since it was part of the public records of Salem, which he pored over, is the fact that his earliest-known maternal ancestor, Nicholas Manning, who came to America in 1662, was brought to trial for incest with two of his sisters. Nicholas's wife and mother testified against him. The wife said she had feared revealing her husband's behavior, though she had witnessed it. The judge in the case was one William Hathorne (1607–81), possibly also a relative of Nathaniel's. Hawthorne spoke of telling secrets in his tales yet keeping "the inmost Me behind its veil."

In your own family, be alert at family gatherings, holidays, and times of family transition—weddings, funerals, birthdays—for which stories get told and how each person is characterized. This is a good starting point for the adventure of exploring your family from a systemic perspective and seeing hidden connections in your family tree. You might also think about the following questions:

■ Have members of your family tended to conform to the middle-class American family life cycle norms? If not, can you see other norms for your family, such as marrying late, not marrying, not having children, living in unconventional groupings, etc.? Can you detect values which these patterns might reflect?

■ Do you see events that are "off time" on your genogram? May–December marriages? Families having children very early or very late? Marrying very early or very late?

■ Can you notice coincidences of life cycle events—births, deaths, marriages, leaving home, onsets of illness—that may have intensified the meaning of particular events in your family?

■ What kinds of rituals does your family maintain? Holiday rituals? Dinnertime rituals? Leisure time rituals? Vacation rituals? Family get-together rituals?

■ What rules are there for celebrating weddings? Funerals? Births? Birthdays? Anniversaries?

■ What are the basic rules in your family (e.g., "Don't trust small men" or "Don't eat ice cream more than once a day")?

■ What are the general stories told in your family?

■ Have there been cautionary tales?

■ Can you figure out from them anything about your family's underlying beliefs, myths, and values?

■ What are the migration stories in your family?

■ What are the death stories?

■ What are the stories about dealing with the outside world?

■ What are the education stories?

■ What are the money stories?

■ What are the holiday stories?

■ What are the betrayal stories?

- What are the survival stories?
- What seem to be the myths in your family?
- What legacies are there in your family? Of strength? Of vulnerability or anxiety? Of success? Of caution?
- In what areas does your family keep secrets? Money? Death? Pregnancy? Sexual behavior? Marriage? Affairs? Parentage? School or work failure?
- How are secrets in your family maintained? Who conveys the messages and how?
- What impact have secrets had on the relationships in your family?

FOUR

FAMILY TIES AND BINDS

"Then you should say what you mean," the March Hare went on.

"I do," Alice hastily replied, "at least—at least I mean what I say—that's the same thing, you know."

"Not the same thing a bit!" said the Hatter. "Why, you might just as well say that 'I see what I eat' is the same as 'I eat what I see.' "

"You might just as well say," added the March Hare, "that 'I like what I get' is the same as 'I get what I like'!"

—Lewis Carroll, *Alice in Wonderland*

While every family is, of course, unique at one level, at another level there are ways of relating that seem to occur in all families across time and across cultures. Families relate in particular ways which can be mapped and studied. To understand your own family, you will need to explore the way the emotional relationships work: Who communicates what to whom? And just as important, who doesn't? In theory, if everything were perfect in a family—if everyone agreed with everyone else about everything, if no one ever left, got sick, or died, and if no one were ever added so that others had to make room for a new member, if no one ever got jealous or angry or sad—in other words, if we were not human beings but some other type of creature, it is possible that families might communicate openly, clearly, empathically, and with tolerance for difference at all times. Family relationships would always be in harmony.

But life being what it is, and this not being the best of all possible worlds, families do not communicate optimally, and relationships, as often as not, do go awry. In fact, some researchers have suggested that as in *Alice in Wonderland,* communication is often used more to obscure than to clarify meaning. Some theoreticians have actually developed an equation that states that to the extent family members are dependent on the reactions of others for their sense of well-being, direct communication will be sacrificed in the service of the relationship system. In other words, the more dependent family members are on the approval of others in the family for their self-esteem, the more likely communication is to be distorted.

RESPONSES TO STRESS

As we know, there is no life without change and no change without disruption, so it is not surprising that family communication and relationships are often stressed by change. And because all members of a family are connected, they react to one another's distress, often compounding their reactions, so that what upsets one ends up upsetting all.

Feeling overwhelmed by the changes that are inevitable in life, family members may try to cling to "the way things were," as if they could prevent the pain and disturbance that are axiomatic with all change. In fact, resistance to change seems to be a natural property of all systems. To a degree, resistance is necessary and healthy. But beyond a certain point a family that resists change becomes rigid and unable to adapt. Extreme resistance to change leads to distorted communication that will weaken the family in the end.

Characteristic ways of coping with stress are usually learned. You tend to do things the way your family did them, just as your family probably handled things the way their families did them. When a family is under stress, there is a tendency to fall into certain types of discommunication: Family members may blame others or themselves for what is going wrong. They may become placaters, denying their own experiences in order to adapt to the needs of others; they may become wishy-washy, rigidly authoritarian, irrelevant, illogical, or silent altogether, whether as Goody Two-shoes or as the "space cadet" of the family, in an effort to cope with their own or the family's distress.

Under stress some families pull together, closing the doors to keep outsiders out and insiders in, demanding a sameness in feelings and behavior, which family therapists call enmeshment. Leaving the family or even disagreeing may be seen as disloyalty.

Other families seem to fall apart under stress. The attitude here is "Everyone for him or herself." Such families cannot organize to handle problems, and outside agencies, such as the police or the health care system, may become overly involved with them in an attempt to superimpose organization on them.

Sometimes family coping patterns may seem to reverse themselves over each generation. If your grandfather was an alcoholic and handled his stress by going to the pub, while your grandmother berated him when he came home, your father's generation may have sworn off alcohol and developed rigid rules for censuring others by silence and avoidance of all emotional issues—drink as well as other problems. Your generation, responding to your father's rigidity, may again turn to drinking and acting out to deal with stress. If we look more closely at the patterns of relating in such a family, we may find a stable pattern of emotional avoidance and a cycle of shame/guilt/repentance that remains the same right down the generations, although superficially the behavior of each looks different.

Families react to many stresses, both internal and external, as they move through the life cycle. As the family therapist Betty Carter has described it, the flow of anxiety through a family has both a horizontal and a vertical dimension. The vertical flow includes patterns of relating and functioning that come down the family tree over historical time.

Generational attitudes, myths, taboos, expectations, labels, and the legacy of trauma that come down a family tree (the vertical stressors) all influence how family members will deal with any experience and what kinds of relationships they will have. This heritage is the given, the hand you are dealt. What you do with it is up to you.[1] The horizontal flow of anxiety comes from the pressures on a family as it moves through time, coping with the inevitable stresses and changes of family development and with the unpredictable stresses, such as economic reversals, untimely deaths, natural disasters, and so forth.

With enough stress on the horizontal or developmental axis, any family will break down. Stressors on the vertical or historical axis may create added problems, so that even a small horizontal stress can have serious repercussions on the system. For example, if a young mother has unresolved issues with her parents (vertical anxiety), she may have a particularly difficult time dealing with the normal vicissitudes of parenthood (horizontal anxiety), which are hard enough in themselves.

By understanding your own and your family's typical responses to stress, you can avoid being automatically caught up in their patterns. This means mapping out current stresses, along with the chronology of previous events and stresses that may have influenced your family's ways of responding in the present.

For example, Theodore Roosevelt, the twenty-sixth president of the United States, had a difficult time handling the launching of his daughter Alice *(Genogram 4:1).* While launching children usually creates some stress on any family, a number of concurrent and prior stressors seems to have intensified this particular transition. For one thing, TR was going through a difficult period as president. Secondly, his favorite son, Teddy, who had had serious physical and emotional problems over the years, was in academic trouble at Harvard. Furthermore, there was a painful history of family losses: Alice's mother (also named Alice), had died, giving birth to this daughter Alice, at age twenty-two, on February 14, 1884. Roosevelt's mother also died on that Valentine's Day night in the same house. Furthermore, this date was the anniversary of the day TR had become engaged to Alice.

Within a year he was secretly engaged to Edith Carew, whom he had known since childhood, though he wrote to his sister Bamie, who disapproved: "I utterly disbelieve in second marriages; I have always considered that they argued weakness in a man's character. You could not reproach me one half as bitterly for my inconstancy and unfaithfulness as I reproach myself. Were I sure there were a heaven, my one prayer would be I might never go there, lest I should meet those I love on earth who are dead."[2] This extraordinary letter was, by the way, suppressed by the family for almost a century. Roosevelt regarded Alice, who was called Baby Lee, as a kind of peace offering to his sister, Bamie, who kept Alice from the time of her birth and gave her back with great reluctance at age three.

Roosevelt remarried in 1886 and fathered five more children. He never mentioned his first wife's name again, and there is not a word in his autobiography to indicate her existence. Alice grew up to bear a remarkable resemblance to her mother, to whom she learned not to refer. Within the family Alice herself also became invisible. TR hardly counted her among the family members.

Starved for attention, she became increasingly flamboyant in her behavior by late adolescence, in spite of a deep inner shyness. By the time she was twenty she was continuously making newsprint for her outrageous pranks: drinking, smoking, racing cars, betting on horses. One might say that she forced her father to pay attention to her by antics that made the newspaper almost daily. As her younger half

The Theodore Roosevelt Family
Genogram 4.1

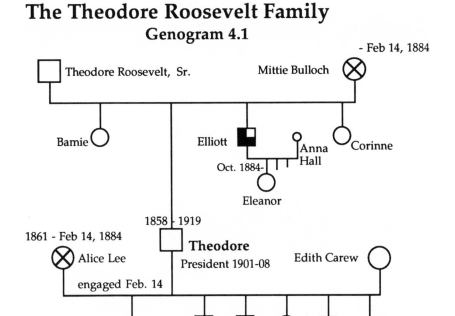

sister later said, she was "a hellion . . . What wickedry she might commit next was felt almost constantly by almost all the family."[3] On February 17, 1906, at age twenty-two, the same age at which her mother had died, Alice decided to marry and leave home.

Both the concurrent stresses in the present and the coincidental

Houghton Library, Harvard University

Theodore Roosevelt and Alice Lee, his first wife, who died after giving birth to a daughter, Alice. Roosevelt's mother died the same night in the same house. He never mentioned Alice Lee's name again and soon married a childhood sweetheart, Edith Carew, with whom he had five children, pictured below. Daughter Alice wears a white hat.

Theodore Roosevelt Collection, Harvard College Library

experiences of the past undoubtedly contributed to Roosevelt's difficulty in letting his daughter go and to her difficulty in leaving him.

Partial Roosevelt Chronology

1880, Feb. 14	TR proposes to Alice Lee.
1884, Feb. 12	Alice gives birth to baby, also named Alice.
1884, Feb. 14	Alice Lee Roosevelt dies at age twenty-two.
1884, Feb. 14	TR's mother, Mittie Bulloch Roosevelt, dies in same house.
1884, Feb. 16	Double funeral is held for Alice Lee Roosevelt and Mittie Bulloch Roosevelt.
1884, Summer	TR submerges grief in adventures out West and presidential politics.
1906	TR has problems as president.
1906, Jan.	Favorite son, Teddy, is failing at Harvard.
1906, Feb. 17	Alice, age twenty-two, marries Congressman Nicholas Longworth, age thirty-four.
1907	Marriage unhappy, Alice and Nick are mostly apart. Nick has serious alcohol problem and is a womanizer.
1923	Alice begins affair with Senator William Borah.
1925, Feb. 14	Alice has baby girl. Wants to name her Deborah, but Nick opposes. Name: Paulina after St. Paul (Alice and William's favorite Bible figure).
1946	Paulina has a baby and names her Johanna.
1952, Nov.	Paulina's husband, Alexander Sturm, commits suicide
1957, Jan. 27	Paulina, age thirty-one, commits suicide.

As Alice departed, her stepmother is reputed to have said: "I want you to know that I'm glad to see you go. You've never been anything but trouble."[4] The launching was not successful, and within a year Alice was spending more time with her father than she was with her husband. This improved relationship with her father was probably what she had been seeking for years.

Her one child, born twelve years later on February 14, was apparently fathered by William Borah, a much older married senator, with whom Alice had been having an affair. Alice wanted to name the girl Deborah, but Longworth refused, so Alice named her Paulina after St. Paul. Paulina led a miserable and neglected life, first attempting suicide when she was in college. She then married someone of whom her mother disapproved, who drank heavily and killed himself when their daughter, Johanna, was six. Paulina, after further depressions, suicide attempts, and hospitalizations, finally took her life when Johanna was ten. At this point Alice, guilt-ridden over her daughter's death, decided to make it up by developing a close relationship with Johanna. They had a happy relationship until Alice died at age ninety-six in 1980.

It might seem that Paulina was "doomed" as the stand-in for the stand-in, the second-generation daughter of loss and neglect, whose life was marked by eerie coincidences of births, deaths, and anniversaries for three generations. Her birth was related not just to unfortunate coincidence but to the secrets of a failed marriage and an affair. Her legal father, Nick Longworth, apparently adored her but died when she was six. Her biological father ignored her completely, though her mother made sure Paulina knew who he was. A most interesting aspect of the story is the loving and generative relationship that resulted between Paulina's neglected daughter, Johanna, and Paulina's neglectful mother, Alice.

THE MARX FAMILY

The immortal Marx brothers *(Genogram 4.2)*, sons of an immigrant German Jewish family that came to New York at the turn of the century, have now charmed three generations with the hilarious antics of their early comic movies. Each brother had his very defined labels and characteristics: Wisecracking Groucho, the "professor," with his glasses, eyebrows, mustache, cigar, and funny walk was a foil for his look-alike brothers Chico and Harpo and played off Gummo and Zeppo in turn as the straight men; Chico had the role and dialect of the uneducated Italian immigrant and played the piano like a magician; Harpo, with his red clown wig, speechless, honking, taking zany outrageous props out of his huge raincoat and playing the harp, played the not-so-foolish fool; Gummo, the fourth brother, named for his Gum shoes, played the straight man but couldn't stand the role. He went into the retail clothing business and later managed the brothers' business. The youngest brother was Zeppo, the baby (no one knows where he got his name), who sang and took over the straight man role from Gummo until he too couldn't stand competing

The Family of the Marx Brothers
Genogram 4.2

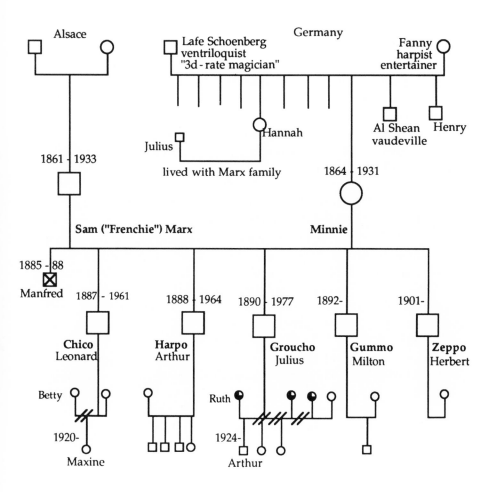

for the limelight. He was, he said, "sick and tired of being a stooge,"[5] though like Gummo, he later rejoined his brothers in a managerial role.

The stage roles of the Marx Brothers characterized them from earliest youth: Chico, whose nickname came from always having "chicks," was the oldest surviving child. A replacement for his mother's first baby, who had died, he became her favorite. He was an irresistible charmer, an irrepressible liar, continuously preoccupied with seducing women, and a perpetual optimist. Though he had less than two years of education, he was brilliant with numbers, which he used primarily in his compulsive gambling.

Harpo, whose name derived from the harp he played with such brilliance, became the solid man of the family: happily married, generous, friendly, understanding. A tranquil soul, Harpo dreamed his way through life: smiling, watching, never needing to top anyone, practicing his harp in the corner, and passing the most contented existence of the five brothers. He finished only the first grade and after that wandered the streets, getting his first jobs from his con artist older brother, who talked his way into so many jobs that he often sent Harpo in his place when he had double-booked himself. Harpo said of himself, "Most people have a conscious and subconscious. Not me. I've always operated on a subconscious and a sub-subconscious."[6] He almost seemed to do just that—to float through life, exuding warmth and contentment.

Groucho, on the other hand, grew up a misanthrope, a pessimist, a skinflint, and a grouch—hence his nickname. He later wrote that Harpo had inherited all their mother's good qualities, and he himself got what was left. But he was also the intellectual, publishing many articles and five books in spite of only a seventh-grade education. Groucho never overcame his resentment that Chico was their mother's favorite. Perhaps Harpo, who was born between them, used his silent smile and outrageous antics as a way not to get caught in the middle.

Where Chico could talk anyone into anything, Groucho sneered and bullied. Where Chico was a spendthrift and a gambler, Groucho was a miser; he was moody, dour, and, unlike his other brothers, not very sociable. His negative behavior probably intensified his mother's temperamental preference for Chico. And Chico's irresponsibility was in part made possible by Groucho's extreme seriousness. In other words, the role each played intensified and exaggerated an opposite role for the other. The more Minnie (the mother) and Chico felt allied against Groucho, the grouchier and more serious he got. His miserliness and seriousness also allowed his brothers to express the carefree, spendthrift side of their personalities; he was always there to protect them financially, as much as he growled about it. Perhaps what Groucho got out of the complementarity was a feeling of moral superiority. What Chico got was the freedom to be irresponsible.

The fourth brother, Gummo, as his shoes suggest, became the prosaic member in the family. Gummo and Zeppo were apparently affable, humorous fellows and decent actors, but that doesn't get you very far when you're trying to share the stage with three great comedians. Actually, Zeppo was considered the funniest of the brothers offstage. He, like most of his brothers except Groucho, was also a gambler. He was also a cold and tough playboy. He had special trouble with Groucho, who hated to share the spotlight.

The Marx family, who were of German Jewish background, came to the United States in 1880. Minnie's father, Lafe, who loved to brag to his grandsons about his sexual conquests, had been a magician, ventriloquist, and circus strongman. Her mother, Fanny, was a small, devout, quiet woman whose main outlet was her harp. In Germany the entire family had been ragtag entertainers. In the United States Lafe became a peddler who repaired umbrellas, while Minnie's younger brother, Al Shean, became one of the all-time great vaudevillians.

Minnie married Sam Marrix (nicknamed Frenchie because he came from Alsace), who had emigrated to the United States to avoid conscription. Taking the advice of a cousin who became a tailor and changed his name to Marx, he did the same. He was a marvelous dancer, and Minnie, though warned of his lechery, fell for him anyway.

Minnie ran the family. The title of a Broadway play about the family, *Minnie's Boys,* conveys the centrality of her mother role. She filled their home with relatives and maneuvered to line up entertainment opportunities for her brother, her sons, and various other relatives. Whether she was viewed as a manipulative conniver or a can-do charmer would depend, of course, on your point of view.

Frenchie Marx was the kind of person who would laugh at a joke even if he didn't understand it. He was playmate to his sons in their card games, but they seem to have disregarded him in any role other than the family chef. Groucho's stories about his parents are typical of what all the sons felt:

> Whatever visitors came for, they always came to my mother—never to my father . . . She engineered loans when they needed money. How she did it was always a source of wonder to me, but she invariably came through. She patched up marriages that were foundering and she out-talked the landlord, the grocer, the butcher and anyone else to whom we owed money. Her maneuvers were a triumph of skill, chicanery and imagination. . . . My Pop was a tailor, but he was no ordinary tailor. His record as the most inept tailor that Yorkville ever produced has never been approached. . . . The notion that Pop was a tailor was an opinion that was held only by him. To his customers he was known as "Misfit Sam." He was the only tailor I ever heard of who refused to use a tape measure.[7]

Another perspective on Frenchie's tailoring was given years later by one of Harpo's sons, who compared it to his own father's virtuosity

with the harp, in spite of the fact that he couldn't read a note of music
and had had no training: "He performed music the way his father,
Frenchie, had performed tailoring, with an unerring feel for fabrics
and color (harmony), but very little for cutting and fitting (melody
and tempo)."[8]

In spite of Frenchie's obvious limitations, Groucho and the others
attributed to him remarkable strengths:

> It's amazing how proficient a man can be in one field and how incompetent in
> another. My father should have been a chef. He usually cooked dinner for all
> of us. . . . He could take two eggs, some stale bread, a few assorted vegetables
> and a hunk of cheap meat and convert this into something fit for the gods,
> assuming that there are any left. Like most women, my mother hated cooking
> and would walk miles out of her way to avoid the kitchen. But my father's
> culinary skill enabled my mother to swing some pretty sharp deals in later
> years. . . . After eating his food the agents were softened up to the point where
> Mother could do business with them on her terms.[9]

Harpo had a similar view of their father, agreeing that with food he
was a true magician but that his failure as a tailor meant he often had
to go off to peddle just to make ends meet, while his mother, with
never a complaint, would hit up her brother for a loan. Harpo says
that Frenchie never ducked his duty as a breadwinner, though he
was the exact opposite of his wife in ambition. "Frenchie was a loving,
gentle man who accepted everything that happened—good luck or
tragedy—with the same unchangeable good nature. He had no ambition beyond living and accepting life from day to day. He had only
two vices: loyalty to everyone he ever knew (he never had an enemy
even amongst the sharpies who fleeced him) and the game of
pinochle. I shouldn't knock Frenchie's loyalty. That's what kept our
family together."[10]

In the early years Minnie and the sons formed a coalition which
excluded the father. Possibly without this coalition and outlet for her
energy the tension between Minnie and her husband might have led
to the breaking point. It is also possible that without the various coalitions the Marx Brothers themselves formed over the years, they
might never have been able to develop their phenomenal comedy
team. Having a good common enemy can make you into a strong
group. When the team broke up, however, it is not surprising that it
was precipitated by Groucho's resentment of his role as the overresponsible one in the family. The overfunctioner in a relationship system is often under the most pressure and may burn out eventually,

Samuel Marx, (left), with his four sons: Harpo, Groucho, Chico, and Zeppo. Minnie Marx (right), their mother was the force behind the show business success of her sons. In their act the four brothers played roles that related to family patterns.

becoming resentful, even if, as was the case with Groucho, the role was self-assumed. His humor itself (unlike that of Harpo, for example) was always a form of "triangling": His jokes involved joining with the audience in ridiculing someone else. It is interesting, though, that he was the only one who managed to continue a career on his own.

The assigned roles in the Marx family played themselves out in the next generation as well. For example, Maxine Marx, the only child of Chico, allied with her father against her mother, Betty, especially after she was sent to live with her grandparents, so that her mother could remain with Chico in his itinerant career. As so often happens with children, Maxine ended up blaming her more visible mother and felt drawn to her romanticized, distant father. As the tension developed in the couple over the years, Maxine tried to move in directly between her parents. "Whenever Daddy, Mother, and I went out to dinner, I would scoot into the booth between them. 'The two of you are disgusting,' Mother would say. . . . Daddy would just laugh. 'Leave her alone,' he would tell her: 'She's just a baby.' "[11]

Later Maxine was able to reflect on what drew her toward her father, illustrating how the facts became subverted in the family emotional process: "I resented Mother's desperate need to stay close to Chico. I didn't realize that he was being unfaithful to her; I simply thought that she wanted him all to herself. . . . He would lie, cheat on Mother, lose all his savings. . . . He always felt that his charms could get him out of trouble. I knew that he was irresponsible . . . and that he was capable of really hurting me, but somehow it didn't matter." She also became aware of the way she intentionally alienated her mother: "As I grew older, I resented it when Mother and I would walk down the street and all the men's eyes were on her. I felt totally inadequate, so I began to lord it over her in another area: education. . . . I lifted my eyebrow in disdain, when she called from the door, 'Maxine, your young swan is here.' 'Mother,' I muttered as I swept out, 'It's "swain," and nobody uses it today anyway.' "

Maxine also became allied with her grandmother Minnie (with whom she lived) against her mother. Not surprisingly, Minnie was not close to Betty; she would probably have felt no wife was good enough for her favorite son. But Minnie and Betty were also opposites in personality. They had clashed from the time Betty and Chico had married. In fact, from the start all the Marx family had a problem with Chico's wife, Betty. She challenged their ways of operating. She had a quick tongue and a frank manner, which seem to have ruffled their seemingly unflappable family. Although the core of the Marx Brothers' humor was wild—outrageous breaking up of a situation—

the family had its own code of acceptable wildness. Betty was pushed into the role of villain by her mother-in-law, her daughter, and the others in the family, who considered her an outsider. As Maxine said, "From early on, Mother had been made the heavy in my family, and being away from her nitpicking and constant rules I felt a great sense of freedom. Minnie was hardly an authoritarian; she was very much like Chico."

Since Minnie had no daughters, it was perhaps natural she would ally with Maxine, her first grandchild. Minnie took Maxine on as a project, as she had taken on so many relatives before, to make her an entertainer, teaching her to recite German poems before she even knew what she was saying. The more grandmother and granddaughter joined together, the more of an outsider Betty became.

But according to Maxine, Chico was attracted to Betty because of the new, different element she introduced into their family: "Chico didn't have the antipathy toward Jewish women that his brothers Harpo and Groucho showed. Betty was just the type of Jewish girl they shied away from. Bossy and abrasive, she knew exactly what she wanted and wasn't afraid to tell you so. Chico admired her 'guts' while his brothers preferred docile *shiksas*. Minnie was manipulative, but never openly bossy, and her sons tended to forget that she was Jewish, too. Not that Betty was shrewish . . . she was just naturally straightforward, whereas the boys were used to Minnie's soft-spoken, devious manner." When Chico brought Betty home, his mother and his four unmarried brothers all resented her. Conflicts ensued. For example, "Minnie was always trying to look very young, with her big blonde wig and chiffon dresses. When the family sat down to eat, she would come sweeping down the stairs in a grand entrance. One evening, Betty, giggling as the grande dame of Grand Boulevard took her seat at the head of the table, whispered a bit too loudly that Minnie looked like the Queen of Sheba. Minnie took this harmless joke well, but the brothers became defensive."

Not surprisingly, when two siblings who have been in conflict marry, their spouses tend to get added to the stew. As typically happens with in-law conflicts, the animosity between the wives of Chico, the ever-careless, irresponsible charmer, and of Groucho, the over-responsible, penny-pinching grouch, reflected primarily the issues between the brothers and within each marriage, rather than differences between the two women themselves. Groucho's wife, Ruth, envied Chico's wife, Betty, for her jewels and furs, because Groucho begrudged her even a new dress. What Ruth overlooked was that Chico often used his generosity and expensive gifts to buy forgiveness for his gambling and other women. In addition, Betty's luxuries might have to be hocked any day to pay Chico's gambling debts—debts which Groucho wouldn't have incurred in a million years.

COMMUNICATION REGULATES DISTANCE

Families generally maintain a stable level of closeness and distance, however much their emotional relationships may seem to fluctuate. This process of distance regulation has to do with who relates to whom and about what. We all know that families may do a lot of talking without becoming intimate. Some families use humor to main- tain distance; others use fighting. Some families can appear very warm and friendly to outsiders, but insiders know that it's all "form" and that if you disobey the rules of "appropriate" behavior, you will be shut out.

Families with a high degree of conflict may also have a high degree of intimacy. Some families share an intensely private language, full of obscure jokes and references. Others communicate their connected- ness through rituals and patterns passed from generation to genera- tion. Take, for example, James Baldwin's description of a ritual family storytelling, illustrating the subtlety of what got transmitted down the generations of his family.

> On a Sunday afternoon, say, when the old folks were talking after a big Sunday dinner . . . maybe somebody's got a kid on his lap and is absent-mindedly stroking the kid's head. . . . He hopes that there will never come a time when the old folks won't be sitting around the living room, talking about where they've come from, and what they've seen, and what's happened to them and their kinfolk. But something deep and watchful in the child knows that this is bound to end, is already ending. In a moment someone will get up and turn on the light. Then the old folks will remember the children and they won't talk any more that day. . . . The child knows they won't talk any more because if he knows too much about what's happening to them, he'll know too much too soon to about what's going to happen to him.[12]

Generally, if something changes the comfortable level of distance established for relationships, the family unit will try to bring things back to the familiar level. At times it almost seems as if family mem- bers were connected by an invisible umbilical cord, operating as one organism, even when separated by thousands of miles. Thus, if one family member becomes sick, the others may come closer to fill the void or decrease anxiety, or they may begin fighting to preserve the familiar distance and avoid too much intimacy. In times of anxiety and change families will try to stabilize themselves by regulating the distance in their relationships.

An amusing example of this process occurred with the Wright brothers Wilbur and Orville when they were trying to design the propeller for the first airplane *(Genogram 4.3)*. The Wright brothers, though seeming opposites, were actually described by their father as "inseparable as twins." Wilbur once wrote: "From the time we were little children, my brother Orville and myself lived together, played together, worked together, and in fact, thought together. We usually owned all of our toys in common, talked over our thoughts and aspirations so that nearly everything that was done in our lives has been the result of conversations, suggestions, and discussions between us."[13] It was said they were so close they often finished each other's sentences. As their work on inventing the airplane developed, the charge in their already close relationship heated up. For six or seven weeks they worked together day and night and argued all the way. (Most likely the arguing regulated their emotional distance to counterbalance the intensity of their collaboration.) Whenever the brothers were in the same room, the shouting started resounding through the house. As their assistant recalled, "One morning following the worst argument I ever heard, Orv came in and said he guessed he'd been wrong and they ought to do it Will's way. A few minutes later Will came in and said he'd been thinking it over and perhaps Orv was right. The first thing I knew they were arguing it all over again, only this time they had switched ideas."[14] Switching sides was probably an attempt to stop the escalation of their fighting, which had then gone too far. Yet agreement would have brought them too close, so they quickly moved back to polarized positions.

The brothers' collaboration on the development of the airplane was one of the most productive partnerships in history, a relationship more binding than most marriages, even to the point where each could use their joint bank account without consulting the other. The brothers often began whistling the same tune while at work in their bicycle shop, as if there were a psychic bond between them. And their voices were so alike a listener could not tell them apart except by seeing them. They attributed this phenomenon to an association of ideas stored in a common memory.[15] Though both were mechanically minded and intelligent, it was their combined abilities and efforts that allowed them to succeed at man-made flight. Only together did they experience genius.

The Family of Wilbur and Orville Wright
Genogram 4.3

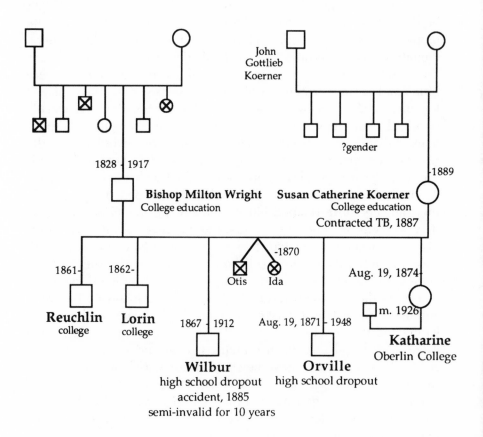

The collaboration of these extraordinary brothers created one of the miracles of our time. On the surface this extraordinary "twinship" is somewhat mystifying. Other sibling pairings in the family might have seemed more natural. Consider the fact that Wilbur and Orville were four years apart in age while their two older brothers were only a year apart. Consider also that both were high school dropouts while every other member of their family, including their mother, went to college. Consider also that Orville and their sister, Katharine, were born three years apart on the same date and were thus linked with each other. As I suggested earlier, I believe their twinship was influenced by the hidden connection brought on by the birth and infant death of twin siblings, Otis and Ida, between the births of Orville and Wilbur. The importance of these twins to the family is shown by the fact that their birthday was commemorated by their father for more than a quarter of a century. Though we know nothing of earlier twins in the Wright family, I wonder if the intensity of the Wright need for twins doesn't also reflect some earlier traumas about other twins in the family.

As we have seen, families that lose children often form a special attachment to the surviving children, who become emotional replacements and have difficulty leaving home. Bishop Milton Wright, the father, actually boasted that neither Orville nor Wilbur ever married or left the parental roof. The reasons for their neither finishing high school nor leaving home remain obscure, leaving one to wonder if there was not some covert message for them not to leave, since both parents and all their siblings did attend college.

Wilbur had sustained a severe injury at age sixteen and withdrew from school to nurse his mother, who was slowly dying of tuberculosis. However, his inability to mobilize himself lasted long after his mother's death and left several family members wondering if he was malingering or depressed. In the Wright family the parental message not to leave may have been intensified by the lost twins and by the fact that Orville and the only sister, Katharine, always called *Schwester* (German for "sister") were born on the same day; these two also had a kind of twin relationship, living as a pair for many years after Wilbur had died. One might almost hypothesize that this family "needed" twins. When the first set was lost, it was replaced by Wilbur and Orville. When Orville no longer had Wilbur, they were replaced by Orville and Katharine. When Katharine finally decided to marry at the age of fifty-two, having hesitated for more than a year to tell Orville of her engagement, he refused to speak to her ever again. As one of the Wright biographers puts it, "Katharine violated a sacred pact. In admitting another man into her life, she had rejected her brother. Katharine, of all people, had shaken his faith in the inviolability of the family ties that provided his emotional security."[16] From a family systems view this example reflects a common family pattern: Fusion leads to cutoff, and cutoff leads to fusion. In other words, if you cut off feelings about one relationship (say, the twins in the Wright family), you may intensify feelings in another (Wilbur and Orville), which got transferred to yet another fusion (Orville and Katharine) and led eventually to another cutoff when Orville's

Wilbur and Orville Wright with their sister, Katharine. "Inseparable as twins," the brothers seem to have been the replacement for twins who died in infancy. After Wilbur's death, Orville and Katharine, who shared the same birthday, lived together in the family house until Katharine's marriage at the age of fifty, at which time Orville cut off the relationship.
Photoworld/FPH International

demand for fusion could not tolerate Katharine's having another intimate relationship.

HANDLING FAMILY PAIN AND CONFLICT

It takes considerable strength and courage to handle conflict, and many families get stuck on this issue. Families with a priority on togetherness tend to avoid discussion of their differences. They cover them over, change the subject, or stifle their own feelings and pretend to agree.

Other families repeatedly erupt in response to anxiety. Disagreements may lead to distance, alienation, and unresolved family resentments. Turmoil can be the basic style of relating, and these families constantly shift the argument without resolution of the conflict.

When a disagreement reaches a certain level, the family shifts to a different battlefront. For example, a marital conflict may arise over the husband's preoccupation with his job. The wife complains that he is unhelpful and unappreciative, while he feels she is insensitive to his work stress. At a certain point, instead of being able to resolve their conflict, they may switch to a disagreement over the son's behavior. When this conflict becomes too intense, they shift to another battleground. The husband says the wife "always" interrupts, and the wife says the husband "never" listens. The son may then distract the parents by picking a fight with his sister. At this point the parents join together to stop the children's fighting. This continual shifting can keep the anxiety level of the family within certain bounds, but relationships remain the same, and conflicts go unresolved. A stable balance may result, though of course, it is quite unsatisfying for the participants.

Sometimes family members, particularly couples, get into a cycle of fighting and making up. There is intense disagreement, maybe even a parting of the ways, followed by a loving reconciliation and a renewed avowal of love. Even when not much is resolved, the intensity of the reconciliations may make the conflict almost worthwhile. Sometimes a person even picks a fight simply to experience the closeness of making up.

Other families live in a "cold war"—no battles, just chronic tension. A contemptuous glance can be the emotional equivalent of a devastating verbal attack. This kind of distancing may not resolve the problems, but it may keep anxiety at a bearable level.

Typically, conflicts between any two family members will affect others in the family. As anxiety rises, conflicts have a ripple effect. Family members become polarized. It is hard to avoid taking sides. Even those who try to remain neutral and above the fray will be seen as having chosen a side by their very silence.

For example, when Kathleen Kennedy, child of Joseph and Rose Kennedy, married a Protestant in England against her parents' wishes and their religion, Rose Kennedy retreated to her room. Joe Kennedy, torn between his wife and his daughter, had his wife admitted to a hospital to protect her from publicity and, perhaps, from having to commit herself publicly to a reaction; Kathleen had to read about the family's response to the marriage in the newspaper and draw her own conclusions. Joe, Jr., the eldest son, on

Kathleen's behalf, finally cabled the parents: "The power of silence is great."[17]

Such responses may temporarily stabilize the family, but they create a situation in which a family will be less well equipped to handle future changes and anxiety.

DISTORTIONS IN COMMUNICATION

Generally people communicate most clearly when they are feeling secure. If there is a problem in the family, they usually distort their messages to protect themselves or others. They may not talk at all, they may blame themselves, they may blame someone else, or they may change the conversation by talking about other subjects.

The level of distortion is a good measure of the overall anxiety and rigidity of family relationships. If two family members always agree, this is probably more their reaction to anxiety than due to the fact that they are soul mates. Conversely, if two family members are always in disagreement, the subjects of their conflict are probably not the real issue. They will end up on opposite sides, no matter what the content of their discussion.

Dysfunctional relationship and communication patterns are most likely to develop in times of stress. Consider how often people stop speaking to each other when there is a death in the family or a financial crisis. If many stresses—death, a move, birth, divorce, and remarriage—all occur at the same time, a family will understandably be overwhelmed and probably won't communicate effectively, at least for a time. The legacy of disturbed relationships and communication becomes most serious when the family communication remains distorted over time. Chronically maladaptive ways of relating ripple out and down the system.

FUSION AND CUTOFF

Under stress, pressure is created for family members to think and act alike—to sacrifice their own identities for the sake of family loyalty. Individuals are forced to give up a part of themselves for the group.

Any independent behavior becomes a threat. Such relationships require family members to maintain a strong degree of illusion about one another. Differences must be ignored or minimized. This kind of closeness is called fusion. The boundaries of each person are lost, and people conform to the needs of others.

There is a profound difference between fusion and a genuinely intimate relationship which respects and affirms individual differences. Fused families often take a stance of "us-against-the-world," limiting their ability to cope. If family members must always follow the "party line," they have difficulty adjusting to change. Closed to outside influences and ideas, they see others as opponents rather than as potential resources. Too much togetherness can lead to enmeshment and finally to devastating cutoffs, when the illusion of total oneness is shattered.

THE O'NEILL FAMILY

Long Day's Journey into Night, Eugene O'Neill's autobiographical play, offers a powerful example of family fusion *(Genogram 4.4).* The O'Neill genogram and the genogram of the Tyrone family in this play are identical in every detail except for the omission of O'Neill's first wife and son and the switching of names between Eugene O'Neill (called Edmund in the play) and his brother Edmund (called Eugene in the play), who died at age four. The central anxiety of the family involves the mother's drug addiction. She has just returned from a sanatorium where she has gone off morphine, and the family fears that she will return to her addiction. Family members lie to her and to one another about their fears or blame themselves, and more often one another, for the problems. Intermittently they distract themselves with other conflicts or with alcohol. The paradox is that their desperate need to distort reality to reassure themselves of their closeness is the very thing that prevents their connection. They are caught up in pretending that everything is all right, preserving their apparent togetherness, even though their inability to be honest with themselves and one another keeps them profoundly isolated. As Eugene O'Neill once said of his family, "We were a very close family—too close."

O'Neill never really resolved the fusion in his original family. He sought closeness and ran from it at the same time. Only weeks after

The O'Neill Family
Genogram 4.4

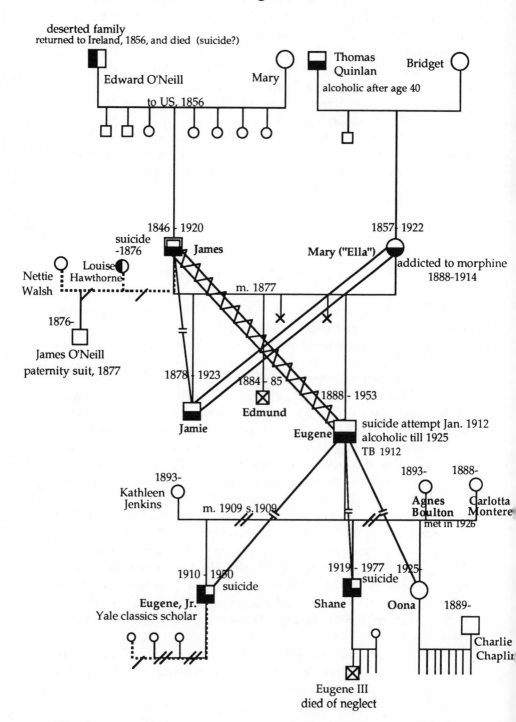

his first marriage he fled, totally abdicating his responsibilities for his wife, Kathleen, and the son she bore (this son, Eugene, Jr., first met O'Neill at age eleven). Following a tortured affair with the wife of a close friend, O'Neill married again. He was extremely possessive of his second wife, Agnes, wanting her (as he always wanted his partners) to be free of children, family, and friends. When Agnes married O'Neill, she left behind a child from her previous marriage, just as he had left his child. He was insanely jealous whenever he saw Agnes with anyone else, saying: "I want it to be not you and me but us . . . in an aloneness broken by nothing. Not even by children of our own."[18]

Even so, the couple did have two more children, Shane and Oona. Eugene ignored the children, and when this second marriage ended, he made Agnes the villain. Fusion, when it disintegrates, typically leads to disillusionment and cutoff. In the years after the divorce, O'Neill cut off not only Agnes but his children as well, refusing even to mention their names.

In his third marriage to Carlotta Monterey, O'Neill's pattern of fusion and cutoff intensified. His first meeting with Carlotta came only a few weeks after the death of his mother in 1922, which probably increased his need for closeness. Their relationship began while he was still married to Agnes. Of their first meeting, Carlotta later said: "He began to talk about his boyhood. He talked and talked, as though he'd known me all his life, but he paid no more attention to me than if I had been a chair. He talked about how he'd had no home, no mother in the real sense, no father in the real sense, and how deprived his childhood had been. Well, that's what got me into trouble with O'Neill; my maternal instinct came out—this man must be looked after, I thought. He broke my heart. I couldn't bear that this child I had adopted should have suffered these things."[19]

It is interesting that Carlotta realized their mutual projections so early. She was an "object" to fill his emptiness, and he was a "child" she could take care of. Carlotta, like O'Neill, had a desperate need to belong. Her previous marriage had foundered because of her husband's continual infidelities.

To justify abandoning his family for someone who would devote herself wholly to him, O'Neill convinced himself that his second marriage had been a fiasco and that Agnes's resentment of his divorcing her was unjustified. But once he and Carlotta were off by themselves, she having left behind her daughter, Eugene was tormented by guilt over leaving his family. Carlotta became increasingly hostile toward friends who showed sympathy for Agnes, and soon all previous relationships were cut off.

Eugene O'Neill with his second wife, Agnes Boulton, and their children, Shane and Oona. Oona married the much-older Charlie Chaplin at the age of eighteen. Archive Photos

Eugene O'Neill and his third wife, Carlotta Monterey, with whom he lived the romantic legend of two-against-the-world, an attitude that extended even to the exclusion of their children.
The Bettmann Archive

As time went on, O'Neill and Carlotta built up a two-against-the-world stance. They isolated themselves further by living abroad. Even after they returned to the United States, Carlotta worked to minimize O'Neill's contact with his children. For the next twenty-six years they developed a romantic legend: of the handsome, remote, château-dwelling O'Neill, secluded in work and in love with his devoted Carlotta. In later years, because of a Parkinson's-like illness, O'Neill was unable to write, and Carlotta's protectiveness intensified. O'Neill, cut off from all three of his children, never saw his grandchildren. Both his sons eventually committed suicide. O'Neill refused to see his daughter, Oona, after her marriage at age eighteen to the comedian and director Charlie Chaplin, who was O'Neill's contemporary. In the last years both O'Neill and Carlotta were seriously depressed; after he died, she went on alone, trying to preserve the legend herself as long as she lived.

THE SYMPTOM BEARER

In times of stress one family member may become identified as the patient or symptom bearer. This person, whom therapists often call the IP or identified patient, may actually serve as a distress signal for the whole family. The symptomatic person provides a focus for the family's emotional energy and distracts them from their own anxiety. There may even be an unconsciousness arrangement among family members for one to be symptomatic so the others have someone to care for. Family members may even take turns being symptom bearer, one person rallying to take care of another. But in rigid families the positions are likely to remain fixed, as in the case of O'Neill and Carlotta. Even when Carlotta herself had to be hospitalized and the roles should have reversed, not to be outdone in his role as patient, O'Neill, managed to get himself hospitalized at the same time in the same facility.

Headaches, depression, anxiety attacks, children's school failure or behavior problems may all provide clues to family problems in which the symptom bearer is peripheral to the primary issue. Often it is the least powerful family members who develop symptoms. When parents are having marital problems, children are likely to become the symptom bearers, particularly if the parents cannot deal with their issues themselves. Women are often the ones who become symptomatic in families, having generally less power to change systems than men, who are socialized not to acknowledge their needs or ask for help.

What this suggests is that responding only to the symptom without exploring the overall context in which it occurs may lead to not understanding what is happening. When a child's stomachaches are responded to only with medication, or school failure only with punishment and remedial help, the response may miss the real issue, which may be the child's distress over family problems.

Symptoms of illness often tell us more about anxiety in the family as a whole than about the sick individual alone. Studies have actually indicated that the time of seeking medical help for a child may have more to do with changes in the parents' anxiety than with changes in the child's state of health.

We can see an example of this in the O'Neill family, when Eugene was diagnosed with tuberculosis in 1912. Earlier in the same year, miserably alcoholic with no money and no career, he had attempted suicide, after his first humiliating divorce. This was a time of dysfunction for the entire O'Neill family. His mother's morphine addiction was severe, as was his brother Jamie's alcoholism, and his father was intensely frustrated about the limitations of his own career. In addition, the family had become increasingly isolated. While the tuberculosis obviously had a biological cause, as we know, we are more vulnerable to illness when our immune systems are stressed.

As it turned out, Eugene's TB symptoms led finally to outside attention: He was forced to enter a sanatorium, where he found supports which helped him transform his life. By the time he returned home a few months later, his goal was to be a writer, and soon he was on his way. Within a year his mother had transformed her life as well, entering a convent, where she finally overcame her twenty-eight year-addiction to morphine. While we know from the later O'Neill history that such transformations did not extend through the family, a new creativity can evolve when a closed system is sufficiently disturbed that it is opened up to new outside influence.

TRIANGLES

Stress can also cause triangular relationships to stabilize, when two people are joined together against a third. The distance or cutoff in one relationship tends to promote the need for fusion in the other. And the closeness of two sets up a conflict when a third enters the scene. Such triangles are commonplace in human interaction, almost inevitable, though they do cause problems. Molly Haskell, a New York journalist, describes the common triangle that developed among herself, her mother, who wanted fusion with her, and her husband, with whom her mother developed a deep sense of rivalry. Even though in her head Haskell knew that mother-in-law triangles are so commonplace as to be material for cartoons and jokes, she could not keep herself from getting hooked into the "ferocity" of the triangle: "It was a tragedy for me that the two people I loved most couldn't get along, yet it was a situation that I, in my own dividedness, had created. Only children . . . expect those they love to love each other, and the child in me persisted long after the adult should have taken over and accepted the inevitable. And yet, beloved of triangles, creators of triangles by our very birth, how is it possible not to keep re-creating them, and reinserting our mediating and trouble-making selves into their midst?"[20] Haskell describes with great clarity how difficult it is to be the third player when two others are alienated, how hard it is not to get caught up in the pattern yourself.

> Basically their pained looks and noises would pass each other by and hit me, like magnetized arrows, and settle in my stomach. The cocktail hour was our Armageddon, the moment when the demons that had been suppressed by sobriety and the presence of outsiders came to the surface. The first drink would pass in a strained facsimile of civilized decorum, but then Andrew, who was partially deaf anyway and whose voice had a tendency to rise with the least emotion, would unwittingly interrupt Mother. Mother would wince; I would feel her wince and cringe; I would be angry with her for her fastidiousness, angry with Andrew for his boorishness as we turned into a Tennessee Williams parody of ourselves. Andrew the elemental brute; Mother the impossibly refined hostess, and me, rigid with the sense of my two halves breaking apart, feeling vaguely responsible.

When such patterns become fixed, we think of them as "triangles" since they usually involve two people who are "close" and "agree" on things and a third who is the rejected outsider—the "bad guy" or the "helpless victim." The rules of triangles can be laid out in almost mathematical fashion: (A) The friend of my friend is my friend; (B) the friend of my enemy is my enemy; (C) the enemy of my enemy is my friend.

As Haskell points out so well, it is exceedingly difficult to be

friends with two people who are at war with each other. The sides of
the triangle have more to do with the emotional needs of the system
than with the characteristics of the players. It was not really Andrew's
"boorishness" that was the problem, but the threat he represented to
Haskell's mother's fantasy of fusion with her daughter. As Haskell
describes it, Andrew represented the antithesis of what her mother
had raised her to be: "the ladylike daughter of the Old Confederacy
who would . . . join the Garden Club and settle down and raise a
family nearby. Andrew was my rejection of that dream staring her in
the face."

A person caught between two others might indeed become symptomatic, shifting the triangle so that the two "enemies" are forced to
join together to care for the symptomatic member.

Triangular relationships are a common response of families to
stress. Two family members begin to gossip about a third. By validating each other's view about how "obnoxious" or "incompetent" the
third person is, the first two shore up their own perceptions, gain a
sense of moral righteousness, and probably lower the anxiety they
each had in dealing with the third person.

Family triangles become particularly problematic when they rigid-
ify into stable relationships. Generally, two-person relationships
seem to be inherently unstable and under stress tend to re-form as
triangles. People are likely to feel threatened by anyone who dis-
agrees with them and then to seek someone else who will validate
their view of things. They see themselves and those who agree with
them as the "good guys" in relation to a third person or several people, who get lumped together as bad, sick, or helpless.

Such triangles in families are quite predictable. Parent-child triangles may resolve marital conflict by focusing on the child, who is
labeled "sick" or "bad." In other cases children are drawn into closeness with one parent and distance from the other. Marital triangles
typically involve a child, an in-law, a friend, a lover, or a job that
becomes the focus of the couple's attention. Three-generational triangles predictably involve grandparent and grandchild siding together,
with the parent in the outside position, labeled "incompetent," "sick,"
"mean," "wrong," or "bad." And sibling triangles most often involve
"the good seed and the bad seed," the star and the loser, or the caretaker and the incompetent in relation to the parents.

In this process one person seeks support in reaction against
another, and each relationship becomes *reactive to* and *dependent on*
the other. People can no longer afford to disagree with their ally for
fear that she or he might then ally with the "enemy." In this way,
triangles become rigid, and the real difficulties between people do

not get worked out. Triangles occur in all human relationships: in work systems, friendship networks, communities, and, of course, international politics. In family relationships triangles can become particularly fierce and painful because members are so dependent on one another for support and self-validation throughout their lives and because families, unlike other systems, are entered only by birth, marriage, or adoption and can be left only by death, if even then.

THE BEETHOVEN FAMILY

The family of the composer Ludwig van Beethoven was dominated throughout by triangles *(Genogram 4.5)*. Ludwig's paternal grandfather and his only surviving son, Johann, formed a close unit excluding the mother, who had been sent to a cloister for her alcoholism. Ludwig's mother, Maria Magdalena Keverich formed an alliance with her mother after the early death of her father. Both of Beethoven's parents were thus tied to their own same-sex parents, who feared losing them and disapproved strenuously of their marriage on the pretext that their partners were unworthy. (Maria had initially married at sixteen, but her first husband and an infant son died soon after.) The marriage of Ludwig's parents thus occurred in the context of two primary triangles with their own parents.

Maria and Johann van Beethoven had seven children, only three of whom survived. The first child, Ludwig Maria, died at six days of age in 1769. The second, also named Ludwig Maria van Beethoven, was born on December 16, 1770, but he grew up always confusing his birth date and that of his dead older brother and namesake. Thus from birth it seems Beethoven felt part of a sibling triangle with his parents and his dead infant brother, whose name he bore and with whom he felt he could never compare. *(Figure 4.2)*.

Beethoven was also involved in a three-generational triangle, with his father and paternal grandfather, also named Ludwig *(Figure 4.3)*. The grandfather was a talented singer, the choirmaster of Bonn, and a successful wine merchant. Though he died when young Ludwig was only three, the boy continued to idolize him with something bordering on hero worship. The grandfather had indeed been talented and successful but also domineering and intrusive toward his only surviving son, Johann, who was amiable and submissive in his youth but lacked talent or initiative. To make matters worse, the grandfather repeatedly broadcast his contemptuous view that Johann would

The Beethoven Family
Genogram 4.5

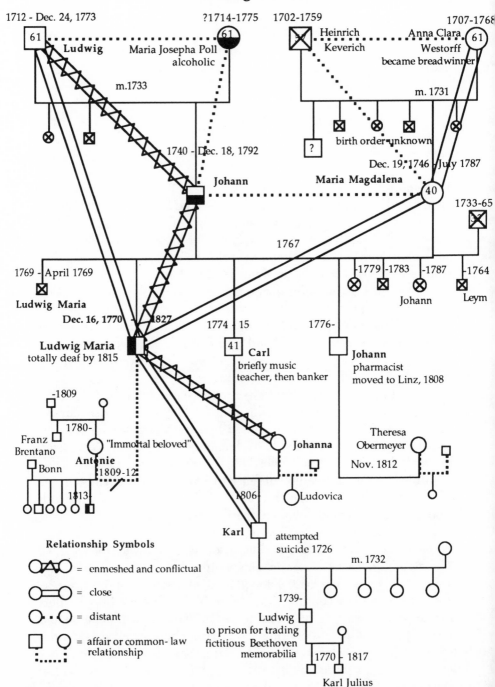

Relationship Symbols

= enmeshed and conflictual

= close

= distant

= affair or common-law relationship

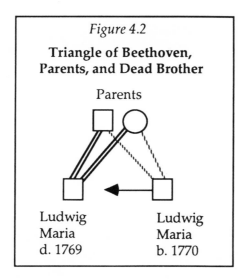

Figure 4.2

**Triangle of Beethoven,
Parents, and Dead Brother**

Parents

Ludwig
Maria
d. 1769

Ludwig
Maria
b. 1770

amount to nothing, calling him Johann the Loafer. Johann fulfilled his father's prophecy by becoming an abusive drunkard, cruel and arbitrary in his demands on young Ludwig to practice, and an embarrassment to the whole family.

In the nuclear family, Beethoven as the eldest child ended up in a painful triangle with his parents. Although he defended his father fiercely against outsiders and intervened desperately when the police came to arrest him for drunkenness, he could hardly have avoided being drawn into a triangle with his parents on the side of his sad,

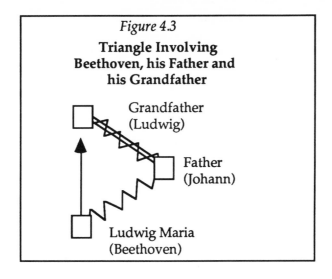

Figure 4.3

**Triangle Involving
Beethoven, his Father and
his Grandfather**

Grandfather
(Ludwig)

Father
(Johann)

Ludwig Maria
(Beethoven)

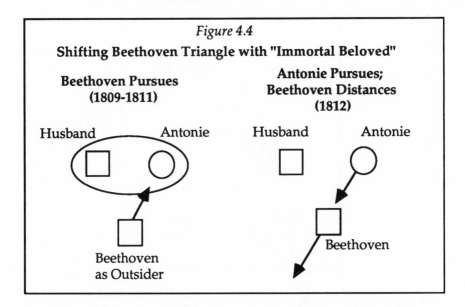

Figure 4.4

Shifting Beethoven Triangle with "Immortal Beloved"

Beethoven Pursues
(1809-1811)

Antonie Pursues;
Beethoven Distances
(1812)

Husband   Antonie

Beethoven
as Outsider

Husband   Antonie

Beethoven

gentle, long-suffering mother, a triangle from which he tried to escape as a child by isolating himself. His mother's death of tuberculosis, when he was seventeen, placed him in charge of the family. The father at this point largely gave up his grip on reality and abandoned himself to his alcoholism. Ludwig became his father's guardian. He was even paid Johann's pension, embarrassing him and greatly humiliating his father. Nowhere in his extensive correspondence does Beethoven refer to his father by name, and when Johann was dying, Beethoven left home.

The relationships of Beethoven's adult life were also characterized by triangles. Early on he became involved with a series of unattainable women (either married or otherwise attached), in which relationships he was naturally the outsider. Sometimes being the outsider in a triangle is preferable because one can play the role of romantic hero without actually having to make a commitment, and this may have been true for Beethoven.

This pattern continued for years until in 1812 he became involved with a married woman, Antonie Brentano, the mother of four children *(Figure 4.4)*. When she finally offered to give up everything for him, Beethoven retreated.[21] Brentano, whose love for Beethoven seems to have developed in the wake of the loss of her father, gave birth to a severely impaired son nine months after the tumultuous ending of their affair. The rest of her life was dedicated to the care of this son. From the time Beethoven broke with Brentano he never

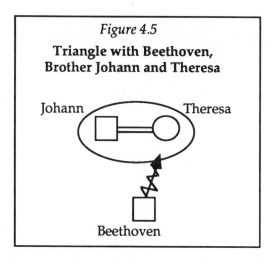

Figure 4.5

**Triangle with Beethoven,
Brother Johann and Theresa**

had another serious involvement with a woman. Instead he turned back on his family of origin and became embroiled in several destructive and intrusive triangular relationships in his brothers' families.

He almost never referred to his youngest brother, Johann, by name, referring to him usually by leaving a blank space or using an epithet such as "pseudobrother," "braineater," "my ass of a brother," or "brother Cain." Immediately after ending the relationship with Brentano, Beethoven traveled to Linz, where Johann was living with a woman, Theresa Obermeyer. In a state of moral outrage he demanded that Johann break off this relationship *(Figure 4.5)*. When Johann refused, Beethoven went to the authorities and obtained a police order compelling Theresa to leave Linz if the relationship continued. Johann foiled this interference by marrying Theresa.

The triangles involving Beethoven and his other brother Carl's family were even stormier. The marriage between Carl and his wife, Johanna, had been full of strife for years. Ludwig had apparently tried to prevent this marriage also, although at other times he played the role of protector to Johanna against Carl's violence. Like their father, Carl often beat his son, Karl, to make him obey, and Johanna was not spared either. In 1811 Carl had denounced his wife, charging that she had stolen money from him. She was convicted and sentenced to a month of house arrest, even though any "stolen" money would have been her own because of the large dowry and inheritance she brought into the marriage.

Beethoven would listen to nothing negative about this brother, though some of his friends believed that Carl was taking advantage of him and even being dishonest. When one friend finally took it upon himself to speak directly about the brother's mistreatment of Beethoven, the latter closed his ears and refused to speak to the friend for ten years.

In 1815, the day before Carl died, he wrote a will providing for Johanna and Ludwig to be coguardians for his son, Karl. Beethoven, learning about this, intervened and compelled his brother to change the will, leaving him sole guardian. Later that day, realizing that Ludwig wanted to exclude Johanna from joint guardianship, Carl added another paragraph to his will, which read: "Having learned that my brother . . . desires after my death to take wholly to himself my son Karl, and wholly to withdraw him from the supervision and training of his mother, and inasmuch as the best of harmony does not exist between my brother and my wife, I have found it necessary to add to my will that I by no means desire that my son be taken from his mother, but that he shall always . . . remain with his mother, to which end the guardianship of him is to be exercised by her as well as my brother."[22]

In spite of this, Beethoven moved immediately after Carl's death to attain sole custody of his nephew and to have Johanna declared unfit even for visiting privileges *(Figure 4.6)*. The struggle went on for years, with the nephew trapped between his loyalty to and affection for his mother and his dutiful respect for his strange but famous and seemingly well-meaning uncle. Ludwig was at this time an unkempt, eccentric bachelor of forty-five, preoccupied with composing, though he had alienated most of his patrons by then. He was totally deaf, often in pain, and in very poor general health, not the best condition in which to take responsibility for a nine-year-old. Over the course of various court battles Johanna won back custody from Beethoven, who continued his pursuit of the boy and retrieved him again. Ludwig was intrusive, abusive, inconsistent, and extremely overprotective of his nephew. He used his brother's earlier unproved accusation of Johanna's embezzlement as justification for obtaining custody. He became convinced that she had destructive powers, saw himself as a divinely authorized and heroic rescuer of his poor, unhappy nephew, and applauded his nephew whenever he repudiated his mother.

It is interesting and perhaps predictable that when on several occasions Beethoven moved toward a rapprochement with Johanna, Karl reacted negatively *(Figure 4.7)*. Such is the nature of triangles that even though they may be hurtful and destructive for all involved, people resist change. Painful as it must have been for Karl to be

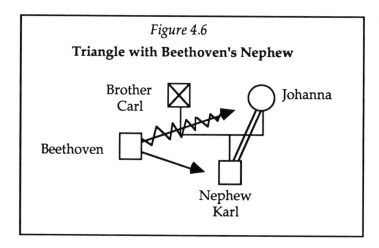

Figure 4.6

Triangle with Beethoven's Nephew

pulled between his mother and uncle, he was also threatened when they seemed to draw together. In 1822, when Johanna became ill and was unable to pay for her medicines, Beethoven took over a portion of a debt she owed and the next year determined to help her financially.

Karl, by then sixteen years old, protested vigorously against this proposed generosity toward his mother and maligned her, in an attempt to forestall a rapprochement between his uncle and her. His fear of closeness between them is understandable. As long as they were fighting over him, his role was pivotal. If they joined forces, he might end up the outsider.

Karl and his mother had become estranged after she gave birth out of wedlock in 1820 to a daughter conceived with a well-to-do man. The child was named Ludovica, an interesting choice of name! Very possibly the intense hostilities between Ludwig and Johanna reflected a strong underlying attraction. As Beethoven continued to move toward Johanna, Karl's feeling of being threatened seems to have diminished also, and for some time there was a note of reconciliation between them. The timing of this reconciliation coincided precisely with his composing the "Ode to Joy" for his Ninth Symphony. This was the most harmonious period in the relationship of Karl and Ludwig. Karl worked as his uncle's secretary and spent weekends and summers with him.

However, by 1825 Beethoven had begun to be suspicious of Karl and fearful that he was again seeing his mother. A number of factors may have intensified the triangle at this particular time. Perhaps their good relationship frightened Beethoven, who seems indeed to have been petrified of closeness, as much as he coveted it. Perhaps Karl's

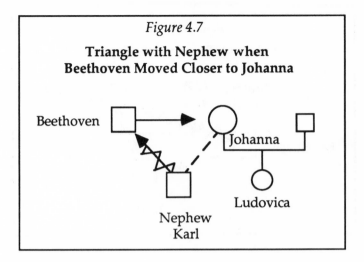

Figure 4.7

**Triangle with Nephew when
Beethoven Moved Closer to Johanna**

becoming a young adult was threatening to Beethoven, or perhaps Beethoven's deafness increased his sense of isolation and power-lessness, in addition to the fact that he was drinking heavily. Perhaps also there were changes in Johanna's life that we do not know about.

The conflicts between uncle and nephew reached a climax when Beethoven began withholding money from Karl, who was now nine-teen, and pursuing him everywhere. Karl then began sneaking visits to his mother, exacerbating Beethoven's worst fears. He would not leave Karl alone. Finally, at the end of the summer, Karl, despairing of any other solution, tried to shoot himself in the head. He survived but was hospitalized, and his feelings of being tormented by Beetho-ven were made public. The crisis seems to have relieved pressure from the system. For Beethoven the dream of fusion with Karl—the dream of being his father—was broken. But the suicide attempt brought in outside influence from doctors, who confronted Beetho-ven with his nephew's feelings. Though Beethoven sought other explanations for the suicide attempt, Karl's explanation was "weari-ness of imprisonment." After this Karl became better able to insist on his right to have his own relationship with his mother: "I do not want to hear anything that is derogatory to her; it is not for me to be her judge. . . . In no event shall I treat her with greater coldness than has been the case heretofore. . . . It is self evident that [seeing my mother] will not prevent you and me from seeing each other as often as you wish."[23] Karl decided to enter the military, and so he did a few months later, with Beethoven's help.

Perhaps anticipating his own mortality, Beethoven seems to have

Ludwig van Beethoven. Beethoven's passion, whether in his music or lived out in his tumultuous personal relationships, was a reflection of intense generational closeness and conflict in his family. Brown Brothers

The mother of Beethoven, after a painting by Caspar Benedict Beckenkamp. Engraving by E. Heinemann. Culver Pictures, Inc.

put his life in slightly better perspective during the last months. He ended on good terms with Karl, who became his sole inheritor, and he also reconciled with Johanna, who was the only family member present at his death. Three days before he died, he wrote a codicil to his will specifying that she would inherit his entire estate if Karl died unmarried, as appeared possible, since he was in the military.

Beethoven's life reflects two classic patterns of triangulation. Prior to 1812 in his romantic relationships with women he played the role of outsider, the "other" lover—a peripheral, safe role which protected him from the responsibility and dangerous power of his childhood triangles. After he gave up the dream of having a family of his own, he intruded himself aggressively into other people's relationships, as with the families of both his brothers, attempting fusion and creating conflict and cutoff all around him, even though he was intending to create a loving family. In the end, possibly through the remedial efforts of Johanna and Karl, he seems to have achieved, for the first time, some sense of connection without fusion or triangling.

Without our knowing the history of triangles in the Beethoven family it would be extremely difficult to fathom Karl's suicide attempt or the stormy pattern of Beethoven's relationship to his nephew. Tracking the patterns of communication, fusion, cutoff, and symptom development in your family can open up new perspectives not only on your family, but one hopes, on your role in family triangles.

Here are questions to consider in trying to understand how the communication and relationships in your family work. As with the questions in other chapters, they are meant to suggest rather than to be exhaustive.

■ What were the rules of communication in your family? Who spoke to whom about what?

■ What topics were taboo? How were the rules of communication transmitted? Who conveyed them? Were they overt or covert?

■ Which family members were extremely close?

■ Which were always in conflict? Who didn't speak to whom? How did others react when two were in conflict or not speaking?

■ Who were the most frequent symptom bearers? What symptoms did they show? How did the family respond to symptoms?

■ What were the rules for each gender in your family? What did they view as the ideal male and the ideal female? Were there family members who broke out of the traditional gender stereotypes? Were there women or men whose symptoms might have reflected their difficulty accepting gender constraints (e.g., a poetic, gentle man who became alcoholic or a feisty, brilliant woman worn down by having no outlet beyond child care and housekeeping)?

■ What were the splits and alliances in the family. Who was in a caretaker-caretakee relationship? A pursuer-distancer relationship? An intense love-hate relationship?

■ How did family members react to change? By silence? Rigidity? Shutting down? Trying to hold on to the past? Escaping into pipe dreams of the future? Blaming others? Blaming themselves?

■ What labels did each family member have: "battleax," "sad sack," "miser," "weirdo"?

■ Were there certain times of great stress and change in your family? Can you track the family story (stories) of those periods? Who could help you get information about those times?

■ How did your family react to stress? Did the members draw together? Did they become more separate? Did certain family members have such strong reactions as keeping silent, talking constantly, changing the subject, or becoming authoritarian?

■ What were the major family triangles? Were there particular types of triangles in your family that repeated over the generations: husband/wife/mother-in-law; husband/wife/affair; father/mother/sick-bad-special child; two close siblings and a third outsider sibling?

LOSS

The Pivotal Human Experience

The single most important thing to know about Americans . . . is that . . .
[they] think death is optional.

—Jane Walmsley, *Brit-Think; Ameri-Think*

If I do not connect myself with my own past . . . I will remain adrift from
it. Those whom I have loved in the past cannot catch hold of me, for they
are dead. It is I who must catch them.

—Audre Lorde, *Sister Outsider*

M ore than any other human experience, loss puts us in touch
with what matters in our own lives. Coming to terms with
death is the most difficult experience we face in life.

Sometimes it seems more difficult to lose another than to die ourselves, for without that other, what do our own lives mean? When
someone important to us dies, it can make us realize how vain our
pursuits are in comparison with the people in our lives—especially
our families. Facing death can be a profoundly life-changing experience, stimulating us to savor our lives more fully and define our prior-
ities more clearly.

We all hope that our deaths and those of our family members will
occur at a point when we are at peace with one another and when
there is a sense of completion about relationships. But we know that
frequently this doesn't happen. Untimely deaths are especially difficult to integrate. Regrets about an unfinished relationship can haunt
a person throughout a lifetime, and when accounts are accounts left
unsettled, a great vacuum may remain. As Robert Anderson's protag-

onist says in the play *I Never Sang for My Father*: "Death ends a life, but not a relationship, which struggles on in the survivor's mind, seeking some resolution which it may never find."[1]

By examining the multigenerational effects of loss, we can learn a great deal about how families operate, what happens when they get stuck, and how we can change these patterns. Loss may strengthen survivors, bringing out their creativity, spurring them on to accomplishment, or it may leave behind a destructive legacy, all the more powerful if it is not dealt with. We may follow patterns of loss set up by earlier generations that we know nothing about.

The images we carry with us of funerals and of the dead are an important part of our heritage and our identity. How our families deal with death is perhaps our best clue to their fundamental values, strengths, and vulnerabilities. We have already seen how pivotal deaths were in the role that Benjamin Franklin and the Wright brothers played in their families. We saw the key impact of early parental death on Queen Victoria and with Franklin the important bearing that coincidental deaths had on other family relationships. We saw the triangles that evolved in the Beethoven family in the aftermath of loss. This chapter will call upon several well-known families, Freud, the Kennedys, the Hepburns, and Elizabeth Barrett Browning, to illustrate the legacy of loss across generations.

In a sense all families are marked by their shared losses. At times of loss, family members are generally required to deal with one another in an intimate way at a vulnerable time. This can be particularly difficult for families that are not close. Siblings who have had little to do with each other for years are suddenly forced to share wrenching experiences. This has the potential to bring a family together, but it can also cause old conflicts to resurface. While a death in the family provides an opportunity to focus on the essential bonds, to reopen relationships that have closed down, to rework old relationships, to risk saying what has until now been left unsaid, such openings can intensify old hurts. As with other pivotal family experiences, if things do not get better, they will usually get worse.

Death, of course, is not the only loss. Marital separation or divorce, chronic illness, lack of a job or a house to live in, or becoming handicapped also involves loss: loss of our dreams and expectations. All change in life requires loss. We must give up certain relationships, plans, possibilities in order to have others. And all losses require mourning, which acknowledges the giving up, transforms the experience to take into ourselves what is essential, and allows us to move on.

Mourning is healthy. When families do not adequately mourn their losses, they cannot get on with life. Instead the feelings go underground. Family members may blame themselves or one another for a death; they may try to mold others into replacements for their lost person or keep themselves from experiencing closeness again. It is not death itself but what happens when families try to avoid the experience that becomes problematic. Families can adapt to even the most traumatic losses. It is when they cannot acknowledge the loss and reorganize that they become stuck.

MOURNING

Our culture's denial of death often means that we do not discuss how we want to die and how we want to be memorialized. A great many people make no wills at all, in spite of the extreme hardship this omission can have on survivors. The quality of dying is ignored in the service of prolonging life by whatever medical means necessary. The end of life often occurs in a cold, sterile medical setting that allows little consideration for the family's intense personal experience. And families are often physically separated and thus even more vulnerable to disruption and isolation in the aftermath of loss.

Learning the facts about a death can be an important first step in coming to terms with it. If facts about the death have not been admitted, family members are likely to develop their own myths about the death.

Sharing the experience of the loss and finding some way to put it in context are also important. A part of this sharing is joint storytelling about the life and death of the dead person. Such sharing helps families integrate the loss by promoting their sense of familial, cultural, and human connectedness and empowering them to regain a sense of themselves as moving in time from the past through the present into the future. To develop a sense of control, mastery, and the ability to survive in the face of loss, family members may need to open up relationships with the living and learn more about the family in general: its history, its culture, and the perspectives and stories of different family members. In some African cultures there is a ritual in which each family member reviews her or his history with the dying family member, including their conflicts, as a part of saying goodbye. I think it would be a good idea if we could institutionalize such a practice because of the way it would normalize the complexity of our intimate relationships—with closeness and conflict mixed together.

Sharing memories and stories of the dead can help family members develop more benign, less traumatic perspectives on the role of loss in their lives. It seems important for families to be free to remember as well as to let go of memories. One of the most difficult aspects of denied or unresolved mourning is that it leaves families with no way to make sense of their experience. If events cannot be mentioned or if the family "party line" cannot be expanded upon, the next generation has no models or guidelines for integrating later losses. Family stories are an important facilitator and enhancer of the integration of loss.[2]

Families also need to find ways to reorganize their system without the dead person, a complex and often painful reorientation process. This may entail a shift in caretaking roles or leadership functions, changes in the social network, shifts in family focus, as when an only child dies, or an emotional reorganization of the generational hierarchy, as when the last grandparent dies.

Finally, moving beyond loss involves a reinvestment in other relationships and life pursuits. Surviving family members, strengthened by the shared experience of loss, can focus more clearly on what they want to do with their lives and relationships.

Most funeral rituals, incorporating traditions that link previous generations, provide family members with a cushion of belonging at the same time that they are experiencing the pain of loss. They provide a special time out of time—that is, an encapsulated time frame which offers an opportunity for experiencing the overwhelming emotions that death evokes, while also containing such an expression. Attending family funerals, like other rituals of family transition, is one of the best ways to learn about your family. They can help you see family history in the making, as the family stories of the death and other deaths get told and retold. As family members gather from near and far, you see who the key definers of your family's stories are, and you see relationships in action that may otherwise be dormant.

There is a story of a Chinese worker who asked his Western employer for permission to attend the funeral of a cousin. The employer granted permission but asked contemptuously whether the worker planned to follow the ancient Chinese custom of leaving a bowl of rice at the graveside. "Certainly," replied the servant. Laughing, the employer asked when the cousin would eat the rice. "Oh," said the worker, "about the same time that your aunt who died last week smells the flowers you placed on her grave."[3]

Cultures differ greatly in their patterns of mourning, in their rituals and the length of time considered appropriate to "complete" the
mourning process. In certain Mediterranean countries, such as
Greece and Italy, women have traditionally worn black for the rest of
their lives after their husbands' deaths. In Italy it is not at all uncommon for family members to jump into the grave when the coffin is
lowered. In India, even into the twentieth century, widows were
expected to throw themselves onto the funeral pyre, sacrifices for
their husbands' lives after death.

At the opposite extreme, some Americans of British ancestry tend
to value a "no muss, no fuss" way of experiencing the loss of family
members. Among such groups, funerals are carried out in a more
pragmatic way. These people tend to experience their last illnesses
in hospitals, where they are not an inconvenience to their families
and where their dependence doesn't force emotional obligations. For
other ethnic groups, however, a death outside the family's emotional
and physical environment is experienced as a double tragedy.

American culture has been moving increasingly toward minimizing
death rituals and expressions of mourning. Through legislation, custom, and public health and work regulations, considerable social control is exercised over the process. Funeral rituals have been taken
over and commercialized by the funeral industry. The allowable leave
for bereavement in the workplace (usually one to three days) severely
constrains families from the traditional attitudes and practices of their
cultural groups. A failure to carry out death rituals can contribute to
a family's experience of unresolved loss, a danger to both personal
health and family relationships.

In the normal experience of acute grief, family members experience a wide range of symptoms: numbness, tiredness, weakness,
digestive symptoms, loss of appetite, a general sense of unreality, a
feeling of emotional distance from others, an intense preoccupation
with images of the dead person, irritability, anger, guilt, restlessness,
aimlessness and searching, and a painful lack of ability to maintain
organized routines of behavior. All these symptoms are normal. It is
when they do not occur or do not stop that we should worry. As seen
in Chapter 4, however, symptoms do not occur in a vacuum. Family
relationships influence symptoms, and symptoms influence family
relationships. We are likely to react, and under the stress of loss to
overreact, to the symptoms of other family members.

Some people may avoid contacts that remind them of the dead
person. Men in particular often develop tension and tightness in trying to keep themselves from "breaking down." If the memories and

feelings do finally break through, the pain may be that much more intense. For example, when the Kennedys lost Joe, their eldest son, Joe, Sr., was the one who handled all arrangements, "protected" Rose, and kept the family together. Sometime later, when he received his son's last letter from the front, his composure disintegrated. Years afterward Rose said that until the letter came, he had been able to block the death from his mind. After that their roles reversed. As she began to recover from her grief, Joe slipped deeper and deeper into depression. Her religious faith helped her find her way, but his faith was not enough to console him. For months he shut himself away, refusing to read the newspaper, listen to the radio, or talk with friends and family.

The emotional and physical burdens that follow death still seem to be "women's work." Women typically handle the social and emotional tasks of bereavement, from the expression of grief and caretaking of the terminally ill to meeting the needs of surviving family members for support and nurturance, while men arrange for the funeral, choose the coffin, pay the fees, and in general handle all the "administrative" tasks of death except for providing the food. While women are free to weep openly, men may deny, withdraw, and avoid their grief, fearing a loss of control. The reactions of each make the other uncomfortable. Men generally take refuge in their work and distance from their wives' open mourning, while women experience their husbands' pulling away as a double loss. This kind of skewed pattern of grieving that is the norm in our culture breeds isolation for family members, who cannot share their experience of loss and are kept from one of the most important healing resources: one another. As one woman put it referring to the pain of the loss of one of her three sons, "Through my eyes flow the tears for our whole family." When a family member must grieve alone, the pain is that much worse.

The movie *Steel Magnolias* has a touching example of a typical gender difference in dealing with death when the mother, at her daughter's funeral, tells the story of her daughter's death to her women friends, the men having left. "They turned off the machines. Drum [the father] left. He couldn't take it. Jackson [the husband] left. It's amusing. Men are supposed to be made out of steel or something. I just sat there. I just held Shelby's hand. There was no noise. No tremble. Just peace. I realize as a woman how lucky I am. I was there when that wonderful creature drifted into my life and I was there when she drifted out. It was the most precious moment of my life." This powerful telling of the story of the death helps the mother and the other women to see the death in the context of the life cycle.

The mother's sense of privilege at being part of the experience of her daughter's death, as agonizing as it is for her, gives meaning to her life. Men in families are often deprived by our culture from sharing in the richness of these nodal life experiences that are seen as women's responsibility. Society's denial of male vulnerability and dependency needs and the sanctions against men's emotional expressiveness undoubtedly contribute to marital distress after the loss of a family member and to the high rate of serious illness and suicide for men following the deaths of their spouses.

The different coping strategies of men and women in dealing with loss can increase marital strain, even for couples with strong and stable relationships.[4] When our culture allows the full range of human experiences in bereavement as in other areas of family life, we will all surely benefit.

FAMILY RESPONSE TO LOSS

If you want to understand your family, you will need to examine how its members have dealt with loss and how losses have influenced your family relationships.

The impact of a death depends on many factors. The untimely death of the young, particularly a child, seems to be the most devastating and incomprehensible loss that a family can experience. It can have a cataclysmic effect on the parents' health and marriage and leave lifelong scars for the siblings. Because small children are so utterly dependent, guilt feelings tend to be especially strong in the survivors. The deceased child is often remembered as perfect and becomes the receptacle of all the parents' hopes and dreams, creating an idealized image which is difficult for surviving children to live up to. For parents also it is probably the greatest loss we can endure. It has been said that when your parent dies, you have lost your past, but when your child dies, you have lost your future. As Joe Kennedy said about the death of his firstborn son, Joe, Jr., "Now it's all over, because all my plans for my own future were all tied up with young Joe, and that has gone smash. . . . When the young bury the old, time heals the pain and sorrow; but when the process is reversed the sorrow remains forever."[5]

The death of a child at any age seems unnatural. However, a death in the "prime of life" also brings special hardships, and the functions the lost person had as caretaker or financial support may be hard to replace. For the spouse there is the loss of a helpmate and companion; for the children there is the loss of a parent, perhaps the breadwinner; for the siblings and friends there is the loss of an age-mate with whom they expected to grow old; for the aging parents there is the wrenching of the death's being "off time."

Not all deaths are equally traumatic. The manner of death also affects the family's response. When we are prepared as much as we can be, when the deceased has lived a long and fruitful life, and when it is an "easy," peaceful death, with minimal pain, recriminations, or unfinished business, the family comes more easily to acceptance.

Sudden death provides little opportunity to prepare or say goodbye. It is almost as if the person has been ripped out of the system. A murder, a suicide, or an accident, where others feel responsible, leaves deep scars on a family. The more sudden, traumatic, or stigmatized the loss, the more widespread its likely impact. Such deaths leave a legacy of stigma, guilt, blame, and anguish for the survivors.

Suicides are particularly catastrophic. The true circumstances of the death are frequently kept secret. This secrecy compounds the emotions the family already feels when a life is ended intentionally and isolates the family further.[6]

At the other extreme are the deaths which drain family caretaking resources and require the family to live in a state of prolonged uncertainty. In such cases the family may come to wish the person dead, to see an end to the pain and agony as well as relief from their burdens. The strain on the caretakers takes energy away from all other relationships and may leave a residue of guilt and ambivalence.

Among the most difficult of all are ambiguous losses, as when a family member disappears. When there is some hope that the person may still be alive, the psychological presence may remain in the family for years. Fantasies develop about the lost person's survival and return. A similar situation is created in the case of Alzheimer's disease or any other catastrophic, degenerative illness or brain injury, in which the person may be physically present but psychologically absent for years before death.[7] Ambiguous losses such as these are extremely difficult to mourn and integrate.

The context in which the death occurs, including the state of family relationships at the time of death and other associated stress factors, will eventually also influence a family's response to death. When there is family conflict or estrangement at the time of death, a family may be left with a bitter legacy which is hard to move beyond.

Historical circumstances may also be important. For example, Robert Kennedy's death in 1968 came at a time of great social upheaval and disorganization in our country, especially among the young. Many of the children in his family were then in their adolescence, a time when their vulnerability to drugs and other reckless behavior put them at much greater risk than was experienced at the time of John Kennedy's death.

When two or more major events occur at the same time, the trauma of the experience is geometrically intensified. For example, the birth of Alice Roosevelt Longworth, discussed in Chapter 4, coinciding with the death of Roosevelt's wife and mother on the same day, surely intensified the meaning of each of those experiences and was, of course, compounded when Alice Roosevelt's daughter was born on this anniversary forty-one years later.

Sometimes such coincidental anniversary events seem to point up almost mystical connections. Both Thomas Jefferson and John Adams died on the fiftieth anniversary of the Declaration of Independence, July 4, 1826. John Kennedy was shot on the exact day that both his paternal great-grandfathers died. Anthropologist Gregory Bateson's middle brother committed suicide on the birthday of the eldest brother, who had died a hero in World War I. Such coincidences intensify the meaning of the death and may perpetuate a legacy of family anxiety around the anniversary date. As individuals we may also fear that we will die at the same ages or same times of year as parents or siblings with whom we have been identified. If deaths have occurred around Christmas or another important family holiday, they may distort the experience of that day for years to come.

The role and function of the lost person in the family and the resources available to fill in for the dead person will also influence the family's ability to integrate the loss. A person who has been a scapegoat may be hard to mourn. An alcoholic father who dies in a car crash may leave a legacy of guilt and resentment in which the death is compounded by the painful years that the family lived through with him. It is also difficult for the survivors to compete with the ghost of a dead hero—a supermother, a successful son—or anyone who has been a central figure in the family.

The loss of a parent or primary caretaker presents the most difficult challenge. Central caretaking functions must be assumed by someone else. Single parents must find someone to care for children while they are at work and must determine how to manage an economic future with just one salary. Replacing the emotional loss of the parent is still another matter. Sometimes an uncle or aunt or grandparents can fill in the gap. If practical or emotional resources are unavailable, the loss can be greatly compounded.

For example, the death of Robert Kennedy left a much greater leadership vacuum in the Kennedy family than did the death of his brother John. After John's death Robert took over the caretaking role for his parents, his sister-in-law and her children, and many others in the family. He even expressed a relief to have the chance to succeed on his own: "Finally I feel that I'm out from under the shadow of my brother. Now at least I feel that I've made it on my own. All these years I never really believed it was me that did it, but Jack."[8]

But when Robert himself died five years later, Ethel was pregnant with their eleventh child, and there was no one who could fill in for him with his children, those of their sister Pat (who had separated from her husband, Peter Lawford, the day John was shot), or the other members of the family who needed support. Ted Kennedy had always been the baby, the "spoiled kid brother." Although he did eventually grow into a family leader, he was not prepared to do so at the time, and the tragedy left a vacuum in the entire extended family. Ted knew himself how tenuous his hold was. He told an aide: "I can't let go. If I let go, Ethel will let go, and my mother will let go, and my sisters will let go. . . ." It had become a house of cards, and he could not assume leadership of the family. A nephew later said: "We felt a lot of bitterness toward him. It was probably unfair. There was no real reason for it except that he couldn't fill Uncle Bobby's shoes and didn't try." What followed for the Kennedy family were years of turmoil and problems for the next generation.

If family members cannot talk to one another or to others outside the family, if myth, secrecy, and taboo surround a death, they will become more vulnerable to future losses. When families communicate openly about the death (no matter what the circumstances), and when they participate together in rituals that have meaning for them (e.g., funeral rites and visits to the grave), death becomes easier to take. Attempts to protect children or "vulnerable" members from the experience are likely to make mourning even more difficult.

THE HEPBURN FAMILY

The Hepburn family (*Genogram 5.1*) provides a striking example of a family's creative responses to the most stigmatizing of all deaths, a

The Hepburn Family
Genogram 5.1

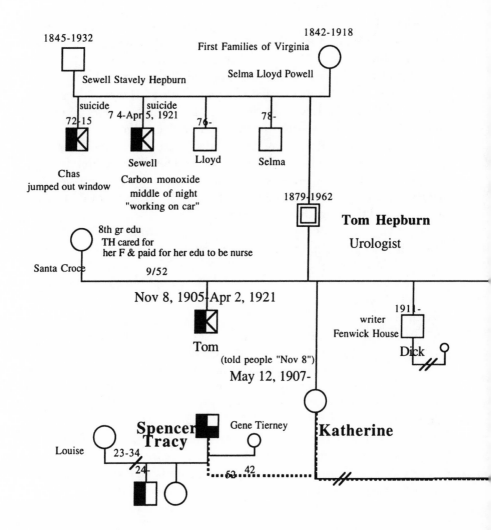

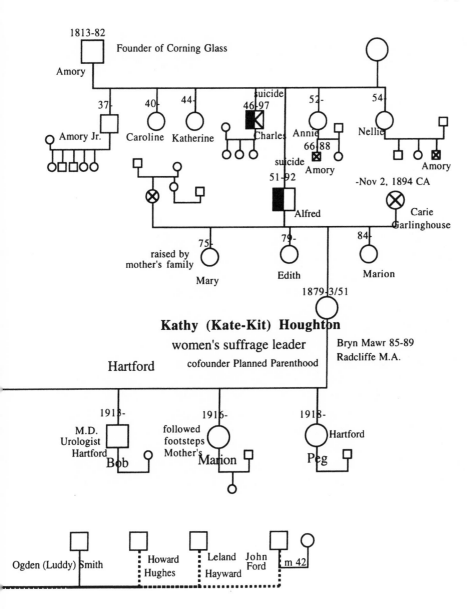

suicide, even as the tragedy constricted their functioning. A most successful and independent thinking family, their roots were in New England and Virginia. They had founded Corning Glass and Houghton Mifflin Publishers.

When Katharine Hepburn was almost fourteen, her older brother, Tom, hanged himself while he and Kate were visiting a close family friend on their Easter vacation. Kate was the one to find her brother's body. He had torn and braided his bedsheet making a rope strong enough to hang himself. That morning the father, a successful urologist, told reporters: "My son was normal in mind and body. The taking of his own life can be accounted for only from a medical point, that he was suddenly afflicted with adolescent insanity."[9] Kate was obsessed with absolving her brother and reminded her father that he had once told a story about a black man who could constrict his neck muscles to avoid dying at the hands of a lynch mob. She recalled that Tom had been intrigued with the story and had tried to hang himself once before, insisting later that he was trying a stunt. Dr. Hepburn then made a new announcement to reporters, explaining away the suicide as an accident resulting from a foolish schoolboy stunt: "I had entirely forgotten that he considered himself an expert in hanging by the neck in such a way as to look as if he were dying, to the entertainment of his brothers and sisters." Dr. Hepburn went on to say that his son must have been "rehearsing" for a performance that night, though the death occurred at 4 A.M., showing the incredible lengths a family may go to to avoid facing a painful reality. In her autobiography, written seventy years later, Kate still says he died "under strange circumstances" and his death "has remained unexplained." She discusses how Tom's death must have tortured her parents, but her mother never mentioned Tom again, and her father also never once discussed the death with her. Hepburn said death seemed to separate her from the world as she had known it.[10]

Tom's suicide, which was obviously excruciatingly painful for the family, drew the family into itself. Tom had always been special but also vulnerable. He was the family's great hope. His father had been pressuring him to follow in his footsteps and enter Yale Medical School that fall, and Tom had been hesitant about attending. Since childhood he had suffered various physical and emotional problems, including bouts of confusion and depression.

The parents had withdrawn Tom early from school to protect him and had withdrawn Katharine as well to serve as his companion. This set a pattern for Katharine as caretaker, though she was the younger of the two siblings.

What Hepburn doesn't mention was that Tom's was the fourth suicide in her family, her father's brother having committed suicide six years earlier, her maternal grandfather when her mother was fourteen, and that grandfather's brother five years later. A fifth suicide, of Katherine's second paternal uncle, Sewell, followed three days after Tom's, on April 5, 1921, before they had even had the funeral for Tom. This death again was explained away as an accident. It was said that Sewell, who killed himself with carbon monoxide in the middle of the night in his garage, "had a heart attack while working on his car." As with Tom's "stunt," the fact that it was the middle of the night was left out.

Another strange fact is that from the time Tom died Katherine began using his birthday as her own and did so for many years, until finally telling the truth in her autobiography a few years ago. The parents apparently went along with this. After the suicide Katherine and her siblings were tutored at home until she left for Bryn Mawr. The family turned more inward in their pain. Indeed, there now developed a kind of cut off between the family and Katherine's maternal aunt, Edith. The two sisters, Kit and Edith, had been extremely close since childhood; this bond intensified when they were orphaned and Kit became the "mother" for Edith. Both had married men who had gone to Hopkins medical school with Edith, and the families had spent summers together for years. But Edith had deeply objected to her brother-in-law's physical punishment of his children, and had felt him overbearing to his son, who was now dead.

Kit and Edith's father, Fred, had shot himself in the head when Kit was fourteen. Thus, Kit and her daughter Kate experienced a suicide at about the same age. The grandfather had felt humiliated in the business by his older brother, Amory, who had inherited the business from his father. Kit's mother, Carrie, died tragically two years later, leaving three orphaned daughters. A fourth daughter, the child of Fred and his first wife, who died in childbirth, was raised by her maternal aunt, who had herself lost an infant daughter. Before she died, Carrie was trying to arrange for her daughters to attend Bryn Mawr, to ensure that they would never be left helpless and dependent, as she had been.

Orphaned by the loss of both parents, Kit and her sisters were left under the financial control of their uncle Amory, who despised them, especially Kit, and refused to support their education. Kit became a fighter, going to court for the right to control her own money, a life-long concern of her mother. She won the right to hire a lawyer to be her guardian. At sixteen she moved herself and her sisters to Bryn

Mawr and went to college while caring for them by herself and in defiance of her uncle. She went on to become a leader in the women's suffrage movement and one of the founders of Planned Parenthood. To give an indication of the uncle's hostility toward Kit, the following is a letter he wrote to Kit when she married Tom Hepburn: "Dear Katherine . . . My opinion of you is the same as it always has been—that you are an extravagant, deceitful, dishonest, worthless person. You have squandered thousands of dollars and left your honest debts unpaid. When you see Tom, please tell him I do not think he could do worse . . . Disgusted, Your affectionate Uncle, A. Houghton Jr."

Katherine says her father's favorite saying was "The Truth will make your free." Indeed, the family was viewed with outrage in their neighborhood, because the parents were so open about sex, allowing Katherine, for example, to watch the childbirth of one of her younger siblings. But one topic could never be mentioned: suicide or any of those who had died by suicide.

There were various messages transmitted by the Hepburn family. One was, "Be independent, successful, and fight for what you want." To this was added the message "Don't ever leave home." In certain ways the family also said, "Let's pretend." Later Hepburn said of her brother's death: "Naturally my brother's death flattened me emotionally. It was a major tragedy. Did it push me further into make-believe? Who knows. I would think it must have."[11]

As often happens with families stretched by tragedy, Katharine and her siblings seem to have found ways to respond to both directives: Be successful and independent, but don't ever leave. Katharine became one of the most successful American screen actresses of all time, yet in a certain sense she never left home. After Tom's death she and the other Hepburn children became a self-contained system, with Katharine, now the eldest, taking much of the responsibility for her younger siblings. She said that her brother's death "threw my mother and father and me very close together, very close." Shortly after the suicide she went through a period of serious behavior problems (vandalism, breaking and entering), symptoms that are not too surprising when we think about the extraordinary ordeal the family had been through and the pressure on her as the oldest surviving child. However, perhaps because of the important legacy of her grandmother regarding women's education, Kate then went off to Bryn Mawr, her mother's alma mater. Here she began to turn her life around. In the end she more than fulfilled her distinguished family's

Katharine Hepburn, (left), with her beloved older brother, Tom, who hanged himself when she was thirteen. She never spoke of his suicide.

demands for high achievement at the same time that she seems to have responded (as did her siblings) to the need of the family to remain close together.

One brother continued to live in the family's summer house. The other followed the father into the practice of urology at Hartford Hospital, living within blocks of the original family home. One sister followed most closely in the mother's footsteps as a nonconformist interested first in politics and eventually became a writer of books on Connecticut history. The other, a librarian, still lives within ten minutes of the family home in West Hartford.

Even though she married briefly and lived three thousand miles away from her family for much of her adult life, Katharine Hepburn always sent the money she made home to her father, who supported her with an allowance for as long as he lived. One close friend says that he could not recall a single conversation with Hepburn in which she did not mention her parents' impact on her life. In her autobiography Hepburn wrote: "We were a happy family. We are a happy family. Mother and Dad were perfect parents." At the same time her loyalty to them must have elicited a price in her personal life. As she said herself, "I never really left home—not really." She kept dolls and stuffed animals on her bed well into adulthood. And even at the age of eighty she spoke of the family home (now owned by her brother) as her home and thought of herself as the dutiful daughter.

Hepburn's twenty-five year relationship with Spencer Tracy seems to have fitted well with patterns evolved in her earlier life. Tracy, an alcoholic, seventeen years her senior, already had liver and kidney damage when they met. One might say he was a doomed man and very moody, reminiscent of the description of her brother's personality. Although separated from his wife for many years, he would never divorce her, in part due to his guilt about abandoning her and their deaf son and in part to his Irish Catholicism. Tracy's wife, Louise, had been heroic in her dedication to the son and received many public awards for her activities on behalf of the deaf. The relationship with Tracy was perhaps ideal for Kate: Its clandestine nature allowed her more privacy than is usually available to stars, while she could maintain her solitary residence and loyalty to her family of origin.

The combination of Tracy's tough masculinity and his vulnerability seemed irresistible. Hepburn's career took second place to his throughout their relationship, and he always got first billing. Between 1942 and 1950 she made ten films—four alone and six with Tracy. The four she made alone were compromises to stay close to him. One senses a repeat of the functional, caring sister. None of this is meant to diminish the love that Hepburn shared with Tracy. Certainly the remarkable chemistry of their screen partnership also gives us a glimpse of an archetypal relationship between a strong woman and a strong man. Yet the family dilemma seems to suggest that an outward manifestation of strength, success, and achievement masked an inner hesitancy about her own home and family. Clearly, the question of how much to focus on the past and how to move into the future was an issue for all the Hepburn children.

DYSFUNCTIONAL ADAPTATION TO LOSS

The process of mourning generally lasts for years, with each new season, holiday, and anniversary revoking the old loss. Even as this process continues, the family must adjust itself to the absence. Roles and tasks are reassigned, new attachments formed, and old alliances shifted. Eventually there comes a time when most families have in a general way come to terms with their loss, although mourning is never totally over. There will always be events that set off the memories of the lost person, but with time and resolution, the pain becomes less raw and intense, releasing energy for other attachments.

When families cannot mourn, they become locked in time—in dreams of the past, emotions of the present, or dread of the future. They may become so concerned about potential future losses that they are unable to engage in the relationships they do have, fearing that to love again will mean further loss. Others focus exclusively on their dreams of the future, trying to fill in the gap left by their losses with new relationships formed on fantasy and escape from the pain. Usually those who cut short their mourning by rushing into the future find that the pain comes back to haunt them when the dreams give way to the realities of the new relationships.

Problems that families have in other developmental transitions, such as marrying, having children of their own, or launching their children, often reflect this stoppage of time. For example, parents may have difficulty accepting a child's marriage if they have not yet integrated another loss. Marriages occurring around the time of a death are also often influenced by the unresolved emotional issues of a loss. Partners may marry primarily out of their sense of isolation or pain after a loss or in an attempt to replace their loved one or fill in the void. Parents may cling to children born at the time of loss out of their own fear and pain, even more than out of love and affection for the child. Unresolved losses even generations before cast their shadow.

Denial and escape are also associated with unresolved loss. In some families the myths, secrets, and expectations that develop around a critical loss may be incorporated and passed down from parents to children. Other families, as we saw with Teddy Roosevelt and as we shall see with the Barretts, stop all mention of the deceased, as if they could thus banish the pain. A family may also make the dead person's room into a memorial or a mausoleum. The mythmaking entailed in such delusional responses binds family members to each other in pathological ways and at the same time may create great psychological rifts among them. Such myths naturally affect the children, who become replacements for family members who have died. Often they are totally unaware of this connection and must discover the mystery behind their identity and find a way of "exorcising" the ghost or dybbuk.

Many of the rigid patterns we routinely observe in families—drivenness about one's activities, affairs, continuous unresolved conflict, alienation, isolation and fear of outsiders, frequent divorce, depression, workaholism, escapism into TV sports or soap operas—may actually be compensations for people's inability to deal with loss, which has finally become their inability to connect with anyone else for fear of further loss.

THE BARRETT BROWNING FAMILY

The romantic story of Elizabeth Barrett Browning (*Genogram 5.2*), the invalid poet, whose love affair with the handsome Robert Browning flourished in poetry before they ever met and who eloped with him from her sickbed to Italy, took place in the context of a family totally unable to deal with loss. One of Browning's distant relatives, who has researched the family extensively, describes their love as fated by mystical connections of their histories: "I was overwhelmingly convinced that there were born into both Robert and Elizabeth seeds of a love which had been unable to grow and bear fruit in a past life. I wondered if ancestors of Robert and Elizabeth respectively had fallen in love only to be torn apart. This would account for the magnetic attraction of souls, as happened with Robert and Elizabeth."[12] However mystical this relative's image of the pattern, the notion that their relationship was influenced by forces far beyond their specific lives is clear.

In all her writings Elizabeth Barrett Browning, wrote only one paragraph about her mother, Mary, who died when Elizabeth was twenty-one, after bearing twelve children: "Scarcely I was a woman when I lost my mother—dearest as she was, and very tender . . . but of a nature harrowed up into some furrows by the pressure of circumstances: for we lost more in her than she lost in life, my dear, dearest mother. A sweet gentle nature, which the thunder a little turned from its sweetness—as when it turns milk. One of those women who never can resist; but, in submitting and bowing on themselves, makes a mark, a plait, within,—a sign of suffering. Too womanly she was—it was her only fault. Good, good and dear—and refined too!"[13]

This powerful, dense, pained assessment suggests a great deal about the family's struggle in dealing with life and death. It is tantalizing to wonder about the impact of the mother's submission, which caused inner signs of suffering, on her brilliant daughter, who eventually used drugs to avoid her own pain. But we have little information about the mother, whose memory could never be discussed in the

Barrett family. The Barretts seemed to feel they would be devastated if they faced the loss directly. When Mary died, her husband refused to speak of his grief. He merely shut up his wife's rooms just as they were, and they were neither entered nor disturbed for years until the family moved. The family simply avoided the reality that the mother was gone, just as she had tried to avoid painful realities while she was alive. "Harrowed" as she was by life's circumstances, the message she conveyed was that we cannot hope to overcome life's difficulties.

Her husband seems to have agreed. Even in the best of times the father had always been a kind of benign dictator with his family. He called their home Hope End, and it represented, indeed, all the hope left to him. With each loss he turned further inward. Determined to maintain the family, he became a tyrant in his own household. He believed his children should never leave him, and the three who married were immediately disinherited and treated as dead.

This family pattern of avoiding whatever was too painful can be traced back to the early life of Edward Barrett, the father of the poet. He came from a distinguished family but had had a very difficult childhood. Two of his siblings died in childhood, leaving a desolate mother. His father deserted the family when Edward was a young child and further embarrassed them by having six children out of wedlock with other women.[14] For the rest of his life Edward never discussed the father who had left him.

He became the oldest and only surviving son and the only legitimate grandson on his mother's side of the family. His position in the family became even more pivotal when his three maternal uncles all died early, leaving only children born out of wedlock. Thus he was the one to inherit his maternal grandfather's fortune, although some of his cousins later contested this. Not surprisingly, Edward was expected to carry on the family legacy, and a great deal of pressure was placed on him to succeed in life. He grew up with a sense of responsibility and self-importance that led to rigidity in his dealings with people. His way was always the right way. Carrying the burden of the family legacy, he probably felt that he could not afford to lose control of his role as family leader. When losses occurred, he could not afford the luxury of his own grief.

At twenty Edward married Mary Graham Clarke, six years older than he. Together they had twelve children. This family meant everything to him. It was an opportunity to make up for the losses of his early family life. When the fourth child, also called Mary, died at age four, the family contained its grief, never mentioning her again. Then, when the youngest child was three years old, the wife Mary died. By that time Edward's response was characteristic: As with his

The Families of Elizabeth Barrett and Robert Browning
Genogram 5.2

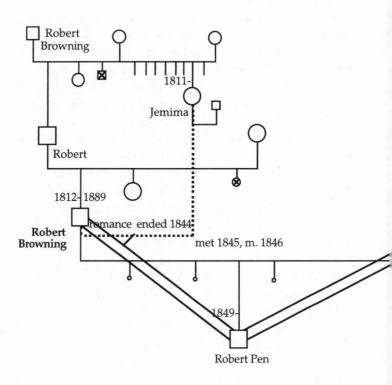

daughter's death fourteen years earlier, the death of his wife became a forbidden topic.

Avoidance and secrecy were a way of life in the Barrett family (see list of key events on Figure 5.1). When threatened with financial disaster, Edward Barrett had kept secret from his wife and family the losses in their plantations in Jamaica, which were the source of their income. When they did finally lose their home, Hope End, Edward refused to speak about it until the very last minute. Once they left, no one could ever mention that home again.

Prior to this and compounding their difficulty in dealing with loss, several family members who had gone to Jamaica to handle family

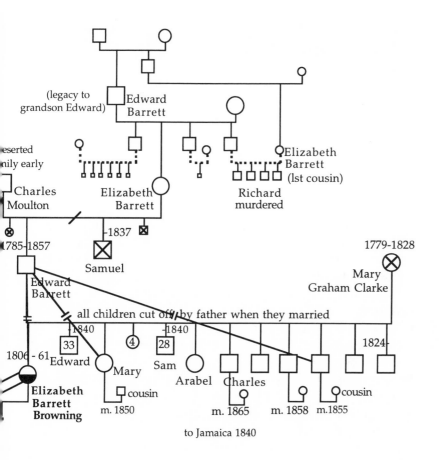

business died tragically. Edward's only brother, Samuel, died there. Then a cousin of the father, Richard Barrett, a man of distinguished career who took over the handling of family property, was mysteriously murdered in Jamaica, the body removed, and no stone ever erected for him. Nevertheless, Edward sent two of his sons to this dangerous locale because maintaining the family's source of income was crucial to their remaining together. First he sent the second-oldest son, Samuel, who died there in 1840. Then he sent the third-oldest son, Charles. The father was not willing to risk his favorite son, Edward, Jr., who was actually the oldest and most qualified to handle the family business.

Figure 5.1   Key Events in Barrett Family

1814   Mary Barrett, Elizabeth's sister, dies at age four and is never mentioned again.

1828   Mary Graham Clarke, Elizabeth's mother, dies and is never mentioned again.

1832   Business losses force Edward Barrett to sell his beloved home, Hope End, which could never be mentioned again.

1837   Elizabeth becomes an invalid. Suffers from tuberculosis and other problems.

1839   Edward's cousin Richard Barrett is murdered mysteriously in Jamaica.

1840   Samuel Barrett, the oldest son, sent by his father to Jamaica to handle the family business, is killed at age twenty-eight.

1840   Edward Barrett sends his third son, Charles, to Jamaica to handle the family business.

1840   July: Edward, Jr., drowns at age thirty-three, while visiting Elizabeth.

1840   Elizabeth suffers a breakdown.

1844   December: Robert Browning's beloved first cousin Jemima becomes engaged.

1845   January: Browning's first letter to Elizabeth, declaring his love without ever having met her.

1845   May: Robert Browning, aged thirty-three, meets Elizabeth Barrett, aged thirty-nine, for the first time.

1846   Couple elopes. Elizabeth's father never speaks to her again.

But keeping him from leaving did not save this son, who drowned the same year (1840) close to home at the age of thirty-three in a freak boating accident. Again, the response to the loss was avoidance, and the family pulled even closer together. Neither the drowning nor Edward's name was to be mentioned again, and the whole family followed its rule of silence.

The death was particularly difficult for Elizabeth, who was only a year older than Edward, and was very close to him. Many years later she wrote that this death was the one event in her life which never became less bitter but returned upon her "like a retreating wave, going and coming again."[15] What made the loss even more difficult to endure was Elizabeth's sense of responsibility and guilt. It was she who had invited her brother to visit her at a seaside retreat where she was recuperating from tuberculosis. The father wanted him to come back to London, but Elizabeth had begged that he be allowed to stay with her. Since no one in the family had ever before dared disagree openly with the father, Edward's drowning left Elizabeth feeling guilty for countering her father's wishes. At a deeper level it may be that Elizabeth's guilt about Edward's death was a displacement for her father's guilt since it was he who had tried to protect Edward by not sending him to Jamaica. From this time on the father managed any open disagreement with total estrangement.

The children developed complicated patterns of secrecy to protect the father from information that would upset him. There was a complicity of silence. They kept the details of their behavior from their father, and the father was willing to turn the other way. When Elizabeth met daily in her bedroom for more than a year with her future husband, Robert Browning, her father chose not to notice. This allowed him to feel self-righteous and betrayed when the two finally eloped, as if he had not known what was going on.

For years Elizabeth had been caught in her family's web of illusion. As the eldest daughter she was expected to lead and care for her siblings under her father's regime. Her only means of individual expression was through her creativity, her poetry. Even here her father played a pivotal role: He would pay for her poems to be published and she would dedicate them to him. She remained ever the devoted daughter. She became an invalid; because of a mysterious illness, she did not leave her bed for days at a time, unable even to walk. She maintained a secret life in her extensive correspondence with the great writers of the era, but she remained firmly attached to her family through her inability to leave her room. For years the sickly Elizabeth lived alone in her room, creating some of the world's greatest poetry and becoming quietly addicted to morphine.

Avoidance of loss can create a siege mentality. And although Elizabeth greatly resented her father's hold on her, she herself developed a similar attitude toward letting other family members go. When her brothers went away, she begged them to come home, complaining that their pleasure for a few days was "disproportionate to the long anxiety of those left at home."[16]

When Elizabeth did eventually leave her father's home to marry Robert Browning, a worldly, attractive, admiring poet, six years younger than she, they planned their elopement with the greatest secrecy. It was by all appearances the perfect love story. Their love began through correspondence, and it was months before they met.

The beginning of their romance related also to a loss that Browning had experienced—of his first cousin Jemima, with whom he had been secretly in love for years. Although he destroyed all material evidence of any association with Jemima,[17] his mysterious love poem *Pauline: A Fragment of a Confession* (1833), which he published secretly and anonymously at his own expense, was apparently written about her. For decades he went to great lengths to preserve the poem's anonymity. Browning could not forget Jemima. Finally, in the summer of 1844, he went to Italy, hoping to remove himself from the temptation of the relationship. He returned to London in December to learn that she had become engaged to someone else. In January 1845 he wrote his first letter to Elizabeth, declaring, without ever having met her, that he was in love with her: "I love your verses with all my heart, dear Miss Barrett . . . I do, as I say, love these books with all my heart—and I love you too."[18] Eventually Browning met with Barrett in her room and nursed her back to health. Finally, when she could walk again and appeared to have given up her drug dependence, Elizabeth eloped to Italy with him. But even though she was thirty-nine years old, she waited until her father was out on business to make her "escape," and her father never spoke to her again. He could not accept any child who had the audacity to leave him. Though Elizabeth wrote many pleading and loving letters to him and kept his picture always opposite her bed, her numerous efforts at reconciliation fell on deaf ears. When she returned home from Italy at the time of her father's death, she found all her letters to him unopened in a packet.

When two of Barrett's other children dared to marry, albeit to cousins, so they were not fully leaving the family, they too were cut off. Three other children waited to marry until their father had died, by which time they were middle-aged.

Even in Italy Elizabeth was never completely able to leave her family behind. She thought of them constantly and was unable to get over her guilt about either the death of her brother or the abandonment of her father. Never feeling entirely comfortable in her marital relationship, she always questioned whether or not she was worthy of her husband: "I cannot help the pain I feel sometimes in thinking that it would have been better for you if you never had known me. . . . May God turn back the evil of me. . . . If I only knew certainly . . . more certainly than the thing may be known by either me or you;— that nothing in me could have any part in making you unhappy—for everything turns to evil which I touch."

Elizabeth Barrett and Robert Browning had one surviving son, Pen, born when Elizabeth was forty-two. She also had four miscarriages. She lived only until her son was twelve, having slipped back into her invalidism and drug addiction long before the end and having drawn Pen into her isolation. The product of one of the greatest romances of all time, Pen could not live up to the expectations that his parents and the world had of him. He remained always more a child than a man, unable to commit himself to a way of life, a job, or a wife. His mother had treated him as an extension of herself, dressing him bizarrely in female clothes, against his father's wishes.

Robert, like his wife's family, had ritualistic ways of dealing with loss. He would not visit his own family home after his mother died, very near the time Pen was born. Later he could not even bear to pass the house where his beloved sister-in-law, Arabel, had died in his arms. Most of all, he could not bear the memories of the home he had enjoyed with Elizabeth in Florence. In all the years of his life he never returned to Florence again. When Elizabeth died, Robert devoted himself to his son, treating him as a reincarnation of his adored wife.

Concern about secrecy continued in the Barrett Browning family. Many years after Pen's death the cousins burned Elizabeth Browning's letters to her father which had never been opened. Burning these letters went very much against Elizabeth's belief that "If the secrets of our daily lives and inner souls may instruct other surviving souls, let them be open to men hereafter, even as they are to God now."[19] Thus it would appear that the pattern of avoiding the pain of loss continued generation after generation in the Barrett family.

THE KENNEDY FAMILY

Another family in which multigenerational patterns of dealing with untimely loss seem to have had a profound impact is the Kennedy family (*Genogram 5.3*). No American who was alive in 1963 can forget the image of John F. Kennedy, Jr., saluting his father's casket on that cold, clear November day. The little boy without a father, three years old, born on Thanksgiving Day two weeks after his father's election to the presidency, reminded us all of the fragility of our lives. We have images of other Kennedy deaths as well: the Mozart Requiem playing at St. Patrick's Cathedral for Robert Kennedy, his ten children all in mourning, Ethel still pregnant with the last, Ted's voice cracking in eulogy for yet another brother.

John Kennedy himself had been a stand-in for his older brother, Joseph Jr., after the latter's death in World War II. A year after the mantle of leadership was passed to Ted, we recall his confused explanation of his role in the death of Mary Jo Kopechne at Chappaquid-

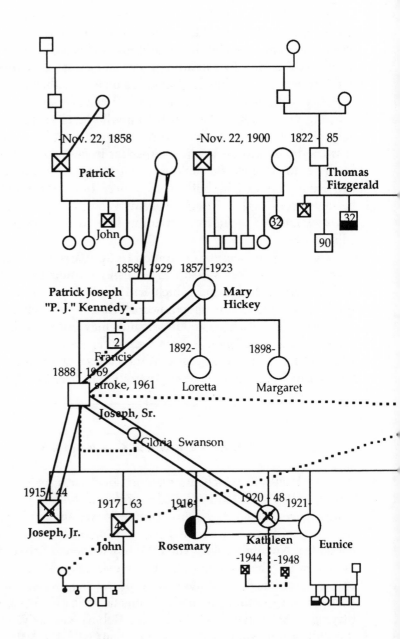

The Kennedy and Fitzgerald Families

Genogram 5.3

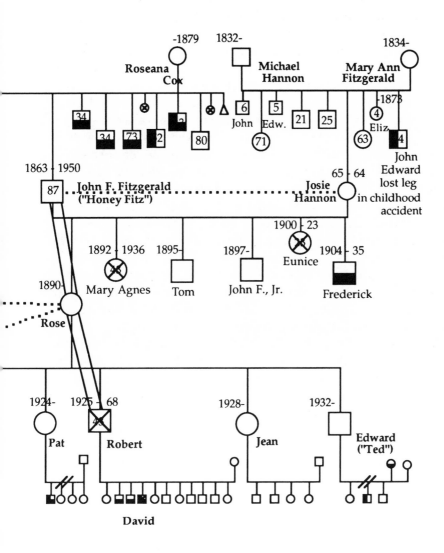

dick. In the next generation there followed the terrible, inglorious death of David Kennedy, whose drug overdose seemed so much the fallout of previous losses.

We are fairly familiar with the losses of the Kennedys in our lifetime, just as we tend to be familiar with the losses in our own families within our lifetimes. Usually we know less about the losses that have gone before, losses that have very much shaped family myths and attitudes. In fact, the Kennedys' history of tragic loss goes back way beyond the children and grandchildren of Joe and Rose.

Joe Kennedy's father, Patrick Joseph ("P. J."), had been the only surviving male in his family. An older brother, John, had died at one year of age, and the father, Patrick, died when P. J. was six months old. These losses must have left P. J.'s mother with special feelings for her only surviving son and a heightened sense of the fragility of life—especially male life. Having come up the hard way—with no father and serving as a replacement for his dead brother—P. J. became a hardworking but cautious man. He "married up" to a clever woman, Mary Hickey, from a successful family. He too was clever, but his insecurities made it hard for him to say no to anyone. He started a liquor business and, like so many of the Irish of his time, moved into politics. He was always a caretaker for the families in his ward, serving eight terms in the state legislature. Mary resented his commitment to helping others as the boss of his district because it intruded upon their own family's success. Yet he must have felt the need to do for others because he identified with them, having been raised as a fatherless child in desperate need himself.

The first child of P. J. and Mary was Joseph P. Kennedy, who again became the only surviving son of his parents. His already privileged position of oldest son was strengthened when his younger brother, Francis, died of diphtheria at the age of two. A granddaughter later said: "The death of the baby was so unexpected and so senseless that [Joe's mother's] only way of coping was to pour even more love onto Joe." Though he had two surviving younger sisters, Joe became the focus of attention for the whole family. Perhaps it is this legacy of specialness of the male survivor, intensifying the general cultural bias toward sons that led Joe to focus his expectations so strongly on his own sons.

Joe grew up to emulate his mother, who believed in putting their family first, and saw his father's support for others as weakness. In the end P. J. was defeated by the machine politics of Boston (very likely he was double-crossed by his son's future father-in-law, Honey Fitz himself!). Though he accepted his defeat with gentle dignity, underneath he grieved like a child who had been unjustly punished.

The lesson his son, Joe, took from this was that political loyalty and generosity were merely commodities. The decision he then made was to trust no one but himself. He developed a will of steel and a calculating, manipulative approach to dealing with others.

It would seem that Joe felt strong pressure to escape the embarrassing identification with his softhearted father, whose kindness, seemingly based on identifying with others who had experienced loss, was repaid with exploitation and rejection. A clue to Joe's relationship with his father is that when P. J. died in 1928, Joe did not attend the funeral but remained in California with his paramour, Gloria Swanson. As much as P. J. longed for a close relationship with his son, he did not succeed in achieving it. Just as P. J., having no father at all, had gravitated to his mother, so Joe's special closeness was to his mother.

Rose Fitzgerald Kennedy's family also experienced overwhelming traumatic losses at critical times in their history. Her father, John Francis, called Honey Fitz, was the fourth of twelve children. The only two daughters both died in infancy, as did the eldest son. Three others had lives totally wasted by alcoholism. Two more, Michael and Edward, had severe alcohol problems as well. The ninth brother, Joseph, had brain damage from malaria and barely functioned. Thus, of the twelve children born in this family, only three, including Honey Fitz, survived in good health. Honey Fitz became the favorite son. After his mother's death, when he was sixteen, his father developed a special ambition for him to become a doctor since illness had caused their family such painful losses. However, after one year at Harvard Medical School, the father died, and Honey Fitz switched his ambitions to politics, which offered an immediate income and an opportunity to provide jobs for his brothers. When he became mayor of Boston, many said that the whole brotherhood of Fitzgeralds actually ran the government. He considered it his responsibility to provide for his brothers, and he did. Later his grandsons would, of course, do the same.

Honey Fitz met his future wife, Josephine Hannon, his painfully shy second cousin, only a few months before the death of his mother. Many said that his bond to her was based on their mutual losses. Josie was the fifth of nine children, only four of whom survived. One brother died of fever at age six, while the mother was pregnant with Josie. Another had died of inflammation of the lung four years earlier. Two other sons died early of alcoholism. The only surviving son had his leg crushed by a train at age thirteen. But the family's most tragic loss was the littlest sister, who drowned with her best friend while Josie was supposed to be caring for them. The devastating loss any

family naturally would feel about the death of a child was compounded by a complex web of guilt and self-reproach that they and
Josie, in particular, had contributed to the death by failing to protect
the children adequately. The family never recovered. Those who
knew the three surviving sisters said that sorrow and withdrawal hung
over them for the rest of their lives.

It is easy to understand what attracted Josie to the confident, force-
ful, adventuresome, and enthusiastic Honey Fitz, whose very nickname reflected his ability to charm others with his words. Honey
Fitz's long courtship of Josie indeed seemed an effort to bring her out
of herself with his humor, his magnetism, and his sociability. Like so
many generations of the family that followed him, he dealt with loss
by mobilizing into frantic activity and trying not to look back. Once
the challenge of winning Josie was complete, the difference in their
natures was overwhelmingly apparent. Or perhaps the very sadness
in Josie which had drawn him to her now became toxic, and he fled
from it. As the years went by, Honey Fitz expanded outward, while
Josie turned further inward. It was his beloved first born daughter,
Rose, who really seemed to replace his mother and sisters. She grew
up as his companion in the exciting political arena of his colorful life;
she went everywhere with him.

She led a charmed life until adolescence, when suddenly it all
changed. Her father's main character flaw—self-centered manipulative ambition, the reflection of his early losses—seems to have led
him to betray her. Perhaps there was also some compulsion to repeat
his experience at sixteen, when he had had to give up his plans for
medical school. He sacrificed her dreams to his personal political
aims. She was a brilliant student, as well as a passionate, untamed
spirit, and her dream was to go to Wellesley, where she had been
accepted at sixteen; but Honey Fitz was in trouble. His political
wheeling and dealing led to charges of fraud and to his being ousted
as mayor of Boston. He made a deal with the leaders of the Catholic
Church that required her to go instead to a Catholic school.

Rose was abruptly sent to a convent school abroad. She was totally
cut off from her family and her exciting social life and put in a rigid
environment, which demanded silence and denied all spontaneous
attachments. Typical of the repression of parochial schools of the era,
there was even a rule against girls' forming "particular friendships."
Rose's response was one she was to manifest again and again in her
long life: She smothered her feelings of resistance, bowed to her
father's will, and forced herself to channel her energies through
adherence to prayer, which was the only avenue open to her. She
forged in that transition a kind of detachment from human relation-

ships which was to characterize all her later life. What she lost was a belief in her special relationship with her father as well as the sense of power to determine her own life. She had to bend to the will of a stronger male. Religion helped her swallow that pill and many other bitter pills to follow.

We are most familiar with the losses of Rose and Joe Kennedy's children by death, but their first loss was not a death. It was of Rosemary, their eldest daughter, who has been institutionalized far from the family and cut off from them (except for Eunice) for the past fifty years. Such a child represents a loss of dreams, an embarrassment, and a pain that does not go away. Wishing to keep her within the family, the Kennedys kept her problems a secret for many years and made every effort to maintain her in as normal a fashion as possible.

By the time Rosemary was in her early twenties her behavior had become disturbing to the family. She had periodic outbursts of anger and had found a way to escape from the convent where she was kept and wander the streets at night. At a certain point Joe decided, while Rose was away, that Rosemary should have a lobotomy although a lobotomy had never been used for retardation before but only for the most chronic and serious mental illness.[20] The operation, which was kept totally secret, worsened her condition considerably. Apparently Joe then had her sent to an institution in the Midwest. He never told his wife—not then or afterward—about the lobotomy. Rose was just told that it would be better if she didn't visit for some time. According to friends and relatives, it was only twenty years later, after Joe's stroke in 1961, that Rose began to piece the story together for herself.[21] Why didn't she insist on visiting this daughter to whom she had devoted herself for so many years? How could she never ask? How could it be that others in the family never questioned the disappearance of one of their members? Did Joe blame himself for what had happened? Did others blame him or themselves for ignoring her for so many years? All we know is that in her memoirs, written thirty-three years after the operation, Rose maintains that she participated in the decision for the lobotomy and fails to mention that she had not visited or asked about Rosemary for twenty years.

The Kennedy family never talked about Rosemary's retardation within the family; the first public mention wasn't until 1960. We do have a suggestion of the long-range impact of the family's inability to deal openly with this "ghost" in an incident described about David Kennedy, the grandson who died of a drug overdose. One day, in the midst of his troubles, he found a magazine story about lobotomies that included a picture of his aunt Rosemary. He is quoted as saying: "She had a new pair of white shoes on and she was smiling. The thought crossed my mind that if my grandfather was alive the same thing could have happened to me that happened to her. She was an embarrassment; I am an embarrassment. She was a hindrance; I am a hindrance. As I looked at this picture, I began to hate my grandfather and all of them for having done the thing they had done to her and for the thing they were doing to me."[22]

The shame and guilt leading to the secrecy and mystification that surrounded Rosemary's disability, lobotomy, and disappearance give this loss a lingering power. In such circumstances other family members are left with the feeling "If she could disappear, I could disappear." And their fantasies fill in the rest of the story with whatever meanings they attach to the pieces of the story they do know.

The ambiguity of Rosemary's loss must have been particularly distressing because it could not be mourned like a death. She remained alive but not physically or mentally present. Rose says in her memoirs that Rosemary remained pleased to see them and recognized them but that she was "perfectly happy in her environment and would be confused and disturbed to be anywhere else."[23] Yet surely other family members, like David, must have wondered whether this was true and questioned her extrusion from the family.

Unfortunately Rosemary was only the first of many children lost to the Kennedy family. In each instance there was a similar tendency toward secrecy about any facts that did not fit with a positive image. Joe, Jr., the "golden boy," programmed by his father to become president, was shot down in an unnecessarily reckless flying mission in June 1944. Only his heroism was mentioned, not his exaggerated risk taking or the fact that he had received a warning that day from his electronics officer that his plane could not possibly make it.[24] The Kennedys also never mentioned that he was living with a married woman, Pat Wilson, at the time of his death. When Wilson wrote a letter of sympathy to Rose, the bereaved mother did not respond.

It is hard to escape the sense that there is a repeated mingling of tragedy, accident and tempting the fates in the Kennedy family. Joe Kennedy, Jr., had been repeatedly carrying out hazardous bombing missions in which he was told his chances of survival were less than than 50 percent. He had already completed his tour of duty but was looking for a mission from which he would return a hero, perhaps because his younger brother John had just received a military medal for his performance in the Pacific. (In that instance John had initially been reported missing in action, and a funeral had been held by the surviving crew members. Joe, Sr., was told this news but kept it from his wife and children for a week, after which he learned that John had, in fact, survived.)

The Kennedy family. From left to right: Pat, Jack, Rosemary, Jean, Joseph, Sr., Ted, Rose, Joe, Jr., Kathleen, Robert, and Eunice. Patterns of dealing with untimely loss shaped the Kennedy family history and behavior over several generations. Dorothy Wilding, John F. Kennedy Library

In this incident and others to follow there are numerous examples of the Kennedys' avoidant ways of dealing with loss. When Joe, Jr., died, his father announced the fact to the children, warned them all to be "particularly good to your mother," and then retreated to his room, while Rose also retreated to her separate room. Rose said that she and her husband "wept inwardly, silently." At the time Joe said, "We've got to carry on. We must take care of the living. There is a lot of work to be done."[25] Rose turned to religion, repeating the rosary over and over, leaving it up to her husband to handle arrangements and respond to correspondence. She was initially consumed by her grief, while he immediately mobilized into action—the usual response of the Kennedy men to loss and consonant with our culture's gender rules.

The second daughter, Kathleen, who had been cut off by her mother for marrying a British Protestant peer in May 1944, lost her husband in the war that September. When the news of his death came, she was in the United States with her family because of her brother Joe's death shortly before. She was out shopping and her sister Eunice went to meet her. Eunice, in typical Kennedy form, complimented her on her purchases and said nothing until they were finished shopping, at which point she suggested that Kathleen call their father before they went to lunch. Joe then gave her the news of her husband's death. That night the family was solicitous of Kathleen, while diligently avoiding any mention of her husband's death! A friend who came to stay with her at the time was appalled by the family's frenetic need to carry on as if nothing had happened.[26]

Kathleen once told another friend that she had been taught that "Kennedys don't cry." When her brother Joe died and his roommate called her to give condolences, she had broken into sobs. Later she wrote him a letter of apology saying: "I'm sorry I broke down tonight. It never makes things easier."[27] Following her husband's death, she left her parents' home and returned to England, where she did allow herself to go through months of overt mourning, staying in the home of her parents-in-law for comfort and support.

Four years later Kathleen fell in love with another Protestant, this time a married British peer, Peter Fitzwilliam, who had a reputation for high living, gambling, and affairs. This time Rose Kennedy said that if Kathleen married, she would not only disown Kathleen but also see that Joe cut off her allowance. Rose vowed she would leave Joe if he refused. Kathleen decided she could not break off the relationship in spite of her mother's threat. In hopes of appealing to her father, she arranged to meet him, while on a weekend trip with Fitzwilliam on the Riviera. In an eerily familiar scenario, Fitzwilliam insisted on flying in a small plane although weather reports were so bad that all commercial flights had been canceled and his pilot strongly urged a delay. Their plane crashed in the storm, and both Kathleen and Fitzwilliam were killed.

Joe, who went to identify the body, said Kathleen looked beautiful and as if asleep, though she had actually been horribly disfigured by the crash. The circumstances of her death with Fitzwilliam were concealed, and she was buried as the widow of the first husband. Her father was the only family member to attend her funeral. Even then he took no role in the funeral arrangements, which were handled by her former mother-in-law, who even wrote her epitaph: "Joy she gave, Joy she has found." The Kennedys and the in-laws joined in a conspiracy of silence about the circumstances of the death.

Friends were appalled that Rose Kennedy sent a mass card with a prayer for those who had not gone to heaven. John and Bobby Kennedy visited Kathleen's housekeeper, drew out all her recollections, and then said, "We will not mention her again." They seem to have kept their word, though Bobby named his eldest daughter for her. Twenty-four years later Rose wrote in her memoirs: "In 1948 [Kathleen] had taken a spring holiday on the Riviera and was flying in a private plane with a few friends to Paris, where her father was waiting to meet her. On the way—a route threading the edges of the French

Alps—the weather went bad, navigation equipment was not adequate, and the plane crashed into a mountainside, killing all on board. Joe was notified and hurried to the scene. He watched as the body of his daughter was brought down the mountainside. We lost our beloved Kathleen on May 13, 1948." All reference to the fiancé was eliminated, as if he had never existed, along with all reference to the fact that Rose had disowned her daughter.

Since then the Kennedys have sustained many other losses and near losses. Three times John Kennedy was given up for dead and was administered the last rites. Twice Ted almost died: a year after John's death, when he broke his back in a plane crash, and a year after Robert's death, when he almost drowned (and his companion, Mary Jo Kopechne, did drown at Chappaquiddick). Was it just coincidence that his near-fatal accidents followed so closely the tragic deaths of his brothers, or is this an example of something that has been documented repeatedly in the research on stress: that loss and other stresses increase our vulnerability to emotional upset, illness, and accident? The most recent family scandal, Willie Smith's indictment for rape, occurred only seven months after his father died.

What leads a family into such reckless and self-destructive behavior? Many people have seen the reckless risk-taking behavior of Kathleen and Joe, Jr., the extremely promiscuous sexual behavior of Joseph and John Kennedy, and the politically dangerous liaisons of several of the Kennedys (John most of all) as a response to their fear of death—living on the edge and, as it were, "tempting fate" to prove to themselves that they were still alive.

When the news came that John Kennedy had been shot, Rose decided to operate on a principle that she and Joe had adopted years before: Bad news should be given only in the morning, not late in the day, because it would then upset your sleep. She therefore arranged for a "conspiracy of kindness" to keep Joe, who had by then suffered a stroke, from learning about the death until the next day. All TVs were unplugged, different stories were told about the relatives and friends who began to appear, and everyone kept up a charade of conversation with him for the whole afternoon and evening. He was told the next morning.

Rose believed that Jackie's composure at the time of John Kennedy's death was an example for the whole world of how to behave. The following week, Rose says, the family "had the Thanksgiving celebration, with everyone of us hiding the grief that gnawed at us and doing our best to make it a day of peace, optimism, and thanks for the blessings that were still left to us." Rose quotes Jackie's praise for how the Kennedy family deals with tragedy:

> You can be sitting down to dinner with them and so many sad things have happened to each, and—God—maybe even some sad thing has happened that day, and you can see that each one is aware of the other's suffering. And so they can sit down at the table in a rather sad frame of mind. Then each one will begin to make this conscious effort to be gay or funny or to lift each other's spirits, and you find that it's infectious, that everybody's doing it. . . . [They] bounce off each other. They all have a sense of humor. . . . It's a little bit irrelevant, a little bit self-mocking, a little sense of the ridiculous, and in times of sadness of wildly wicked humor of irreverence. . . . They bring out the best. No one sits and wallows in self-pity.

Commenting on the death of her third son, Robert, nearly five years after Jack's, Rose said that the grim reality of the second assassination was so incredible it would seem beyond fiction to imagine. She says others commented on her composure, her bravery, and her self-possession at the funeral, but also that her waving a greeting to others was somehow "inappropriate." She responded: "As for my being composed—I had to be. If I had broken down in grief, I would only have added to the misery of the others and possibly could have set off a chain reaction of tearfulness. But, in fact, it was not just I who set an example of fortitude. They all set it for one another."[28]

Grief is a personal matter. Every family must find its own ways of handling grief. The Kennedys showed many strengths in their handling of an incredible series of tragedies, and they also showed glaring vulnerabilities, particularly in facing up to losses that were embarrassing and not heroic. The remarkable thing about this family is their ability to persevere even after the most devastating losses.

Families like the Kennedys that have experienced so many traumatic, untimely deaths may develop a feeling of being "cursed" and unable to rise above the experience, or they may come to see themselves as survivors, who can be struck down but never beaten. For all their difficulties in handling feelings, the Kennedys have shown an amazing life-force and courage in overcoming tragedies. It is almost as if their sense of the family mission carries them through.

THE FREUD FAMILY

The Freud family (*Genogram 5.4*) provides another interesting example of pattern repetition which appear to have been a legacy of loss.

Sigmund, the oldest of his mother's eight children, was born in 1856 in Freiberg, Moravia. In addition to being the oldest, he was the only son for many years. He had an intense relationship with his mother, Amalia, who always referred to him as her "Golden Sigi." By all accounts, he was the center of the household. He was followed by a brother who died, then by five sisters, and finally by a brother ten years younger.

Sigmund's specialness for his father was probably intensified by the death of his paternal grandfather three months before his birth. This grandfather, Schlomo, was a rabbi, and Sigmund, in his fervency for his new belief system, psychoanalysis, has been compared with a religious leader and thus, in his own way following in this grandfather's footsteps. Sigmund's father, Jacob, had also lost two children in his first marriage, though we know no details about them. Such losses tend to intensify the meaning of children who come after, particularly the next in line, who in this case would have been Sigmund.

Sigmund's brother, Julius, born when he was seventeen months old, lived for only seven months. In Sigmund's case, his closeness to his mother may have become even more important after the death of her second son. The loss of this infant would itself have been intensified by the fact that exactly one month before his death, Amalia's youngest brother, also named Julius, died at the age of twenty from pulmonary tuberculosis. Probably she had known that her brother was dying when she named her son for him seven months earlier since it is not generally the Jewish custom to name a child for a living family member. In later life Sigmund said that he had welcomed this brother with "ill wishes and real infantile jealousy, and his death left the germ of guilt in me."[29] In addition, at this time Sigmund's nursemaid was dismissed from the household and the family moved twice, apparently because of financial difficulties. His nephew John and both half brothers emigrated to England shortly afterward. Furthermore, he soon had to share his parents' affection with a new sibling, Anna, with whom he was never to get along. Freud's sense of his own specialness and his religious fervor about his beliefs, as well as the relationships that evolved in the Freud family, were undoubtedly influenced by this pileup of losses near the time of his birth.

Another critical period occurred when Freud was forty and his father died. This death occurred just after the birth of Freud's last child, Anna, named not for his sister but for the daughter of his high school Hebrew teacher and mentor, Samuel Hammerschlag.[30] Perhaps it is not surprising that this last child, Anna, born the year Freud's father died, became his favorite, his primary follower, and by far the most emotionally linked to him of all his children. He also

The Freud Family

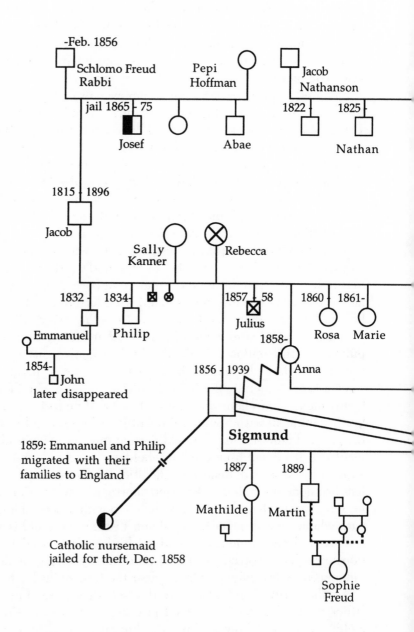

Genogram 5.4

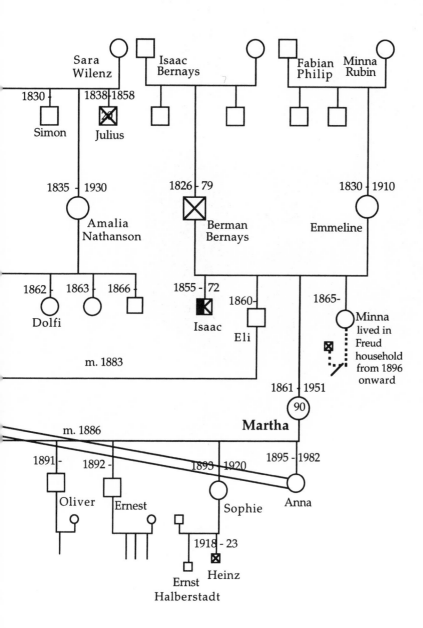

Sigmund Freud as a young boy with his father, Jacob. (top left) Freud with his wife, Martha Bernays (bottom left). Minna Bernays, Freud's sister-in-law, who came to live with the Freuds (right). Freud in 1922, with his grandsons Ernst and Heinerle (below). Mary Evans/Sigmund Freud Copyrights

drew closer to his sister-in-law Minna, who moved into the household at this time. She became his intellectual and emotional companion for many years. In a letter to his then closest friend, Wilhelm Fliess, Freud describes Minna during these years as "otherwise my closest confidante."[31] He often traveled alone with her, while his wife stayed with the children, and there is speculation that he became sexually involved with her,[32] a pattern that is not uncommon in families following a loss, even though the connection between the death and the affair remains out of awareness.[33] Even more fascinating is the possible repetition of this pattern of an affair with a sister-in-law in the next generation—between Freud's oldest son, Martin, and his wife's sister.[34]

Jacob Freud, like his son Sigmund, had been forty when his father died. While mere coincidence may be at work here, an exploration of family history often reveals such coincidences. In any case, Freud seems to have had a special identification with his father. He called his father's death "the most important event, the most poignant loss, in a man's life."[35] When his father died in 1896, Freud wrote: "By one of those obscure paths behind official consciousness the death of the old man has affected me profoundly. I valued him highly, understood him very well, and with that combination of deep wisdom and romantic lightheartedness peculiar to him he had meant a great deal to me. His life had been over a long time before he died, but his death seems to have aroused in me memories of all the early days. I now feel quite uprooted."[36]

His reaction to this death contrasts with that to his mother, who died at the age of ninety-five in 1930: "No pain, no grief, which is probably to be explained by the circumstances, the great age and the end of the pity we had felt at her helplessness. With that a feeling of liberation, of release . . . I was not allowed to die as long as she was alive, and now I may."[37]

Her death, as he said, provided a relief that she was out of her pain, and since Freud himself had been suffering from cancer for seven years, he was spared the life cycle reversal he dreaded: that he might die before she did. He did suggest there might have been other effects on him "in deeper layers" of his consciousness. We do know that he did not attend his mother's funeral but sent his daughter Anna as "the family representative," in what might well have been an avoidance of his feelings.

It is also significant that when his mother died, he was seventy-five and basically dying himself, whereas when his father died, he was only forty and around the time of this death he went through a major life crisis with symptoms of depression, "pseudo" cardiac problems, lethargy, migraines, and various other somatic and emotional concerns. He began his famous self-analysis and constructed the edifice of a new theory which led to the publication of *The Interpretation of Dreams*. It was at this time also that he both formulated and then recanted his seduction theory. Many have viewed this recanting as a response to a sense of guilt over the thought that his theory could apply to his father.

Sigmund Freud provides an interesting example of the differences in reaction to loss depending on the life cycle timing, the role of the person, and the nature of the death. Some deaths have more impact on a family than others. Particularly traumatic are untimely deaths, such as the early death of Sigmund's brother Julius. A similar example two generations later was the death of Sigmund's four-year-old grandson Heinz, who had been orphaned as an infant by the death of Freud's daughter Sophie. The grandson was apparently extraordinarily intelligent. Freud wrote of him: "He was indeed an enchanting little fellow, and I myself was aware of never having loved a human being, certainly never a child, so much. . . . I find this loss very hard to bear. I don't think I have ever experienced such grief; perhaps my own sickness contributes to the shock. I work out of sheer necessity; fundamentally everything has lost its meaning for me."[38] For more than three years he was apparently in a depression and unable to enjoy life. His strong reaction seems to be due partly to its coinciding with his own diagnosis of a cancer that was eventually fatal. He wrote to the child's father three years later: "I have spent some of the blackest days of my life in sorrowing about the child. At last I have taken hold of myself and can think of him quietly and talk of him without tears. But the comforts of reason have done nothing to help; the only consolation for me is that at my age I would not have seen much of him."[39]

LOOKING AT LOSS IN YOUR OWN FAMILY

Considering the anomie and disconnection of our society, the very experience of sharing a loss can help families to expand the context in which they see themselves—to experience continuity from past to future and to see the connection to one another, to their culture, and to other human beings. The death and their whole lives come into better perspective, and they are strengthened for the future. Family rituals are excellent ways to promote healing and transformation. A toast made at a wedding or an anniversary party, or even a eulogy at another family member's death, may help keep the dead person in the context of family relationships. One young man, making the family toast at Thanksgiving, ended a two-year silence about his sister-in-law by giving thanks for the happy memories they all had of her. She had died two years before in an automobile accident, and the family had become so tied up in the pain of her loss that it had stifled all their relationships. In another case a woman held a memorial service twenty-five years later for her brother, who had committed suicide on his birthday. She thus began a process of reconciliation around a loss that had gone unacknowledged for a quarter of a century. Such evocations to integrate loss may occur long after the death, even after a generation or two. The healing process can benefit the family in profound ways.

Questions, again, are the most powerful tool for gaining a new understanding of losses. In your family are dates of death remembered or barely honored? How comfortable are family members in talking about the deceased and the circumstances of the death? Are both good and bad memories accessible?

Consider the dealings with funeral directors, the rituals observed, who speaks at the service, and who doesn't. All this information indicates how family members relate, what they believe, what they fear, and what they cherish. You might also think about the following:

- How did various family members express their reactions to death? Tears? Withdrawal? Depression? Frantic activity? Did they talk to one another about the loss?
- Who was present at the moment of death? Who was not present who "should have been"?
- How were family relationships at the time of death? Were there unresolved issues with the person who died?
- Who arranged the funeral? Who attended? Who didn't? Who gave the eulogy?
- Was the body cremated or buried? If cremated, what happened to the ashes? Is there a marking of the grave?
- Did family conflicts or cutoffs occur around the time of death?
- Was there a will? Who received what bequests? Were there family rifts because of provisions in the will?
- Do family members visit the grave and how often? Who men-

tions the dead person and with what frequency? What happened to the belongings of the dead person?

- Was there secrecy about the cause or circumstances of the death? Were facts kept from anyone inside or outside the family?

- What mythology has been created in the family about the dead person? Has she or he been made into a saint?

- What would the history of the family have been like if the dead person had survived longer?

- Do family members feel stigmatized by the death (e.g., a suicide, a death from AIDS)?

- How have the survivors' lives been influenced by their relationships with the person? What do they carry with them from this person?

- What are the family beliefs about afterlife, and how have these beliefs influenced an understanding of the meaning of loss?

- What other beliefs do family members have that may help sustain them in the face of loss e.g., a sense of family or cultural mission, a sense of survivorship?

WHERE DO WE COME FROM?

Parents and Children

My mother . . . is monumental, really. . . . Probably she is exactly like me; otherwise we wouldn't so hanker after one another whenever we are wise enough to keep apart. Her letters are things I dread, and she always asks for more of mine (I try to write monthly; but we haven't a subject we dare be intimate upon).

—T. E. Lawrence, letter to Mrs. G. B. Shaw

My mother is 72. We visit often. I have to see about her and she thinks she has to see about me. But it's a curious thing, because I was taken from my Mom to be raised by my grandmother when I was 3 and except for a disastrous bitter visit when I was 7, I didn't see her again until I was 13. I'm often asked how I got over that without holding a grudge. I see her as one of the greatest human beings I've ever met. She's funny and quite outrageous really.

—Maya Angelou, conversation with Stephanie Stokes Oliver

No one can ever replace your parents. They provided for you when you were an infant and helpless, and throughout life you depend on them in one way or another. There is a debt you can never repay. Yet in the complex web of the family many people feel little joy in the connection to parents. And few of us really get to know our parents as people. We may be too busy "fending off" what seems to be parental intrusiveness or wishing for connections we never had.

However, by seeing your parents in the context of their lives—as children, siblings, lovers, friends—and by exploring family patterns of parent-child relationships, you may come to a different understanding. The more fully you relate to each parent's life, the more you will understand—and perhaps sympathize with—their influence on you.

You can start simply by talking to your parents about their lives.

What were their dreams? Were those dreams realized? How did they feel about their own parents? What do they remember about childhood? You can also interview other family members about your parents: What were their impressions of your parents as children, siblings, friends, workers, lovers (though this may be touchy!)?

For some people the relationship with parents is the most difficult one they will know. Experiencing themselves as victims, they feel misunderstood, mistreated, abandoned in dangerous places, required to perform adult tasks at too tender an age, like Snow White, Cinderella, or Hansel and Gretel. They fantasize that they were adopted, once belonging to some other saner, kinder, more "normal" father and mother. And for some people it is impossible to mature beyond those childhood experiences of intimidation and powerlessness.

Later the parent-child roles may reverse: As parents age, they lean on their children more, become dependent, and the children's responsibility increases. This can be a gratifying time of human connectedness or, if earlier resentments persist, a time when problems intensify. It is often difficult for children, even as adults, to develop a clear sense of their parents, one that goes beyond early larger-than-life expectations of "mother" and "father." And it is also essential to realize that we as children have a tremendous power to hurt our parents. When Maya Angelou's son chided her, "Mother, I know I'm your only child, but you must remember this is my life, not yours," she wrote: "The thorn from the buds one has planted, nourished and pruned pricks most deeply and draws more blood."[1] We must remember that what we say to our parents taps into their profoundest feelings about themselves and about what we mean to them.

Most of us grow up with very different feelings about mothers and fathers because of the profoundly different roles each is "supposed" to play in our culture. A typical illustration of the different expectations is expressed by the son and daughter in Robert Anderson's play *I Never Sang for My Father:*

> SON: I just do not want to let my father die a stranger.
> DAUGHTER: You're looking for something that isn't there, Gene. You're looking for a mother's love in a father. Mothers are soft and yielding. Fathers are hard and rough to teach us the ways of the world, which is rough, which is mean, which is selfish and prejudiced.
> SON: What does it matter if I never loved him or he never loved me? And yet, when I hear the word "father," it matters.[2]

Perhaps we should consider the different problems and roles for daughters and for sons, for mothers and for fathers. Traditionally fathers have been more often unknown and unknowable, while mothers, more overtly present, get the brunt of our anger and more of our love. Mothers are often perceived as being overly present, offering too much advice and wanting too much intimacy. As one young woman has described it, "Our fathers worked six days a week, twelve hours a day, and when they came home they were too tired for our exuberance and need. Or they were absent, or travelling, or dead. We remember them as people we hungered to know better, yet if they are with us now we refrain from asking the hard questions that make our hearts a battleground. These questions we keep for our mothers, with whom we seem locked in an unending arms-length minuet of impassioned love laced with fierce anger."[3]

To understand parents fully, we need to question how the culture has often prescribed distance between fathers and children and between mothers and sons. We need to consider the constrictions traditional gender roles had on our families. This means expanding our view of men beyond the idea of the dominant male and the selfless female. We need to develop an appreciation of the men in our families who were able to admit doubts or to become nurturers and the women who dared defy conventions by expressing their strength directly.

The ideal for all of us would be to have a comfortable, trusting person-to-person relationship with each parent. But this ideal is rarely achieved. Because it takes two adults to create a child, everyone starts out as part of a three-person system (at least), and this threesome generally becomes the central triangle in life. If everyone gets along, things are fine, but if there are conflicts, this triadic pattern can become problematic. In "real" life the basic triad often fails to remain in place. Current estimates are that more than one-third of this generation's children will live in a single-parent household before the age of eighteen, while many others will be raised by grandparents, gay or lesbian couples, or foster or adoptive families and in many other types of households.

The classic parent-child triangle involves the child or children siding with one parent, while the other is the outsider. The children may feel close to their mother, who is seen as nurturing and reasonable, while the father is seen as withholding and unreasonable. Or they may see their mother as intrusive and nagging and the father as Mr. Nice Guy. It is hard to be equally friendly toward both parents if one of them is always angry with the other. Children will end up taking sides without even realizing what they are doing.

Such a classic good guy/bad guy triangle can be seen in Eleanor Roosevelt's family *(Genogram 6.1)*. Both her parents died when she

The Family of Eleanor Roosevelt
Genogram 6.1

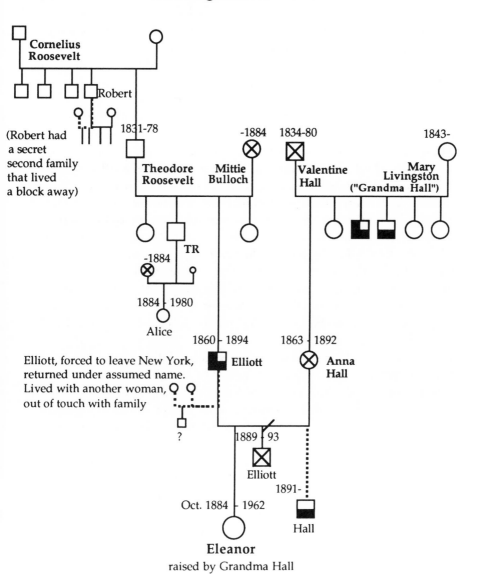

Eleanor
raised by Grandma Hall

was quite young, and that fact probably locked her childhood view of the triangle in place, since there could be no adult experiences to counteract the intense early memories. Had Eleanor's father lived, she might have developed a very different relationship with him, demanding a different kind of love—one with consistency and accountability. She might have become fed up with his inconsistent behavior. At best, Eleanor Roosevelt might have developed a more realistic view of her father and her mother, accepting both their flaws and their virtues. As it was, she was a remarkable person who showed amazing fortitude in dealing with difficult circumstances and relationships. However, throughout her life she is said to have been initially enthusiastic in personal relationships, but later disillusionment often set in.

Eleanor's relationship to her father, Elliott, was very close. She was his first child, "a miracle from heaven," he had said,[4] born eight months after the double tragedy in the family, discussed earlier, when her uncle Theodore Roosevelt lost both mother and wife on the same night. Perhaps Eleanor was a consolation for her father's grief. He certainly identified with her, giving her the same nickname, Nell, that he had been called as a child, and she in turn adored him. Though he died when Eleanor was only ten, she carried his letters around with her for the rest of her life. In her autobiography, written when she was in her seventies, she wrote: "He dominated my life as long as he lived, and was the love of my life for many years after he died. With my father I was perfectly happy. . . . He was the center of my world. . . . With his death went for me all the realities of companionship which he had suggested for the future, but . . . he lived in my dreams and does to this day."[5]

In contrast with the intense bond with her father, Eleanor's relationship with her mother was not close. She saw her mother as distant and unsympathetic. She saw herself as homely and was sure that her mother concurred in this assessment. She recalls in her autobiography: "My mother was one of the most beautiful women I have ever seen. I felt a curious barrier between myself and . . . [my mother] . . . I can still remember standing in the door, often with my finger in my mouth, and I can see the look in her eyes and hear the tone of her voice as she said 'Come in Granny.' If a visitor was there she might turn and say, 'She is such a funny child, so old-fashioned that we always call her "Granny." ' I wanted to sink through the floor in shame."

Eleanor's world had begun to disintegrate before her father died. When she was five, Elliott, a disturbed and erratic alcoholic, abruptly left the family. Although from a background of wealth and success, Elliott never lived up to his potential, dropping out of school in his teens. Despite his reputation as an adventurer, his amiability, good looks, and social position led to marriage with Anna Hall, a highly sought-after debutante. For the first few years of their marriage, his

Eleanor Roosevelt, with her beloved father, Elliott, and two younger brothers. When her father died at an early age, Eleanor carried his letters with her for the rest of her life. Franklin D. Roosevelt Library

charm, intelligence, and inherited wealth stood him in good stead, although he did not himself provide much income for his family. Then, after a painful injury to his ankle, Elliott was transformed rather quickly into a depressed addict and alcoholic. Sometimes hostile and even suicidal, he would disappear, leaving his young wife and small children alone and unsure of his whereabouts. When he did finally reappear, there were drunken sprees and bouts of violence. Even then Eleanor favored her father. In describing one of his returns, she remembered almost guiltily: "My father had come home . . . and I am sorry to say he was causing a great deal of anxiety, but he was the only person who did not treat me as a criminal."

The family made various efforts to help its wayward son, persuading him to undergo several sanitarium stays. Finally, to protect his estate, the family moved to have him judged insane, and he was not allowed to live with his wife and children. For a time he made a partial recovery, working in a small southern factory town as part of his rehabilitation. During this time he lived with different women, and his family did not know where he was. (There is an interesting parallel in the previous generation of this family when Elliott's uncle

Robert maintained two separate families almost around the corner from one another and two sets of children. When his wife died, he apparently moved his second family in with the first.) Then Eleanor's mother took ill with diphtheria and died suddenly. Even here Eleanor's first thoughts were of her father: "Death meant nothing to me, and one fact wiped out everything else—my father was back and I would see him very soon."

There was, however, no storybook ending. Elliott continued to drink and could not care for his two small children, who ended up living with their kind but stern Grandma Hall, who disapproved of their father. Elliott wrote Eleanor letters full of promise and hope but rarely visited. Once when he did visit, he took her to his club but abandoned her in the vestibule. Hours later she had the humiliating experience of watching him be carried out drunk. Despite such painful experiences, Eleanor continued to believe that one day he and she would go off blissfully together. She remembered his reassurances: "He began . . . to explain to me that . . . he and I must keep close together. Some day I would make a home for him again; we would travel together and do many things. Somehow it was always he and I. I did not understand whether my brothers were to be our children or whether he felt that they would be at school and college and later independent."

The letters he wrote raised her hopes that he was coming home, only to disappoint her when he did not. Within a short time he moved back to New York under an assumed name and lived out of touch with the family. In 1894, when Eleanor was ten years old, and only two years after his wife's death, he died of his alcoholism.

Later she wrote about her childhood: "I acquired a strange and garbled idea of the troubles around me. Something was wrong with my father, but from my point of view nothing could be wrong with him. If people only realized what a war goes on in a child's mind and heart in a situation of this kind, I think they would try to explain more than they do, but nobody told me anything." When she was a teenager, an aunt in an argument told her the truth about her father's drinking and affairs, but her love for him remained unshaken. It seemed even to strengthen her belief that she and he had needed each other and that he had been as vulnerable as she was.

Eleanor's one-sided loyalty provides a good example of how an unrealistic view of parents can be imprinted early, lasting throughout life, if the need to preserve it is intense. In Eleanor's case it was as if she allowed her imagination to fill in his absences with the father she wished she had. Of course, by doing that, she never really knew the father she did have.

Nor did she ever gain a clear view of her mother. With the tremendous reservoir of affection she reserved for her father, there was little left for her mother. Her mother's judgmental attitude may have seemed responsible for her father's problems. Young children often see things this way. Most likely, the more she expressed her loyalty to her father, the more she felt rejected by her mother, who must have sensed Eleanor's preference. In turn, the more distant she was from her mother, the more she valued her special relationship with her father. In the end she was not able to see either parent for who he or she really was.

For many years Eleanor's daughter, Anna, named for her mother, was caught in a similar triangle in which she saw her father, Franklin, as the hero and her mother as the villain. She writes: "It is no wonder that my Father was my childhood hero. . . . He talked about all sorts of things I liked to hear about—books I was reading, a cruise we might be going to take. . . . [Mother] felt a tremendous sense of duty to us . . . but she did not understand or satisfy the need of a child for primary closeness to a parent."[6]

Eleanor's son James writes: "Having gained no useful knowledge on the subject from her own unhappy years as a child, mother was absolutely terrified to find herself a parent. . . . [Her] fear of failure as a mother in turn hurt her as a mother. For many years—until it was too late for her to become a real mother—she let our grandmother act as our mother."

Eleanor herself seems to have agreed about her difficulties as a mother. That was not surprising, considering her own wretched childhood: "It did not come naturally to me to understand little children or to enjoy them . . . because play had not been an important part of my own childhood."[7]

Anna's husband later reported that she used to tell him that her mother was unpredictable and inconsistent: sweet and lovely one hour and the next hour critical and demanding. Luckily for both mother and daughter, they lived long enough and worked hard enough to move past their conflicts and problems. Eleanor was to write later: "Today no one could ask for a better friend than I have in Anna, or she has in me. Perhaps because it grew slowly, the bond between us is all the stronger. No one can tell either of us anything about the other, and though we might not always think alike or act alike, we always respect each other's motives, and there is a type of sympathetic understanding between us, which would make a real misunderstanding quite impossible."[8]

Many children never reach this type of mature understanding with their parents. They never give up trying to mold their parents into the unconditionally loving caretakers they felt they never had. As adults they may do this by continuing to seek parental approval or by continuing to act needy. In both cases they are likely to be disappointed.

THE FAMILY OF FRANZ KAFKA

Some, like the Jewish Czech writer Franz Kafka (*Genogram 6.2*), never get past their preoccupation with whatever didn't work out in their relationships with their parents. Kafka was obsessed all his life by his problems in relating to his father. He made a well-known but failed attempt to reconcile with his father, as well as to change him, in a letter he never delivered. In this letter he said: "My writing was all about you; all I did there, after all, was to bemoan what I could not bemoan upon your breast."[9] Not surprisingly Kafka wrote about people caught up in terrifying situations where they were the victims of a senseless, impersonal, all-powerful, persecuting world.

Kafka saw his father as a loud, overpowering, hot-tempered man, self-centered, hypocritical, and incapable of providing emotional support, yet sabotaging his children's efforts to break away. He believed his father intended to frighten him into being less timid and unmanly, a tactic that never worked. Always terrified of his father, Kafka blamed him for his own lack of confidence and sense of guilt.

Kafka viewed his mother as everything good—a peacemaker, kind and considerate, who buffered the tensions between father and son. But in the end he felt she sided with his father, and ultimately Kafka felt unprotected by her, saying that she loved her husband too much and could not act as an independent spiritual force on her son's behalf. Kafka's father was the villain, and his mother the unwitting, if well-intentioned, accomplice; he had fleeting awareness of his own provocations in the pattern, always turning to his mother as intermediary and never dealing with his father directly.

In Kafka's letter to his father, written when he was thirty-six, he tried to insist that no one was to blame for their relationship—from the beginning a mismatch of natures: "I too believe you are entirely blameless in the matter of our estrangement. But I am equally

The Family of Franz Kafka
Genogram 6.2

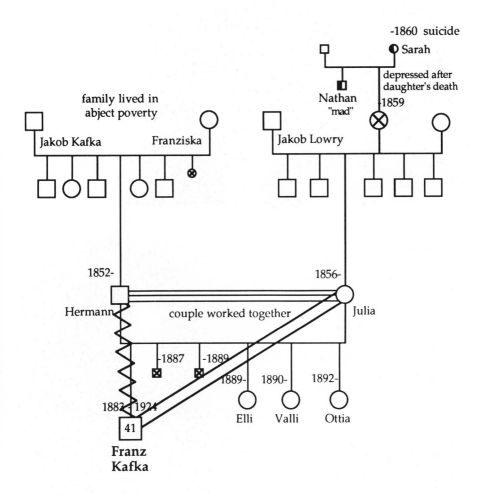

entirely blameless. If I could get you to acknowledge this, then what would be possible is—not, I think, a new life; we are both much too old for that—but still, a kind of peace; no cessation, but still, a diminution of your unceasing reproaches."

Kafka proceeded to list incident after incident of his father's insensitivity. He blamed his stammering on his father for not allowing him to contradict. He said his father expected him to do poorly, and sure enough, in his nervousness he fumbled. He said his father expected him to marry yet insisted that no one he proposed to marry was good

Franz Kafka with his two younger sisters. Two brothers, born between Kafka and his sisters, died in infancy. Throughout his life Kafka felt intimidated by his father (below) but saw his mother, (right), as the embodiment of goodness and kindness.
Archiv Klaus Wagenbach, Berlin

enough. Kafka even predicted that his father would dismiss his letter with "Is that all you're so worked up about?"

Kafka's letter provides an astute analysis of the role played by the "good" parent, in this case his mother, in perpetuating a parental triangle: "Mother unconsciously played the part of a beater during a hunt. Even if your method of upbringing might in some unlikely case have set me on my own feet by means of producing defiance, dislike, or even hate in me, Mother cancelled that out again by kindness, by talking sensibly . . . , by pleading for me; and I was again driven back into your orbit, which I might perhaps otherwise have broken out of, to your advantage and to my own. But no real reconciliation came about. Mother merely shielded me from you in secret."

In his view his mother's peacekeeping efforts kept the conflict between his father and him unresolved. Her failure to confront the father made him feel justified. Kafka impeded his own efforts at coming to terms with his father by relating only through his mother. He never managed to see his father as anything but a tyrant and a bully, failing to go beyond the surface behavior to understand his father's perspective.

Hermann Kafka had been the fourth of six surviving children in a family so poor they lived in a one-room shack. At fourteen he left home to make his own way, and he did that by determination and single-minded ambition. He married Julia Lowry, who came from better circumstances, but whose mother had died when she was three, leaving her with heavy responsibility for her younger siblings. Like her husband, she was vigorous and ambitious. They looked to each other for the love and caring they had missed in childhood. By all accounts they had a devoted marriage, working together in their dry goods business and socializing in the evening.

From Franz Kafka's viewpoint as the eldest child of six, the children were left out of this arrangement. They were raised by caretakers while the parents worked to establish the father's business. Probably Kafka felt powerless to make up to his parents for family losses (two brothers died of childhood diseases). Things may look one way to children, until they become parents themselves—often the time when such reevaluation first takes place.

No matter how well off he became, Hermann Kafka had a lifelong worry about survival. He could not understand his children's complaints, especially those of his sensitive, ever-fretting son. His prime concern was to give them economic security, and they failed to appreciate this.

Franz Kafka, who died at the age of forty-one, never could bring himself to marry. He feared that marriage and parenthood might make him more like his father. Even worse, he might have children who would resent him as he resented his father. In his letter Franz admitted that he was a difficult, obstinate child who tended to be oversensitive and that there were times when he deliberately provoked his father by taking a contrary opinion.

In a remarkable ending to the letter, Kafka provided a detailed rebuttal of all his own arguments, anticipating his father's criticisms. He was sure his father would mistrust the letter, seeing it as full of veiled recriminations, and would chide him for continuing to accept money while criticizing him.

Despite the professed desire for reconciliation, the tone of the letter was bitter. By itself the letter probably would not have improved the relationship between father and son, though it would probably have been the most honest communication they had ever had. However, true to the family triangle, instead of giving the letter to his father directly, Kafka gave it to his mother to deliver. The mother returned it to her son, who then kept it to himself. Family therapist Tom Fogarty calls this pattern a "Two Step"—a dance in which even when an effort toward change is made, we are called back into line, and we accept the rebuff. One wonders what might have happened if Kafka had then given the letter directly to his father.

The opposite side of the "parent as villain" is the "parent as saint." When the idealized image of one parent gives way to disappointing reality, the previously excluded parent may then be seen as all good and the previously favored parent as all bad. This is an equally unrealistic view, again showing how triangles can distort relationships. Whether a parent is vilified or idealized, a transformative process is necessary to understand the parent's story, adding new perspectives that include other points of view.

THE DICKENS MARRIAGE

When Charles Dickens (*Genogram 6.3*), after twenty-two years of marriage and twelve children, decided to leave his wife, Catherine Hogarth Dickens, for his eighteen-year-old mistress, Ellen Ternan, he justified his behavior by establishing his wife as the villain of the piece. Declaring he had never loved her, he blamed her for destroy-

The Dickens Family
Genogram 6.3

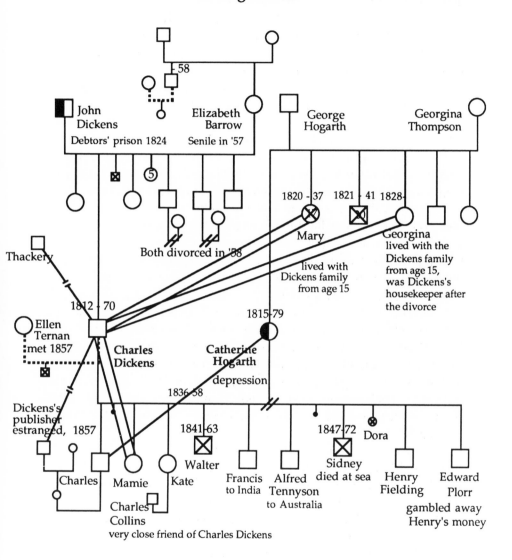

ing their marriage, though the real precipitant of their separation was
his affair with Ellen. In this context he reassessed the many years of
their marriage: "I believe my marriage has been for years and years
as miserable a one as ever was made. I believe that no two people
were ever created with such an impossibility of interest, sympathy,

confidence, sentiment, tender union of any kind between them, as there is between my wife and me."[10] She was, not surprisingly, depressed and lacking in confidence. His first direct act of separation was to wall up the connection between their bedroom and his dressing room, which he now took as his own bedroom. He then set her up as the villain, saying that if her sister Georgina had not lived with them and become the energetic, intelligent, inventive, and attractive "mother" to the children, they would have had no mother. He said that his wife was the only human being he had ever known with whom he could not get along or find common interest; indeed, he said, no one, not even her own mother, could get along with her.

Dickens's affair and sudden separation from his wife triggered disruptions with relatives, friends, and colleagues. Though he tried to blame everything on his wife and took elaborate efforts to protect the secrecy of his affair, his actions had a profound impact on his children. One son, Walter, left for India shortly before Dickens met Ternan and never returned. All but one of the other Dickens children, always adoring of their father, sided with him at first. This was not surprising. Dickens was entertaining, famous, and magical. He created numerous lively family festivities.

Catherine Dickens, on the other hand, was passive, quiet (probably seriously depressed), and not especially responsive. The children blamed her for losing their father's love. Initially only the oldest son sided with his mother, stopped talking to his father, and defiantly announced his engagement to the daughter of Dickens's estranged publisher. Dickens was given custody of all the other children, moving them in with his wife's sister Georgina, who became the family caretaker.

However, only a few months later Dickens sent his son Henry, age eight, to join his three older brothers in boarding school and for the first time left them at the school for the Christmas holidays, which had been the most festive of Dickens's family celebrations. Indeed, in his story *The Christmas Carol* one of the saddest memories evoked is of being left as a child in boarding school over the Christmas holidays. The older daughter, Mamie, became her father's caretaker and never left him. The younger sister, Kate, assisted her sister but married relatively soon, clearly to get away from home. It is interesting that Kate chose to marry the younger brother of one of Dickens's closest friends, Wilkie Collins, who himself had a separate menage with a young mistress.

Years later Catherine Dickens gave Kate the letters Dickens had written her, hoping for some understanding of how wronged she had

Top left: Catherine Hogarth Dickens in 1857, the year that Charles Dickens left her for a clandestine relationship with Ellen Ternan (above), an eighteen-year-old actress. (Below), Charles Dickens in 1859.

been and to show that he had indeed loved her. Kate consulted with George Bernard Shaw about the letters, and he helped her revise her view of her parents, particularly of her mother. Shaw said her view that her parents' marriage as a case of "the man of genius tied to a commonplace wife" had been rudely upset by a writer named Ibsen. He predicted that history would sympathize more with Catherine, who had sacrificed her life, to the extent of bearing Dickens twelve children in fifteen years, and that her only real sin was "that she was not a female Charles Dickens." Kate eventually cooperated in the publication of the story of the Dickenses' marital separation from her mother's point of view[11] and dedicated it to the memory of her mother.

The Dickens marriage involved a triangle from the start, since Catherine's younger sister Mary moved in with the couple right at the beginning. After Mary's death the next year Dickens so idealized her that he wrote: "I have lost the dearest friend I ever had. . . . The very last words she whispered were of me. . . . I solemnly believe that so perfect a creature never breathed. . . . She had not a fault."[12] He bought a double cemetery plot, hoping to be buried beside Mary, and celebrated the anniversary of her death all his life. Several years later Catherine's younger sister Georgina, who bore a striking resemblance to Mary in both personality and physical appearance, joined the Dickens household. She was fifteen, the same age Mary had been when she moved in. Her resemblance to her dead sister was so strong that their mother said: "So much of Mary's spirit shines out in this sister, that the old time comes back again at some seasons, and I can hardly separate it from the present."

Over the years Dickens felt entitled to include other women in his marriage. Twice when Catherine suspected his affairs, he accused her of pathological jealousy and made her apologize to his mistress. As time went by, he became increasingly convinced that his wife was boring and useless. As one of our most perceptive critics of marriage, Phyllis Rose, has said in her book *Parallel Lives*, "Marriage and career, family and work, which so often pull a woman in different directions, are much more likely to reinforce one another for a man."[13]

Dickens was a case in point. He, whose father had lived in a debtors' prison, married "up." Catherine Hogarth Dickens was the daughter of a successful journalist. In the early years Dickens appears to have been extremely happy with her. He wrote of the early days of his marriage, "I shall never be so happy again . . . never if I roll in wealth and fame."

THE DILEMMA OF WOMEN'S ROLES
IN FAMILIES

As you consider your own family tree, note the roles that women have played over the generations, and be sure to see them against the prevailing cultural constraints of their times. Traditionally women have been evaluated primarily by their beauty and their mothering and housekeeping skills. Their creative work has often had to be accomplished, as Mary Catherine Bateson has put it, "in scraps of rescued space and time in marginal roles that have to be invented again and again."[14]

A woman who is not cut out to be a good caretaker has never had an easy time. In the past a woman who wanted to have a life of her own, with its own adventures and quests, often developed an "eccentric story" in order to free herself from the strictures of marriage and family.[15] George Eliot, for example, removed herself from conventional expectations by her decision to live with a man who could not divorce his legal wife. By one act that was considered outrageous she escaped social demands and made up for her despair at being considered unattractive.

Illness, even to the point of invalidism, has sometimes been the only way women could see out of the "slavery" of traditional roles. We saw this with Elizabeth Barrett Browning, whose invalidism freed her from conventional expectations and allowed her a degree of flexibility to focus on her poetry, though with the trade-off of being confined to her room.

Sonya Tolstoy provides another example of the "womanly" role. After forty years of catering to her "genius" husband, Leo, she wrote: "Geniuses must create in peaceful, enjoyable, comfortable conditions; a genius must eat, wash, dress, he must rewrite his work countless times; one must love him, give him no cause for jealousy so that he has peace, one must raise and educate the innumerable children who are born to a genius, but for whom he has no time." Providing such an atmosphere for genius was a constant struggle for Sonya Tolstoy since like her husband, she was brilliant, passionate, volatile, sensitive, easily jealous, and prone to self-analysis. She asked ironically, "But for what would I, an insignificant woman, need an intellectual and artistic life?" and replied: "To this question I can only answer, I do not know. But always suppressing my needs to care for the material needs of a genius is a great hardship."[16] Sonya questioning of her life and purpose will seem familiar to many women even today.

Because women have been valued mainly for their caretaking roles, we must rewrite the narratives of our families if we are to understand them in context. In the Tolstoy family it was many years before Sonya's son Sergei was able to appreciate her importance: "I understand better than I did then the importance of my mother in our family life and the great value of her care for us and for my father. At the time, it seemed to me that everything in our life went on of its own accord. We accepted Mother's care as a matter of course. I did not notice that beginning with our food and clothes to our studies and the copying for father, everything was managed by her."

FINDING YOUR PARENTS AS YOU LOSE THEM

In the normal course of events we realize that our parents will most likely die within our lifetime, yet knowing this and fully realizing it are two different things. If the relationship with a parent has been estranged or stormy and much is left unsaid or unresolved, his or her loss will be even greater. But it is also possible that in the consciousness of a parent's dying, we may achieve understanding between the generations.

For most of her life Simone de Beauvoir *(Genogram 6.4)* had devalued her mother as critical, unsophisticated, bourgeois, and guilt-inducing. She dealt with her by avoidance. But as her mother was dying, Simone came to reevaluate her, realizing that her mother had been raised to "live against herself." She recognized that a full-bodied, spirited woman lived inside her mother but was a stranger to her. Her mother had spent all her strength in repressing her desires, squeezing the armor of principles and prohibitions over her heart and mind, as she had been taught to pull the laces tightly around her body.

De Beauvoir shows remarkable insight into the ways in which this constriction developed in her mother. Simone's father had studied law although he spent much of his time as a dandy, having used his marriage to improve his status. But shortly after the marriage Simone's maternal grandfather, who had been a wealthy banker, was sent to jail for fraud, and the family experienced a very public and humiliating bankruptcy.

As Simone thought about her mother's life, she realized that her mother's concern for convention and her desire to please were com-

De Beauvoir Family
Genogram 6.4

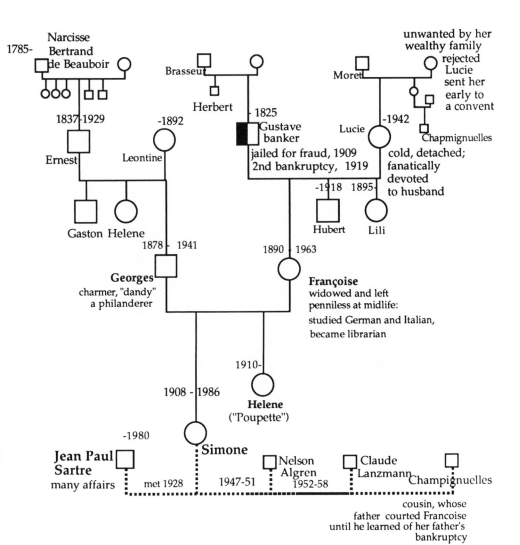

pensation for the shame she felt about her father. She felt guilty all her life that her husband had never received the dowry he expected. She saw her husband as noble for not blaming her for her family's poverty after the bankruptcy, though the husband was not much of a provider, and the family struggled for many years just to survive. As

Simone thought about her father's extramarital affairs, she began to appreciate how difficult life had been for her mother and how strong her mother had been.

De Beauvoir also developed an appreciation for the way her mother had recovered after her husband's death, which left her penniless at the age of fifty-one. Françoise, apparently, had not been trapped by her past but had taken advantage of her late-life freedom to take courses, receive a certificate to work as a Red Cross librarian, learn to ride a bicycle, study German and Italian, reestablish ties with friends and relatives who had been driven away by her husband's surliness, and she was able to satisfy one of her earliest longings— to travel.

As de Beauvoir reevaluated her mother, she perceived with touching clarity the tragedy of her mother's limited options: "It is a pity that out of date ideas should have prevented her from adopting the solution that she came round to twenty years later—that of working away from home. . . . She would have risen in her own esteem instead of feeling that she was losing face. She would have had connections of her own. She would have escaped from a state of dependence that tradition made her think natural but that did not in the least agree with her nature, and no doubt she would then have been better equipped to bear the frustration that she had to put up with."[17]

Although as a child Simone de Beauvoir had been very close to her mother, her adolescence became a stormy battle for independence, and the conflict continued in her adult life. When she learned that her mother had contracted terminal cancer, this information took her by surprise. That her mother would die one day was a fact devoid of meaning for de Beauvoir—one of those things we all know but imagine to take place in some other "legendary" time. As she began to face the reality of her mother's impending death, she decided to attempt a reconciliation. But there, watching her mother in the hospital, she felt an intense desire to distance herself: "The sight of my mother's nakedness jarred me. No body existed less for me: none existed more. As a child I had loved her dearly; as an adolescent she had filled me with an uneasy repulsion, all this was perfectly in the ordinary course of things and it seemed reasonable to me that her body should retain its dual nature, that it should be both repugnant and holy—a taboo. But, for all that, I was astonished at the violence of my distress." In time she achieved more perspective. She was no longer worried by her mother's nakedness and instead became afraid of hurting her. More important, she began to see her mother as a person.

She was capable of selfless devotion for my father and for us. But it is impossible for anyone to say "I am sacrificing myself" without feeling bitterness. . . . She was continually rebelling against the restraints and the privations that she inflicted upon herself. . . . She flung herself into the only other course that was available to her—that of feeding upon the young lives that were in her care. "At least I have never been self-centered; I have lived for others," she said to me later. Yes, but also by means of others. She was possessive; she was overbearing; she would have liked to have us completely in her power.

Gradually Simone saw her own part in the earlier alienation with her mother, though it was difficult to overcome her negative reactions. She would promise herself to find common ground with her mother, but then she would be irritated by her mother's clumsy use of language. Even so, as she sat with her mother in the hospital, she gradually developed the patience to listen to her mother's story for the first time and to admire her courage: "[Mother] . . . said very firmly, 'I would not admit that I was old. But one must face up to things; in a few days I shall be seventy-eight, and that is a great age. I must arrange my life accordingly. I am going to start a fresh chapter.' I gazed at her with admiration." In absorbing her mother's story, Simone realized she did not have the power to eradicate the early unhappiness of her mother that had led her to make her children unhappy and to suffer herself for having done so. She realized that if her mother had embittered Simone's childhood, Simone had more than paid her back.

Françoise had had an unhappy childhood herself. She was also the older sister in her family, had grown up feeling that her mother was cold and that her father favored the younger sister, Lili. Realizing that Françoise had wanted from her children what she did not receive from her parents, Simone began to comprehend the intensity of her mother's investment in her as the intellectual older sister.

In the end Simone managed to retrieve her relationship with her mother, which had been short-circuited so long before: "I had grown very fond of this dying woman. As we talked in the half-darkness I assuaged an old unhappiness; I was renewing the old dialogue that had been broken off during my adolescence and that our differences and our likenesses had never allowed us to take up again. And the early tenderness that I had thought dead forever came to life again."

Unfortunately too many people wait until it is too late before achieving such understanding. It is, of course, much easier to reconcile with your parents if they are still alive. But even if they are not, you can better understand yourself and your family by trying to discover as much as you can about them.

The goal of reconnecting is to share yourself with your parents, not just to find out about their lives. Parents may resist one-way questions if they feel they are being "investigated." They are more likely to respond if you express interest in family stories. Your own self-disclosure, along with nonthreatening, specific questions, will encourage them to flesh out the details that help you see them as people trying to get by as best they can.

Many people think, "Not my father, he's too intimidating," or, "I could never talk to my mother; she's too domineering and intrusive." From this perspective, whatever your parents' behavior, the challenge is to understand how they got to be that way. Parents who act controlling got that way somehow. Such behavior typically reflects a sense of insecurity or inadequacy rather than a willful attempt to harm a child. Once parents believe they still have something to offer, such as information about their own lives and experiences, the need to be so controlling may lessen.

Accepting your parents means giving up your efforts to change them. As family therapist Tom Fogarty says, "It helps you improve your relationship with a parent if you lower your expectations to zero." This isn't to say that you do not keep working to understand your parents and trying to communicate more effectively. But instead of building the relationship on the basis of an expected "payback" from the parent, you put the emphasis on how it is *you* want to relate.

QUESTIONS ABOUT PARENTS

■ What kind of relationship did each of your parents have with each of their parents? Their siblings? Their grandparents? Their aunts and uncles? How did they like school? Did they do well? Did they have friends? How did they spend their time? How did the family spend holidays and vacations?

■ Were there critical life experiences that changed things for them: a death, an illness, a move, a change in financial circumstances? What do they remember of those experiences?

■ What about when they were growing up? How did they experience adolescence? Did their parents approve of their friends? What were their dreams?

■ When your parents met each other, how did their parents react? Were there conflicts over the wedding? Did their parents disapprove of their child-rearing practices?

■ What was it like for them to become parents? What did they want to do differently from their own parents? What do they remember of your behavior as a child? Were you hard to discipline? What were the good memories? What did they find most difficult about parenting? What do they remember about times when you or your siblings had problems?

■ Were there times when they were raising you that were particularly difficult for them? Your adolescence? Hard times financially?

■ Were there ways that your mother or other women in the family did not conform to the stereotypes of mother? Did your mother work outside the home? Did she want to? What about your aunts and grandmothers? What were their dreams? How did they manage or react to the socially approved women's roles in their time? How did others react to them?

■ Were there ways in which your father or other men in the family did not conform to the stereotypes of father? Were they affectionate? Caretakers? Talkers or storytellers? Emotionally involved with other family members? Were these men able to show their vulnerabilities? How did they manage against the constrictions of men's roles in their time?

■ What were the best models of parent-child relationships in your family? Why do you think so? What were the typical patterns of parent-child relationships for each gender? What were the rules for parent-child relationships at each phase of the life cycle: infancy, childhood, adolescence, launching, young adult, maturity? Are there clear expectations for how close parents and children ought to be ideally in your family? Are parents and children expected to spend leisure time together? Holidays? To share intimate thoughts?

■ Could you tell your parents what you appreciate about what they gave you and forgive them for what they were not able to give? What would you have to forgive?

SEVEN

SISTERS AND BROTHERS

I don't believe that the accident of birth makes people sisters and brothers. It makes them siblings. Gives them mutuality of parentage. Sisterhood and brotherhood are conditions people have to work at. It's a serious matter. You compromise, you give, you take, you stand firm, and you're relentless. . . . And it is an investment. Sisterhood means if you happen to be in Burma and I happen to be in San Diego and I'm married to someone who's very jealous and you're married to somebody who's very possessive, if you call me in the middle of the night, I have to come.

—Maya Angelou

You got to hold onto your brother and don't let him fall, no matter . . . you may not be able to stop nothing from happening, but you got to let him know you's there.

—James Baldwin's mother in "Sonny's Blues"

My dearest friend and bitterest rival, my mirror and opposite, my confidante and betrayer, my student and teacher, my reference point and counterpoint, my support and dependent, my daughter and mother, my subordinate, my superior and scariest still, my equal.

—Elizabeth Fishel, *Sisters*

Our sibling relationships are generally the longest relationships we have in life. While parents are our first caretakers, from whom we learn about trust and independence, it is our brothers and sisters to whom we first relate as partners and equals. In some ways we have more in common with our brothers and sisters—beginning with the fact that we shared our parents, our family history—than we will ever have with others. In some families, siblings remain one another's most important relationship. In others, their rivalry and conflict causes families to break apart. Katharine Hepburn said of her sisters and brothers: "They are so much a part of me that I simply know I could not have been me without them. They are my 'box'— my protection."[1] Siblings can become the models for future relationships with friends, lovers, and other contemporaries. In our modern world spouses may come and go, parents die, children grow up and leave, but siblings are always there if we hold on to our convictions.

Surprisingly, the importance of siblings has been overlooked in much of the psychological literature. Freud completely ignored sibling relationships. His early colleague and follower Alfred Adler did focus on sibling patterns in personality development, but when the two came to a parting of the ways, it was Freud whose ideas became more dominant. Freud, incidentally, viewed Adler's defection as the act of an ungrateful younger brother.

But the evidence is that sibling relationships matter a great deal. According to one important longitudinal study of successful, well-educated men (the Harvard classes of 1938–44), the single best predictor of emotional health at age sixty-five was having had a close relationship with one's sibling in college, more predictive than childhood closeness to parents, emotional problems in childhood, or parental divorce, more predictive, even, than having had a successful marriage or career.[2]

We've already taken a look at two celebrated siblings, the Wright brothers, Wilbur and Orville, a duo so linked that one is never spoken of without the other. Obviously not all siblings are as close as they were. Childhood rivalries and hurts carry over into adulthood. At family get-togethers everyone tries, at least at first, to be friendly and cordial. But beneath the surface old conflicts may simmer. The eldest sister, once the responsible caretaker, may still resent her "bratty and irresponsible little brother," now a successful six-foot-two executive. She soon finds herself falling into an old pattern of giving him advice. And he is immediately on the defensive because the old family script triggers his memories of being bossed around and feeling impotent. A younger sister who felt dominated or abused by her older brother, who teased her mercilessly throughout childhood, may feel uncomfortable even sitting at the same table with him. All the old unpleasant memories flood back. Two brothers who spent their childhoods competing in sports, in school, and for parental attention may find themselves subtly competing in the holiday dinner table conversation. Even if there are no major flare-ups, family members may leave the dinner feeling bored or vaguely dissatisfied, glad that such occasions occur only a few times a year.

Unfortunately parents sometimes make things worse. This is particularly true when siblings see one another only at the parental home or when adult siblings hear about one another only through the parents, especially the mother, who becomes the family "switchboard." Whether deliberately or inadvertently, parents can perpetuate old sibling patterns. A mother may compare one child with another, perhaps chiding one for not calling as often as another does. A father might talk repeatedly about how proud he is of his son, not realizing he is ignoring his daughter. A parent may elicit the support of one sibling in an effort to "shape up" another. Siblings themselves may even encourage this parental interference since this is the customary family pattern.

Sibling experiences vary greatly. An important factor is the amount of time brothers and sisters spend together when young. Two children who are close in age, particularly if they are of the same gender, generally spend a lot of time together, must share their parents' attention, and are usually raised under similar conditions. Siblings born farther apart obviously spend less time with each other and have fewer shared experiences; they grow up in the family at very different points in its evolution and in many ways are more comparable to only children.

In today's world of frequent divorce and remarriage there may be a combination of siblings, stepsiblings, and half siblings who live in different households and come together only on special occasions. There are also more only children, whose closest siblinglike relationships will be their playmates. And there are as well more two-child families, in which the relationship between the two children tends to be more intense for the lack of other siblings. Clearly the more time siblings have with one another, the more intense their relationships are likely to be.

Siblings who have little contact with outsiders grow to rely on one another, especially when parents are absent, unavailable, or inadequate. Charlie Chaplin and his half brother Sydney, four years older, provide an example of an unusually close and lifelong bond (*Genogram 7.1*). Sydney was less than three months old when his mother married Charles Chaplin, Sr., who became responsible for his support, though he did a very poor job of it. Chaplin, Sr., separated early from the boys' mother, became an alcoholic, and more or less abandoned them. Their mother suffered repeated bouts of insanity throughout their childhood and had to be institutionalized. Their aunt once said of the boys' relationships: "It seems strange to me that anyone can write about Charlie Chaplin without mentioning his brother Sydney. They have been inseparable all their lives, except when fate intervened at intervals. Syd, of quiet manner, clever brain and steady nerve, has been father and mother to Charlie. Charlie always looked up to Syd, and Sydney would suffer anything to spare Charlie."[3] At one point in their childhood when the brothers were separated, Sydney became concerned that Charlie was not re-

The Chaplin Family
Genogram 7.1

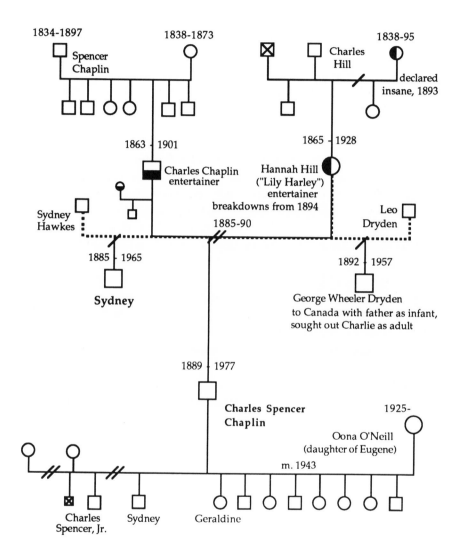

sponding to his letters; this was so partly because he could not spell well. Sydney reproached Charlie and touchingly recalled the misery they had endured together: "Since Mother's illness, all we have in the world is each other. So you must write regularly and let me know that I have a brother."[4] From early childhood they had to fend for themselves and move about from place to place—to the workhouse, an orphanage, and a series of apartments—having at times to help their mother receive care. Late in life Sydney, who had performed with his brother and then became his manager, wrote to Charlie: "It has always been my unfortunate predicament, or should I say fortunate predicament, to concern myself with your protection? This is the result of my fraternal or rather paternal instinct."[5]

Actually, Charlie Chaplin had another half brother, three years younger than he, Wheeler Dryden, whom Chaplin never mentioned in either of his autobiographies. Dryden's father abducted him away from his mother as an infant, and he never met Chaplin again until 1918, at which point Wheeler had to make many efforts to reconnect before Chaplin would even see or speak to him. Chaplin apparently got him to agree not to acknowledge their brotherhood, possibly to protect their mother's memory, since Chaplin does not mention that Sydney had a different father either. In later years Dryden worked for Chaplin and was more than a devoted follower. He seems to have revered his brother totally, following him around from a deferential distance, saving every scrap of memorabilia about him.

The extraordinary Brontë family discussed in Chapter 3, which produced three of the world's most remarkable authors, Charlotte, Emily, and Anne Brontë, also provide a touching illustration of the power of sibling relationships to compensate, when other relationships are problematic in a family. Charlotte Brontë once wrote: "The value of sisters' affections to each other: there is nothing like it in this world." The Brontës also show an incredible creativity, faced with the constrictions of women's roles. The sisters became one another's primary support. If they had not had one another in this way, the world might not have had the remarkable literature this sisterhood created.

Their mother died very early, leaving the children reliant on one another. When her two older sisters also died, Charlotte, at age nine, became leader and caretaker, the functional eldest. *(Genogram 7.2)*. It was she who invented racy and dangerous games and who in later years became the primary spokesperson for the family, encouraging her sisters to write and publish and handling all family business with the outside world. Next came the family "genius and prodigy," Branwell, the focus of parental energy and expectations, who was scheduled for glory but could not live up to family expectations. The two younger sisters, Emily and Anne, although a year apart in age, grew up almost like twins in closeness, though in personality they were very different. Emily was intense, athletic, often in a bad temper, and her imagination knew no restraint. Anne, the baby, was less drawn to the imagination than her older siblings, hiding a deep sadness behind

Museum of Modern Art

Charlie Chaplin with his brother, Sydney. Their aunt once said of them: "They must have been inseparable all their lives, except when fate intervened at intervals. Syd, of quiet manner, clever brain, and steady nerve, has been father and mother to Charlie." (Left) Hannah Chaplin, mother to Charlie and Sydney.

Roles of the Brontë Siblings
Genogram 7.2

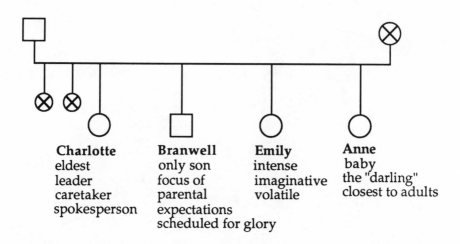

Charlotte
eldest
leader
caretaker
spokesperson

Branwell
only son
focus of
parental
expectations
scheduled for glory

Emily
intense
imaginative
volatile

Anne
baby
the "darling"
closest to adults

a gentle exterior. The roles the Brontë sisters played are common sister roles: Charlotte, the director and social organizer, whose dramatic imagination directed the play of the other children; Emily, the isolationist, the stubborn, independent one; and Anne, the darling, the sweet one; but also, a baby when the tragedy of the mother's death occurred, the one to grow up with the deepest attachment to an adult, her aunt Elizabeth. It was said of the other siblings that they believed only in the reality of childhood, while Anne had a skepticism about their romantic fantasies.

TWINS

The ultimate shared sibling experience is between identical twins. They have a special relationship that is exclusive of the rest of the family. Twins have been known to develop their own languages and maintain an uncanny, almost telepathic sense of each other. Even fraternal twins often have remarkable similarities because of their shared life experiences.

The major challenge for twins is to develop individual identities.

The Lederer Family
"Ann Landers"/"Dear Abby" Family

Genogram 7.3

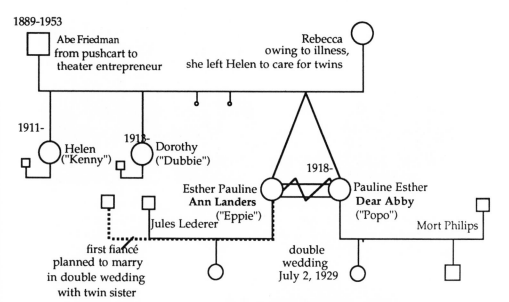

Both sisters were in love with Mort
Eppie met Jules while buying wedding
dress for 1st fiance and became engaged
in order to have a double wedding

Since they do not have a unique sibling position, there is a tendency to lump twins together. This becomes a problem especially when as adolescents they are trying to develop their separate identities. Sometimes twins have to go to extremes to distinguish themselves from each other.

Esther Pauline Friedman and Pauline Esther Friedman, identical twins, better known as Ann Landers and Dear Abby *(Genogram 7.3)*, were born seventeen minutes apart on July 4, 1918. With almost identical names, these famous twins demonstrate both the extremes of shared closeness and the intense, bitter competition of siblings. At times the bond between them was so strong that even their husbands felt like outsiders, but then, when the rivalry got too intense, they went for years without speaking. Still, their lives followed almost

"Dear Abby" and "Ann Landers," identical twins originally named Lederer, with other sisters at a family wedding. A double wedding had celebrated the marriages of the twins, who each became a famous columnist in her own right. AP/Wide World Photos

identical lines in an uncanny way, each pursuing exactly the same course as housewife-turned-advice-columnist. When they came together again, it was in some ways as if they had never been apart.

The twins did not begin to separate until the question of marriage arose. Interestingly, both women were attracted to the same man. It was Abby who won out, and when she decided to marry, Ann found herself another groom, so they could marry in a joint wedding. She even switched partners midway through the wedding plans, when the first marital choice did not work out, lining up a new mate in time for the double wedding with her twin sister. The two husbands were even connected, working in the same business organization for many years.

After the wedding the two couples left together for a double honeymoon. Unfortunately for Ann, her husband ran out of money midway through the trip, and the twins were forced to part. From this point on their lives began to diverge, although the closeness and the competition continued.

Some years later, bored with being a housewife and without work experience or a college degree to back her up, Ann talked her way into becoming the writer of the Ann Landers advice column. Initially she called on her sister for help, but in less than three months Abby had moved to the West Coast and was involved with her very similar (Dear Abby) advice column. She had exactly the same lack of credentials. The competition now began in earnest, and an extraordinary rivalry soon developed, with questions even being raised about one's plagiarizing the other—so similar was their work. Abby became widely syndicated, and that rankled Ann, who had had the idea to start with. Over the years, including many years of total cutoff, the two sisters have both been highly successful. Not surprisingly, their public has not always found it easy to distinguish between them since their opinions about real-life problems are so similar. In one area they do disagree. Abby said she thought being a twin was marvelous. Ann said it was not easy.

Sisters generally have been treated differently from brothers in families. The Wright brothers' father, Bishop Wright, for example, wrote to his youngest child and only daughter, then fifteen: "You have a good mind and good heart, and being my only daughter, you are my hope of love and care, if I live to be old. . . . But for you we should feel like we had no home."[6] Katharine Wright was even called *Schwester* (Sister), defining her primary role even in her nickname. While both parents and all the children except Wilbur and Orville attended college, Katharine was the only one who went to Oberlin, where her work was outstanding. After college, however, she returned and obediently took on the role of caretaker for her father and brothers, devoting herself to them for the next thirty years. We can only wonder about the price the Wright family and other families have paid in the lost talents of their daughters.

There are many reasons for the complexity of sister relationships: the familial bonds, the length of these relationships, the caretaking responsibilities sisters share, and their competitiveness for male attention and approval. There is also a special intricacy and intimacy in sister relationships. It is almost as if women saw in their sisters a reflection of aspects of themselves, while they view men from a greater distance, often a very great distance. Women are led by that distance and by the patriarchal power structure to romanticize and idealize men. On the other hand, women's response to women, and to sisters in particular, is influenced by their closeness and by sharing the culture's general devaluation of female characteristics.

Much of our literature has denied the sharing of sister relationships. As Louise Bernikow has pointed out, if we think of the most famous sisters in literature—Rachel and Leah in the Old Testament, Cordelia and her sisters in *King Lear*, Cinderella and her "wicked" stepsisters, or Chekhov's *Three Sisters*—a man always stands between the sisters, who are not supportive of each other. And mothers are hardly mentioned at all, unless divisively, as in *Cinderella*. Older sisters in literature are usually depicted as evil, while the youngest is "Daddy's Girl," the infantilized baby and favorite, receiving Daddy's love and wealth in return for her loyalty and willingness to be his "love object." The price she pays of conflict with her mother and sisters and loss of their affection is overlooked. As Bernikow says, "They do each other no good, these female siblings, if the stories are to be believed. One would be better off without them. In this masculine vision, all women would be better off without other women, for the woman alone—motherless, sisterless, friendless—can fix her eyes solely on father, brother, lover, and therefore peace will reign in the universe."[7]

But the truth is our parents usually die a generation before we do, and our children live on for a generation after us; it is rare that our spouses are closely acquainted with our first twenty or thirty years or for friendships to last from earliest childhood until the end of our lives. Thus our siblings share more of our lives genetically and contextually than anyone else, and sisters even more, since sisters tend to be emotionally more connected and to live longer than brothers. In fact, we can divorce a spouse much more finally than a sibling.

Luckily it is rare for siblings to break off their relationships or lose touch completely with one another. Sister pairs tend to have the closest relationships of all. Sisters seem to provide a basic feeling of emotional security in life. They can provide role models for successful aging, widowhood, bereavement, and retirement. They act as caretakers and exert pressures on one another to maintain values.

Sisters not only do more caretaking but also tend to share more intimacy and to have more intense relationships, as well as more family responsibility, although they typically get less glory than brothers. From childhood on, most sibling caretaking is delegated to older sisters, with brothers freed for play or other tasks. In the classic story of childhood *Peter Pan,* the only sister, Wendy, is immediately inducted into the role of mother, not only for her own brothers but for Peter Pan and for all the "lost boys."

It is important in exploring the life choices of the women in your family to take into account the constraints of the particular time and culture in which these choices were made. A woman who wants to avoid a move made necessary by her husband's job in order to remain near her sister is considered strange indeed. She will probably be labeled "enmeshed" or "undifferentiated." And yet the sister was there at the beginning, before the husband, and she will most likely be there at the end, after he is gone. In fact, a strong sense of sisterhood seems to strengthen a woman's sense of self.

Historically the "weak or ill" role may have been a type of rebellion. Emily Brontë and Elizabeth Barrett Browning, for example, seem to have used their illnesses in a way to avoid conventional social behavior. Both had brothers for whom the father had extremely strong expectations, and both lost sisters and their mothers at an early age. This probably increased their conflict as strong women who by temperament could not accommodate to the roles society prescribed for women.

In early childhood sisters are often caretakers of one another and of their brothers, as well as rivals and competitors for parental attention. Parents may, with the best of intentions have conveyed very different messages to their sons than their daughters. Here, for example, is a description by Jackie Robinson of his daughter, Sharon, the middle child with two brothers *(Genogram 7.4)*, and the role of his wife, who had had the same sibling constellation.

> She was just such an ideal and perfect child in our eyes and in the opinion of virtually everyone who came in touch with her that she sometimes seemed a little too good to be true. While fathers may be crazy about their sons, there is something extraordinarily special about a daughter. It's still the same—our relationship—perhaps even deeper. . . . Rachel had been brought up with the same family pattern—a girl in the middle of two boys. She was the busy, loving, but not necessarily always happy, mainstay of her family, who took care of her younger brother. With a kind of grim amusement, I recall our assumption that Sharon was strong enough to cope well with whatever she was confronted with. We took her development for granted for many years. She rarely signaled distress or called attention to her problems by being dramatic.[8]

In certain cultures, such as Italian and Hispanic, daughters are more likely to be raised to take care of others, including their brothers. Some cultural groups, such as Irish and African American families, may, for various historical reasons, tend to overprotect sons and underprotect daughters. Other cultural groups have less specific expectations. WASPs, for example, are more likely to believe in brothers and sisters' having equal chores.[9] But in general, it is important to notice how gender roles influence sibling patterns in understanding a family.[10]

Sisters of sisters tend to have very different sibling patterns from sisters of brothers, because of our society's strong preference for sons. If the brother is older, he is often idolized and catered to. If the

The Jackie Robinson Family
Genogram 7.4

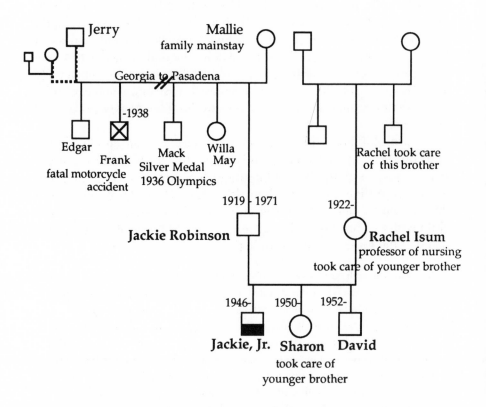

brother is younger, he may be envied and resented by the sister for his special status.

As Gloria Steinem, one of our leading feminists, has described it, A boy and a girl can come out of the exact same household with two very different cultures. While there has not been a great deal of research done on the subject, there are a few interesting findings on the differences between brothers and sisters. It appears that sisters of brothers are more likely to adopt opposite-sex characteristics than are their brothers, probably because male attributes seem more prestigious in our society. By contrast, brothers of sisters may, if anything, have intensified male characteristics, probably out of a desire not to be identified with the sisters.

Because women tend to be so central in maintaining the emotional relationships in a family, sisters may focus their disappointments more on one another or on their sisters-in-law than on their brothers,

Jackie Robinson with his wife, Rachel, and their three children, David, Jackie, Jr., and Sharon. Robinson later wrote: "While fathers may be crazy about their sons, there is something extraordinarily special about a daughter." Sharon, like her mother, was a middle child between two brothers.
AP/Wide World Photos

who are often treated as superior and not responsible for support when caretaking is required. Brothers may be expected to give financial support, but their work often provides an excuse for their lack of actual participation, while for sisters neither family commitments nor even work commitments are seen as an excuse for not taking responsibility for the needs of others.

Older women are especially likely to rely on their sisters as well as their daughters and even their nieces for support. Often they live together. Sisters are the ones most often turned to by older widows, more often than to children, even when they live at a distance. Thus siblings, especially sisters, take on added significance for women as confidantes, caretakers, and friends after they have been widowed. Having a relationship with a sister stimulates elderly women to remain socially engaged with others as well. Although the relationships of sisters tend to be invisible in the value structure of the culture at large, sisters tend to sustain one another in time of need throughout life. In old age they become indispensable. As Margaret

Mead described it, "Sisters draw closer together and often, in old age, they become each other's chosen and most happy companions. In addition to their shared memories of childhood and their relationships to each other's children, they share memories of the same house, the same homemaking style, and the same small prejudices about housekeeping."[11] Mead's comment is interesting in its focus on details. Especially as we grow older, it is the details—of our memories, our housekeeping, or our relationships with one another and with one another's families—that may hold us together.

The oldest sister can hardly avoid becoming the surrogate mother to her younger siblings. Margaret Mead (Chapter 10), who was followed by a brother and then by three sisters, describes having been enlisted by her grandmother (who lived with them) to take notes on her younger sisters' behavior: "I learned to make these notes with love, carrying on what Mother had begun. I knew that she had filled thirteen notebooks on me and only four on Richard; now I was taking over for the younger children. In many ways I thought of the babies as my children, whom I could observe and teach and cultivate. I also wanted to give them everything I missed." But unlike oldest sons, who typically have a clear feeling of entitlement, oldest daughters often have feelings of ambivalence and guilt about their responsibilities. Whatever they do, they feel it is not quite enough, and they can never let up in their efforts to caretake and to make the family work right.

The oldest child's experience is very different from that of the youngest, and middle children have their own unique experiences. While birth order can profoundly influence later experiences with spouses, friends, and colleagues, a particular birth order does not guarantee a particular type of person. There are many other factors that influence sibling roles, such as temperament, disability, looks, intelligence, talent, gender, and the timing of each birth in relation to other family experiences: deaths, moves, illnesses, changes in financial status, and so on.

For these and other reasons, parents may have a particular agenda for a specific child, such as expecting him or her to be the responsible one or the "baby," regardless of that child's position in the family. Children who resemble a certain family member may be expected to be like that person or to take on that person's role. Children's temperaments may also be at odds with their sibling position. This may explain why some children struggle so valiantly against family expectations—the oldest who refuses to take on the responsibility of the caretaker or family standard-bearer or the youngest who strives to be a leader. In some families it will be the child most comfortable with the responsibility—not necessarily the oldest child—who becomes the leader. Parents' own sibling experiences will affect their children as well. But certain typical patterns often occur that reflect each child's birth order.

OLDEST SONS AND DAUGHTERS

In general, oldest children are likely to be the overresponsible and conscientious ones in the family. They make good leaders, since they have experienced authority over and responsibility for younger siblings. Often serious, they may feel they have a mission in life. In identifying with their parents and being especially favored by them, they tend to be conservative even while leading others into new worlds, and while they may be self-critical, they do not necessarily handle criticism from others well.

We have already noted in Chapter 5 the specialness of Sigmund Freud's family position (*Genogram 5.5*) in relation to the surrounding deaths of his paternal grandfather, two older half siblings, the infant brother who followed him, and a maternal uncle. Other factors influencing Freud's special position in his family include the fact that shortly after his birth the family developed financial problems which forced them to migrate from their home in Moravia to Vienna, after which time the father seems never to have had a secure financial base again. Sigmund's prerogative in relation to his five younger sisters and brother was astounding. The household was organized around his needs. He was the only one of the children who had a special space set aside for him to work. The family story goes that when his sister Anna wanted to play the piano, their mother bought one, but she immediately got rid of it because Sigmund complained that the noise bothered him. That was the end of the sisters' music education! As in many cultures, the Freuds favored their son over their daughters. Sigmund's special position was further demonstrated when the family gave him the privilege at the age of ten of naming his younger brother after his hero Alexander the Great.

Sigmund apparently did not think much of his siblings, particularly his sisters. He once said to his younger brother, Alexander: "Our family is like a book. You and I are the first and last of the children, so, we are like the strong covers that have to support and protect the weak girls who were born after me and before you."[12] More significantly, he did not mention his siblings once in his autobiographical writings about his own development. So it is not surprising that sibling patterns play no role in his psychological theories. He does, however, mention his one-year-older nephew John, who for the first few years of his life was like a brother: "Until the end of my third year we had been inseparable; we had loved each other and fought each other and . . . this childish relationship has determined all my later feelings of intercourse with persons my own age. My nephew, John, has since had many incarnations, which have revived first one and then another aspect of character and is ineradicably fixed in my conscious memory. At times he must have treated me very badly and I must have opposed my tyrant courageously."[13]

Children often do have more intense feelings about a slightly older sibling than about a younger one. Sigmund Freud was never to have a true equal again. In later life he became a powerful leader, but as is so often the case with firstborns, he had difficulty sharing the stage with colleagues who would not accept his leadership in every idea, bringing about a falling-out with most of his followers (Adler, Jung, Stekel, Ferenczi, and others) as soon as they challenged him.

A major characteristic of the oldest is liking to lead others and assume responsibility for them, working hard to elevate the group to an elite position. George Washington, our first president (*Genogram 7.5*), is an outstanding example of this.[14] Washington's leadership ability was surely a major factor in the formation of the United States. At the age of twenty Washington joined the Virginia militia and quickly distinguished himself, becoming commander in chief of all Virginia forces by the age of twenty-three. He had a seemingly miraculous ability to lead his men into battle and emerge unscathed. A brilliant leader, he kept a single-minded focus on his objectives and his obligation to duty, regardless of the sacrifices involved.

Washington's leadership skill, determination, and sense of responsibility were undoubtedly intensified by his father's sudden death when he was only eleven, which left him responsible for his mother and four younger siblings. His thirteen-year-older half brother, Lawrence, then returned from abroad and became George's guardian and mentor. But unfortunately Lawrence died when George was only twenty, leaving him even more alone in his role as family leader. Though he could never have children of his own, he became a devoted stepfather to his wife Martha's two children and to numerous other relatives, whom he supported, mentored, or even raised. As a brother he was caring and responsible. He wrote of one of his own brothers late in life: "I have just buried a Brother [John] who was

The Washington Family
Genogram 7.5

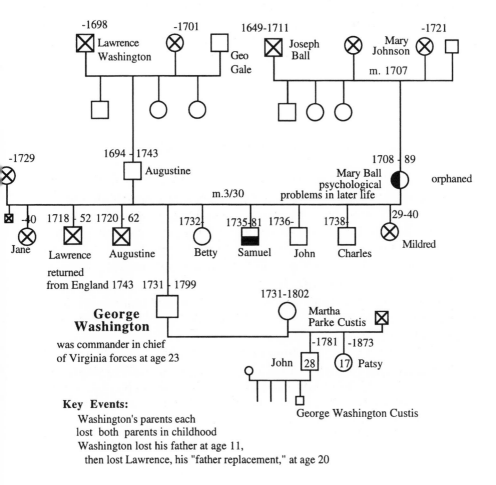

Key Events:
Washington's parents each
lost both parents in childhood
Washington lost his father at age 11,
then lost Lawrence, his "father replacement," at age 20

the intimate companion of my youth, and the friend of my ripened age."[15]

Being the firstborn can be a mixed blessing. As the answer to parents' dreams and as a beginning of a new family, the firstborn may receive an intensity of interest and devotion denied to the children that follow. But the burden may be heavy. Even when firstborns explicitly reject family expectations, uneasiness and guilt may plague them for not living up to their appointed role.

Monica McGoldrick

The oldest daughter often has the same sense of responsibility, conscientiousness, and ability to care for and lead others as her male counterpart. However, daughters generally do not receive the same privileges, nor are there generally the same expectations to excel. Thus they may be saddled with the responsibilities of the oldest child without the privileges or enhanced self-esteem. When siblings are all female, oldest sisters may have certain privileges and expectations urged on them that would otherwise go to sons.

THE YOUNGEST CHILD

The youngest child often has a sense of specialness, which allows self-indulgence without the overburdening sense of responsibility of the oldest. This pattern may be more intense the more siblings there are in a family. The younger of two probably has more a sense of "pairing" and twinship—unless there is a considerable age differential—than the youngest of ten. Freed from convention and determined to do things his or her own way, the youngest child can sometimes make remarkable creative leaps leading to inventions and innovations, as in the examples of Thomas Edison, Benjamin Franklin, Marie Curie, and Paul Robeson.

Thomas Alva Edison, a youngest son *(Genogram 7.6)*, invented the phonograph, the microphone, the motion-picture camera and projector, the typewriter, and the light bulb, made the telephone practical, and devised more than eleven hundred other inventions. He very much followed his own path in life. Like another famous youngest, Benjamin Franklin, Edison left home in adolescence. Edison's special position, like Franklin's, may have been reinforced by the deaths of two older siblings in infancy and a third at the age of five. Besides being a youngest child, Edison came from a long line of independent, stubborn, ambitious, determined individualists. His great-grandfather, John Edison, was forced into exile at the time of the Revolutionary War because of his Tory allegiance. His grandfather was voted out of the Baptist Church for ridiculing and refusing to obey its rules. His father had to flee back to the United States after participating in a rebellion against the Canadian government. Edison too was an individualist, as well as an amazing innovator, despite (or, some have argued, because of) his having had only six months of formal education.

The Edison Family
Genogram 7.6

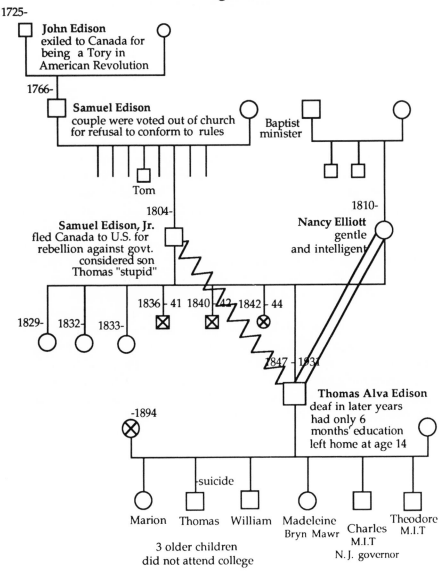

1725-

John Edison
exiled to Canada for
being a Tory in
American Revolution

1766-

Samuel Edison
couple were voted out of church
for refusal to conform to rules

Baptist
minister

Tom

1804-

Samuel Edison, Jr.
fled Canada to U.S. for
rebellion against govt.
considered son
Thomas "stupid"

1810-

Nancy Elliott
gentle
and intelligent

1829-   1832-   1833-

1836 - 41 1840 - 42 1842 - 44

1847 - 1931

Thomas Alva Edison
deaf in later years
had only 6
months' education
left home at age 14

-1894

suicide

Marion   Thomas   William   Madeleine   Charles   Theodore
                                 Bryn Mawr   M.I.T   M.I.T
3 older children   N.J. governor
did not attend college

In adult life Edison was eccentric. He dressed in baggy, shabby
clothes although eventually he was a multimillionaire; he slept little
and worked incessantly; and he was curious about everything. He
developed into an extraordinarily good businessman, rewarding inge-
nuity and hard work but caring little for bureaucratic regularity. His

concern about money was purely for the freedom it allowed him, a typical attitude among youngest sons.

Other general characteristics of youngest children are readily apparent. Since the youngest has older siblings who have often served as caretakers, he or she is more used to being a follower than a leader. The youngest may remain the "baby," a focus of attention for all who came before, expecting others to be helpful and supportive. Youngest children may feel freer to deviate from convention. Youngests may even feel compelled to escape from being the "baby"; this may cause a rebellion, as with Edison and Franklin, who both ran away in adolescence.

Given their special position as the center of attention, youngest children may think they can accomplish anything. The youngest may feel more carefree, more content to have fun rather than achieve. Less plagued by self-doubt, they are often extremely creative, willing to try what others would not even consider. They can also be spoiled and self-absorbed, and their sense of entitlement leads at times to frustration and disappointment. In addition, the youngest often has a period as an only child after the older siblings have left home. This can be an opportunity to enjoy the sole attention of parents, but it can also lead to feelings of abandonment by the siblings.

Often the youngest child can seem almost underresponsible in certain ways. John Adams, a good and typical eldest son, saw Benjamin Franklin, the youngest son of two youngests and the last of five generations of youngest sons, as too much amused by frivolous pleasures and remaining noncommittal so that everyone would like him: "Although he has as determined a soul as any man, yet it is his constant policy never to say yes or no decidedly, but when he cannot avoid it."[16] Franklin was indeed self-indulgent and rather underresponsible, particularly when it came to his family. He left his fiancée (who later became his wife) to go to England, writing to her only once in a whole year, and he was later negligent of the feelings and needs of his wife and daughter, leaving them for years at a time for his social life of diplomacy abroad.

Like many youngest children, Benjamin Franklin was a rebel. All his life he was an iconoclast, fighting the conventions that did not make sense to him. Having been a major figure in the Revolution, he was still a major force for change at the age of eighty-one, when he became a primary framer and signer of the U.S. Constitution, a most remarkably unconventional document. He was not so much a leader of men as an indirect influencer of events, negotiating through diplomacy and guiding through his brilliance.

A younger sister tends to be protected, showered with affection, and handed a blueprint for life. She may be either spoiled (more so if there are older brothers) and have special privileges or, if she is from a large family, be frustrated by always having to wait her turn. Her parents may have just run out of energy with her. She may feel resentful of being bossed around and never taken quite seriously. If she is the only girl, the youngest may be more like the princess, yet be the servant to elders, becoming, perhaps, the confidante to her brothers in adult life and the one to replace the parents in holding the family together.

Marie Curie *(Genogram 7.7),* born Manya Sklodowska in Poland in 1867, the only person ever to receive two Nobel prizes—for her research on radiation—was another extraordinary youngest. As the last of five children, with one brother and three sisters, the oldest of whom died in childhood, she showed an independence and lack of concern for convention from early childhood. Determined to follow her own path, she was perhaps, the extreme noncaretaker, a common characteristic of youngest children. Like Edison, who had little interest in his appearance or surroundings, Marie pursued her interest in science to the extreme. Shortly after she went to France to study, she was found unconscious on the street, weak from starvation, because she was too preoccupied with her work to bother with food.

Marie Curie (née Sklodowska) with her siblings: from left to right, Zosia, who died at fifteen, Hella, Marie, Jozio, the only brother, and Bronya, who eventually became Marie's caretaker. Mme. Curie was the only recipient of two Nobel Prizes. Archives Curie, Paris

The Curie Family
Genogram 7.7

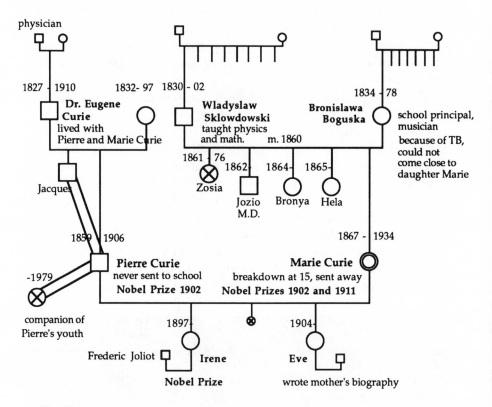

Key Events:

1867 Russian section of Poland stripped of its name
Father (WS) has new job
Mother (BBS) feels forced to give up her job for family move
Nov. 7, birth of Manya Sklowdowska (Marie Curie), 5th child
Mother has first symptoms of TB - can no longer hug the children
1873 Father demoted by hostile Russian authorities.
1874 Father invests all savings in speculative venture and loses
(Felt he ruined the family)
1876 Zosia and Bronya contract typhus. Zosia dies at age 14
1878 Mother dies after 11-year illness

One can imagine what can happen when two youngests get together, as was the case with Marie and her husband, Pierre. The story goes that when they were first married, Marie in an effort to develop domestic skills—which interested her not at all—asked her older sister's advice about cooking chops. Later, when Marie asked her husband how he enjoyed his lamb chop, he gave an astonished look and said, "But I haven't tasted it yet," not noticing his empty plate."[17] Marie Curie pursued science with no interest or ambition for success or honor, much less any desire to lead others, but with a need to answer her inner questions. Einstein once said of her that she was "of all celebrated beings, the only one whom fame has not corrupted." Her younger daughter, Eve, who wrote her biography, described her as remaining to her last day "just as gentle, stubborn, timid and curious about all things as in the days of her obscure beginnings."[18]

Paul Robeson *(Genogram 7.8)*, another brilliant and creative youngest, was the multitalented star in his family. Outstanding athlete in every sport, Phi Beta Kappa in college, lawyer turned world-famous singer and actor and then political activist, Robeson was deeply aware of the importance to him of each of his siblings in his life. He said everyone lavished an extra measure of affection on him and saw him as some kind of "child of destiny . . . linked to the longed-for better days to come."[19] This is a common role for a youngest, especially when the family has experienced hard times. The oldest Robeson brother, William Drew, was named for the father and followed in the father's footsteps, attending the same college, Lincoln, before going to medical school. According to Robeson, William was the most brilliant of the children and the one who taught him to study. William Drew never reached his potential largely because of racism. Reed, the next brother, too overtly angry to survive easily in their community, became the "lost" middle child, though Paul felt he got toughness from this brother. The third son, Ben, became an outstanding athlete and role model for Paul. He became a successful minister like the father. The fourth, the only girl, Marion, became a teacher, like the mother, and was noted for her beatific spirit. For Paul, Ben and Marion—those closest to him in age—were his most important mentors: "reserved in speech, strong in character, living up to their principles—and always selflessly devoted to their younger brother." This support was all the more important because his mother died tragically in a fire when he was only five.

There were lessons also from Reed, who carried a little bag of stones for self-protection should he encounter a dangerous situation. Robeson admired this "rough" older brother and learned from him a quick response to racial insults and abuse. Robeson had a special feeling for this middle brother, who did not live up to the father's high expectations of the Robeson children. Robeson later wrote: "He won no honors in classroom, pulpit or platform. Yet I remember him with love. Restless, rebellious, scoffing at conventions, defiant of the white man's law. I've known many Negroes like Reed. I see them every

The Robeson Family
Genogram 7.8

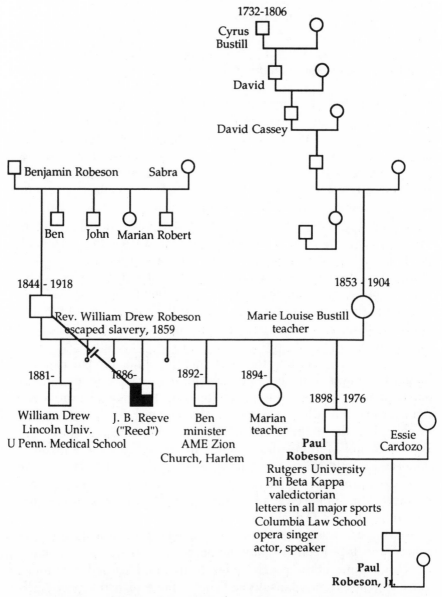

day. Blindly, in their own reckless manner, they seek a way out for themselves; alone, they pound with their fists and fury against walls that only the shoulders of many can topple. . . . When . . . everything will be different . . . the fiery ones like Reed will be able to live out their lives in peace and no one will have cause to frown upon them." Although Reverend Robeson disapproved of Reed's carefree and undisciplined ways and eventually turned him out for his scrapes with the law, Paul saw Reed as having taught him to stand up for himself. In a one-man play written about Robeson's life, the character of Robeson says there was one conversation he and his father could never finish—about this brother, Reed: "Aw Pop, how could you pretend one of your sons didn't exist. Reed did exist. He was your son too." Remembering the night his father turned Reed out, fearing he would set a bad example for his younger brother, Paul imagines getting together with his father and brother Ben to go looking for Reed to bring him home. He imagines his response to his father: "Aw Pop, don't change the subject. . . . Reed was not a bad influence. Only horrible thing he said to me was, 'Kid, you talk too much.' All he ever told me to do was to stand up and be a man. 'Don't take low from anybody, and if they hit you, hit 'em back harder.' I know what the Bible says, Pop, but Reed was your son too! You always said you saw yourself in me. Pop, you were in all your sons."[20] This dramatization expresses eloquently the connectedness between siblings and how much it matters if one is cut off, even though others in the family may not realize it.

MIDDLE CHILDREN

The middle child in a family is in between, having the position of neither the first as the standard-bearer nor the last as the "baby." Middle children thus run the risk of getting lost in the family, especially if all the siblings are of the same sex. On the other hand, middle children may develop into the best negotiators, more even-tempered and mellow than their more driven older siblings and less self-indulgent than the youngest. They may even relish their invisibility. Henry Adams liked to say he had the good fortune to be born the fourth of seven children, which gave him a status so trifling he could fritter away his life and "never be missed."[21]

The middle sister is under less pressure to take responsibility, but she needs to try harder to make her mark in general because she has no special role. She remembers running to catch up with the older sister from childhood and running frantically from the younger one, who seemed to be gaining on her every minute.[22] The position of middle can stimulate competitive feelings and leaves her vulnerable to maladjustment if she cannot find a place to stand. She is the com-

The Lincoln and Todd Families
Genogram 7.9

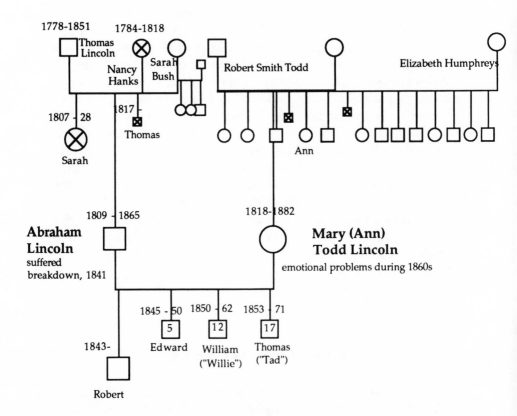

promiser, the go-between and tends to be gregarious and a good negotiator if she can define a middle path, a compromise between extremes.

Follower to the oldest and leader to the youngest, middle children are less likely to show extremes. Without the rights and prerogatives of the oldest or the privileges and benefits of the youngest, they often feel somewhat lost and unappreciated, unless the middle child is the only girl or only boy. On the positive side, in intense, highly fused families, the somewhat removed middle child may become the nego-tiator, the one who avoids getting pulled into the family vortex.

Mary Todd Lincoln (*Genogram 7.9*), the wife of Abraham Lincoln, was a middle child who sought recognition all her life. Named Mary Ann, she was the third daughter in the large Todd family. Her father was the third son, "lost" among twelve children, who became a rest-

An idealized rendition of the Lincoln family after the painting by Francis B. Carpenter, 1861. All three sons died in childhood or early youth.
The Granger Collection

less and often absent parent. Her mother was also a middle child, timid and unassertive. When Mary Ann was eleven months old, she was abruptly weaned and lost her place as youngest to a first son. When she was four, a second baby brother died. At five she lost her middle name, Ann, to a younger sister. At six her mother died, giving birth to a third brother. By the time she was seven a new wife absorbed her father's attention.

Nine more children were born to the second family. All of Mary's siblings may have felt disoriented in this family drama, but she seems to have been the most affected. Her two older sisters had already formed a strong alliance with each other. Ann, the youngest sister, was the namesake and favorite child of the aunt who took over the family after their mother died until the father remarried. And the two surviving sons held a special place in their father's and uncles' affections.[23]

Thus Mary was the neglected middle child, whose response was a pervasive sense of insecurity. She was extremely vulnerable to slights, rejections, and the sense of being ignored. Understandably, having felt invisible as a child, Mary developed a great determination to be recognized. She was a highly intelligent student, much better educated and socially sophisticated than her husband, a superb horse-woman, and an outstanding hostess. She was very ambitious for her husband and played the role of "the woman behind the man." Her husband referred to Mary as his "child wife" and "mother," suggesting perhaps that she vacillated between both roles. Lincoln's opponents criticized Mary for her extravagance, flamboyance, "interference" in politics, and unwillingness to accept the passive womanly role, all possible characteristics of a middle child who seeks attention. Later, when she was institutionalized in a mental hospital against her will, she managed to engineer her own release through great efforts to bring others to her cause. This was perhaps the supreme example of the resourcefulness of a middle child.

ONLY CHILDREN

Like middle children, only children show characteristics of both old-ests and youngests. In fact, they may show the extremes of both at the same time. They may have the seriousness and sense of responsi-bility of the oldest and the conviction of specialness and entitlement of the youngest. Not having siblings, only children tend to be more oriented toward adults, seeking their love and approval and in return expecting their undivided attention. The major challenge for only children is to learn how to get along with others their own age. Only children often maintain very close attachments to their parents throughout their lives but find it more difficult to relate to friends and spouses.

The French philosopher Jean-Paul Sartre was an interesting exam-ple of an only child. His father died when he was just over a year old, and he spent his early childhood with his mother and her parents. All the adult attention of this household became focused on him. By his own account, Sartre was a spoiled and pampered child: "My mother was mine; no one challenged my peaceful possession of her. I knew nothing of violence and hatred. Not having been bruised by its sharp angles, I knew reality only by its bright unsubstantiality. Against whom, against what, would I have rebelled? Never had someone else's whim claimed to be my law."[24]

In fact, only children often become highly sensitized to the con-flicts and needs of the adults around them. The dynamics of this three-generational household of only child, single parent, and aging grandparents who provide the support for the family is a typical one. It was Sartre's grandmother, Louise, who punctured his mother and grandfather's charade that he was the perfect child prodigy. She would order him to stop "smirking and smiling." He would disobey. She would demand an apology. He would refuse to apologize. His grandfather would side with him. His grandmother would then storm off to her room. Sartre's mother, who feared her own mother, would then accuse her father of causing a quarrel. After that, the grandfather would storm off. The mother would then beg Sartre to ask his grandmother's forgiveness. Sartre, playing his role as "perfect child," would now make a casual apology.

Sartre thus learned to wend his way through the complex and convoluted relationships of the adults in his world. His life as an only child was compounded by lack of contact with children his own age until he was twelve. He had only three adults against whom to develop a sense of self. He was successfully conscripted into a family drama and played the part of obedient child prodigy, a common role for only children.

Trouble began for Sartre at the age of twelve, when his mother remarried and he was sent off to school. "He was an irascible, cantankerous, quarrelsome boy, most unpleasant toward his peers," remembered one of his classmates.[25] Sartre's classmates felt only contempt for this pompous, affected child, who was always trying to be the center of attention. At times he tried to buy friends or impress them by lying or by a spectacular misdeed. He was often beaten up and rarely asked to join the various teenage groups. He spent much of his time alone, creating his own world through reading and writing. Eventually Sartre did adapt to his new situation and found a kindred soul in another only child who liked literature and writing stories. He never did lose his sense of self-importance or confidence in his ability to do great things. It is interesting that this only child was one of the founders of a philosophy that focuses on the importance of individual consciousness, the basic existential solitude of humanity, the absurdity of life, and the necessity for each individual to create his or her own reality.

SIBLING POSITION AND MARRIAGE

Sibling relationships can often pave the way for couple relationships—for sharing, interdependence, and mutuality, just as they can predispose partners to jealousy, power struggles, and rivalry. Since siblings are generally your earliest peer relationships, you're likely to be most comfortable in other relationships that reproduce the familiar sibling patterns of birth order and gender. And generally marriage seems easiest for partners who fit their original sibling pattern—e.g., an oldest marrying a youngest, rather than two oldests marrying each other. If a wife has grown up as the oldest of many siblings and the caretaker, she might be attracted to a dominant oldest, who offers to take over management of responsibilities. But as time goes along, she may come to resent his assertion of authority because by experience she is more comfortable making decisions for herself.

All things being equal (and they seldom are), the ideal marriage based on sibling position would be one in which the husband was the older brother of a younger sister and the wife was the younger sister of an older brother. This pattern replicates not only their own family patterns but the favored pattern in society, with the man dominant and the woman in a junior position. However, the complementarity of caretaker and someone who needs caretaking, or leader and follower, does not guarantee intimacy or a happy marriage.

In addition to complementary birth order, it seems to help in marriage if one has had siblings of the opposite sex. Most difficult might be the youngest sister of many sisters who marries the youngest brother of many brothers since neither would have much experience of the opposite sex in a close way, and they might both play "the spoiled child" waiting for a caretaker.

Eleanor Roosevelt (*Genogram 7.10*), an oldest, and her cousin Franklin, an only, are a good example of two strong-willed spouses whose marriage seems to have survived only because each evolved separate spheres. Leaders in their own separate worlds, they came to live apart except for holidays. Early in the marriage Eleanor generally subordinated herself to Franklin and his powerful mother, Sara Delano Roosevelt, who played a major role in their lives. However, as she became more self-confident and developed interests of her own, she began to show the determination of an oldest. The crisis came when Eleanor discovered letters revealing Franklin's affair with Lucy Mercer. Apparently it was Franklin's mother who negotiated a contract between them for Eleanor to return to the marriage. Since oldests and only children are oriented to parents, Sara may have been the only one who could have kept them from separating, and she did.[26]

The Roosevelts remained married but began to live separate lives, with politics as their common ground. After Franklin's paralysis as

The Family of Eleanor and Franklin Roosevelt
Genogram 7.10

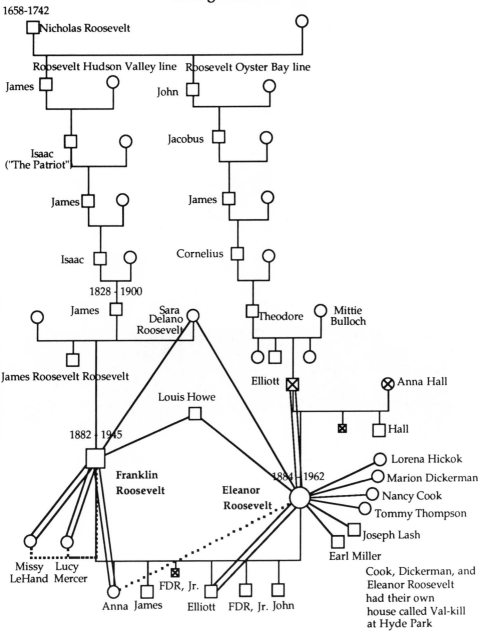

1658-1742

Nicholas Roosevelt

Roosevelt Hudson Valley line   Roosevelt Oyster Bay line

James   John

Isaac ("The Patriot")   Jacobus

James   James

Isaac   Cornelius

1828 - 1900
James   Sara Delano Roosevelt   Theodore   Mittie Bulloch

James Roosevelt Roosevelt   Elliott   Anna Hall

Louis Howe   Hall

1882 - 1945   Lorena Hickok
Marion Dickerman
Franklin Roosevelt   1884 - 1962   Nancy Cook
Eleanor Roosevelt   Tommy Thompson
Joseph Lash
Earl Miller

Missy LeHand   Lucy Mercer   FDR, Jr.

Anna   James   Elliott   FDR, Jr.   John

Cook, Dickerman, and Eleanor Roosevelt had their own house called Val-kill at Hyde Park

Franklin D. Roosevelt, at sixteen months, on his father's shoulder. James Roosevelt died before his son reached adulthood. (Below), The Roosevelt family at Campobello in 1920, with FDR's mother, Sara Delano Roosevelt, centrally located between Eleanor and Franklin. The children, from left to right: Elliott, Franklin, Jr., John, Anna, and James. Underwood & Underwood, The Bettmann Archive

the result of polio, Eleanor became essential to his political career. She nevertheless had her own political views and activities, her own living space in a separate house at Hyde Park which she shared with her friends, and her own intimate relationships. Eleanor Roosevelt, whose creative ability to master the most horrendous experiences of her childhood has already been discussed, managed to make the most of her life. But she did not fail to realize the price she was forced to pay. Many years after learning that her husband had been elected president of the United States, Eleanor Roosevelt wrote: "I am sure that I was glad for my husband, but it never occurred to me to be much excited. . . . I felt detached and objective, as though I were looking at someone else's life. This seems to have remained with me down to the present day. I cannot quite describe it, but it is as though you lived two lives, one of your own and the other which belonged to the circumstances that surround you."[27] Eleanor's description of this experience not only reflects the gender bias that has for so long required women to give up their own lives for their husbands but also suggests the creative solution she and Franklin worked out to their difficult dilemma in marriage, probably based in part on their child-hood sibling roles. The remarkable thing about Eleanor is her effec-tiveness in creating a life of her own. After Franklin Roosevelt's death in 1945, her career flourished even more, including her assignment as U.S. ambassador to the United Nations.

In contrast, Richard Burton and Elizabeth Taylor, who married and divorced each other twice, provide a dramatic example of two youngest children who competed to be "junior," both seeking a care-taker. Burton was the second youngest of thirteen children but was treated like a youngest since he was raised apart from his younger brother. In very large families several of the younger children will often have the characteristics of a youngest. Elizabeth Taylor was the younger of two, with an older brother whose needs were often sacri-ficed to her stardom; this, of course, solidified her special position. Burton and Taylor were known for their histrionic love quarrels, each outdoing the other in demanding and childish behavior.

There are, of course, many other possible sibling pairings in mar-riage. The marriage of two only children might be particularly diffi-cult since neither has the experience of intimate sharing that one has with a brother or sister. Middle children may be the most flexible since they have experiences with a number of different roles.

If you have struggled in your own sibling position, you may over-identify as a parent with a child of the same sex and sibling position as yourself. One father who was an oldest of five felt that he had been burdened with too much responsibility, while his younger brothers and sister "got away with murder." When his own children came along, he spoiled the oldest and tried to make the younger ones toe the line. A mother may find it difficult to sympathize with a youngest daughter if she has always felt envious of her younger sister. This was how Simone de Beauvoir described the relationship of her mother (the older of two sisters) with herself (also the older of two sisters) and her sister: "Until I began to reach adolescence Maman ascribed to me the loftiest intellectual and moral qualities: she identified herself with me and she humiliated and slighted my sister—Poupette was the younger sister, pink and fair, and without realizing it, Maman was taking her revenge upon her."[28] Parents may also identify with one particular child because of a resemblance to another family member. Whether these identifications are conscious or unconscious, they are normal. It is a myth that parents can feel the same toward all their children. Feelings will depend on each child's characteristics and unique position in the whole family constellation.

Problems arise when the identification is so strong that parents perpetuate their old family patterns or when their own experience is so different that they misread their children. Two sisters may get along quite well although their mother expects them to fight like cats and dogs the way she and her sister did. And a parent who was an only child may assume that normal sibling fights are an indication of trouble.

BROTHER-SISTER RELATIONSHIPS IN ADULT LIFE

Sibling relationships can be a most important connection in adult life, especially in the later years. However, if negative feelings persist, the care of an aging parent may bring on particular difficulty. At such a time siblings may have been apart for years. They may have to work together in new and unfamiliar ways. The child who has remained closest to the parents, usually a daughter, often gets most of these caretaking responsibilities, which may cause long-buried jealousies and resentments to rise to the surface.

Once both parents are no longer living, siblings are truly independent for the first time. From here on out whether they see one another will be their choice. This is the time when estrangement can become complete, particularly if old rivalries continue. The focus become complete, particularly if old rivalries continue. The focus may be on concrete disagreements: Who should have helped in the care of their ailing parent? Who shouldered all the responsibility? Who was more loved?

Strong feelings can be fueled by all the old unresolved issues and conflicts. But the better relationships the siblings have, the less likely it is that this and other traumatic family events will lead to a parting of the ways.

QUESTIONS ABOUT SIBLING PATTERNS IN YOUR FAMILY

■ Do members of your family conform to the generalized characteristics described for birth order—e.g., the oldest as leader, the youngest as rebel, the middle seeking recognition? If not, are there mitigating circumstances that may have influenced sibling patterns, such as a child with special needs or characteristics, other changes in the family around the birth of a child, and so forth?

■ How were siblings in your family expected to behave: To be pals, "blood brothers," rivals, partners, opposites?

■ Have family legacies influenced sibling roles and relationships?

■ Are any siblings especially close in your family? Are any in business together? Are any estranged, and if so, what were the issues involved? Caretaking of a parent? Rivalries about careers, money, spouses, who was the preferred child or whose children were more special? Do any specific sibling patterns run throughout the family?

■ Did your parents tend to identify with the child of the same sex and sibling position as their own?

■ Can you figure out in each sibling group which child was the most "triangled," and do you have any hypotheses about why this child was "it"?

■ Can you tell anything about the family values and patterns by the labels that different siblings had: The star and the loser? The angel and the villain? The strong one and the weak one? The good seed and the bad seed? Can you figure out any reasons why such labels might have been given, beyond the obvious?

COUPLE RELATIONSHIPS

How soon the character of the race would change if pure and equal real marriages could take the place of the horrible relations that now bear that sacred name.
>—Lucy Stone to Henry Blackwell, July 27, 1853

This fellow spirit has been so woven into mine that nothing could quite tear us asunder.
>—Antoinette Brown about her marriage to Samuel Blackwell, 1854

At the most only one bad woman exists in the world. It is unfortunate that each man considers his as being this unique one.
>—Gotthold Lessing (1729-1781) circa 1780

Marriage is one of the most fascinating relationships to explore in learning about your family. What makes marriage work? How did your parents and grandparents do it? And how can anyone do it nowadays, especially with the profound complexities of divorce, remarriage, and the current pattern of two employed parents, who must provide support to both children and aging family members in our highly mobile society. Finding out how and when your parents, grandparents, and other couples in your family met, getting them to tell you the stories of what attracted them to their spouses and how they decided to marry will get you started learning about the marital patterns in your family.

Some cultures have no expectation that marriages will be intimate. Marriages are contracted between the fathers for the economic and social stability or betterment of the family. In our culture marriage is thought to be a matter of individual choice of the partners for reasons of spiritual, emotional, and physical intimacy. This creates many problems since the main need society has for marriage is for the production and nurturing of children. Thus we have many potentially conflicting goals at work in any particular family when it comes to the place of marriage in the family as a whole.

A particular problem in marriage is that it is the only family relationship in which exclusivity is expected. We can love more than one child, sibling, parent. But we are not supposed to love more than one partner (at least not at one time). Also, while marriage is the weakest relationship in the family, as our current divorce rate of 50 percent attests, it is the only one we swear is forever. Indeed, it would probably be a good idea if we made that promise about our parents, our siblings, and our children. Maybe the very fragility of the marriage bond is the reason we have to swear that our marriage vows are till death do us part. Indeed, the most powerful experiences human beings have of intimacy—along with the most common sense of disillusionment—are probably in couple relationships. Being "in love" is more disorienting than any other relationship, and it is the most mysterious of emotions, as well as the one that most often fools us. It can make a blithering idiot out of the sanest person. Women have traditionally lost even their names, not to mention their identities in this relationship. And both men and women have often been willing to give up everything for a love, who is presumably a hoped-for marriage partner, although we are less likely to give up as much for a long-term marital partner as for a new romance. Our confusion between lust, love, companionship, loyalty, friendship, and sexual intimacy runs deep. And no other relationship is so linked up with our very sense of who we are.

For these and other reasons some marriages are so full of intensity they seem intolerable. But marriages lacking in intensity also have their problems. Eugene O'Neill, whose difficulties with marriage and other relationships we have already discussed, had the following dream for the perfect marriage: "My wife and I will live on a barge. I'll live at one end and she'll live at the other, and we'll never see each other except when the urge strikes us."[1]

But the conflicting goals, the intensity, and the difficulties of gender arrangements are not the only reasons marriage is so complex. It has often been said that what distinguishes human beings from other animals is the fact of having in-laws. Human beings are the only animals that tend to develop highly intense relationships with their in-laws. The joke that there are six in the marital bed is really an understatement. In the animal kingdom mating involves only the two partners, who usually mature, separate from their families, and mate on their own. But for us it is an entirely different proposition. Indeed, marriage places no small stress on a family to open itself to an in-law—an outsider who now becomes an official member of the family, often the first new member in years.

Naturally it is often hard to enter a family because of its long-shared history of which the new spouse is not a part. And it is hard to include a new person, who does not share your memories, private jokes, code words, and the traditions you have in common as a family. Shortly after George Bernard Shaw married his wife, Charlotte, he described the problem of prior history for the new spouse in a letter to a woman friend: "You do not understand the nature of Charlotte's objections to you; she has exactly the same objection to . . . everybody who forms the past in which she has no part. The moment you walk into the room where I am, you create a world in which you and I are at home and she is a stranger. It is just the same with me: the moment her old friends call I become a mere chance acquaintance."[2]

Marriage shifts the relationship of a couple from a private twosome to a formal joining of two families. Issues that the partners have not resolved with their own families will tend to be factors in marital choice and are very likely to interfere with establishing a workable marital connection in the context of the extended families. It may even be that much of the intensity of romantic love is determined by patterns in the families of origin. From this perspective Romeo and Juliet might have felt intensely attracted to each other precisely *because* their families hated each other. In idealizing the forbidden person, Romeo and Juliet, like many other romantic couples, including Tristan and Isolde, were spared any broader perspective on their relationship, by their untimely deaths, which also saved them from possible later conflicts over who would pick up the socks and how to handle the mother-in-law. In everyday life the outcome of such forbidden love affairs is not always so romantic. If couples marry expecting the other to solve their problems, they may soon be disappointed.

Marriage is indeed a difficult proposition. Yet our culture's mythology portrays marriage, along with parenthood, to which it has long been the symbolic precursor, as the easiest and most joyous life cycle transition. Our society's myths about marriage may add to its difficulty. Marriage, more than any other rite of passage, is viewed as the solution to loneliness or turmoil, the fairy-tale ending "And they lived happily ever after." On the contrary, in the context of the multigenerational family life cycle, marriage comes in the middle of a complex process in the structure of two families, as they are transformed by new roles and relationships.

Courtship and weddings are fascinating nodal points to explore in learning how your family process works. By examining the marriages, you can see how your family tends to deal with change, with outsiders, with gender roles, and how successful people are at finding partners who complement them.

The tendency for relationships in a family to become polarized during the stress of a wedding can be intense. The new spouse may be subtly rejected as "not our class, darling," or of the "wrong" cultural or religious background. Parents may see their child's involvement with a partner who is "not our type" as a personal rejection. The tears that frequently are shed on the wedding day may reflect the profound stress of the changes taking place in the family, rather than distress over the photographer's ineptitude, the guest list, the seating arrangements, the bridal gown, or the usher's cummerbund. Family conflicts around weddings can be fascinating indicators of underlying family values, alliances, and fears. And of course, eloping or having a wedding without key family members may indicate family patterns just as clearly.

Given our culture's idealization of marriage, couples often define their problems primarily within the marital relationship, ignoring the need for other relationships: with parents, siblings, aunts, uncles, children, or friends. There is a tendency to put all our eggs in one basket. Spouses may overfocus on marital issues as the source of their happiness or dissatisfaction in life. If they feel dissatisfied, they may blame the partner—"He let me down; he doesn't love me"—or blame themselves: "I'm no good; I'd be able to satisfy her if I were." Once this personalizing process begins, it is very difficult to keep the relationship open.

The increasing interdependency of couples over time leads them to interpret more and more facets of their lives within the marriage. For example, if one partner becomes depressed during courtship, the other is not likely to take it too personally, assuming "There are many reasons to get depressed in life; this may have nothing to do with me." Such an assumption of not being responsible for the other's feelings permits a supportive response. After several years of marriage, however, this partner has a much greater tendency to view the other's emotional reactions as a reflection of his or her behavior and think: "It must mean I'm not a good spouse or I would have made my husband/wife happy by now."

Of course, this sense of responsibility for the other's well-being is more of a problem for women since the culture also tends to hold them responsible for the happiness of others. But once partners start taking responsibility for each other's feelings, more and more areas of the relationship may become tension-filled and therefore avoided. The wife may feel inadequate, guilty, and resentful. She may decide to avoid dealing with her husband because she does not want to arouse his irritability or blame, or she may become protective of him and stay silent to keep from making him upset. He may avoid raising issues that create tension out of fear of her annoyance. In either case, the more the reactions of each are a response to the other, the more their communication will become constricted in emotionally charged areas and the less flexibility there will be in the relationship.

Married couples who find it threatening to have direct conflicts with each other may lower their anxiety by focusing their energy on their children, who oblige them by becoming the "problem," which allows the parents to form a united front.

The failure of partners to become mature individuals before marriage leaves both spouses needing to build self-esteem in the marriage. Both may fear communicating with the other. He may think: "I must never let her know how worthless I am or I will lose her, since my parents never really loved me either, and I shall never tell her that at times all her talk is boring." Meanwhile, she is thinking: "I mustn't let him know how I am really worthless or he will leave me, the way my father did. And I mustn't let on that his endless silent watching sports and TV is boring. He has nothing to say."

In such couples each puts the other in charge of his or her self-esteem: "I am worthwhile because you love me," which means the converse would also be true: "If you don't love me, I am worthless." Thus couples may become bound up in a web of evasiveness and ambiguity, because neither can dare to be straight, for fear of things' turning out unhappily, as they think happened in their families of origin. Messages between them become more and more disguised. They may finally end by doing things neither wants to do because each thinks the other wants it that way. As Groucho Marx put it:

> Lying has become one of the biggest industries in America. Let's take, for example, the relationship that exists between husband and wife. Even when they're celebrating their golden wedding anniversary and have said "I love you" a million times to each other, publicly and privately, you know as well as I do that they've never really told each other the truth—the real truth. I don't mean the superficial things like, "Your mother is a louse!" or "Why don't we get an expensive car instead of that tin can we're riding around in?" No, I mean the secret thoughts that run through their minds when they wake up in the middle of the night and see imaginary things on the wall.[3]

As you explore the couple relationships in your family, pay particular attention to any couplings that have not received the sanctions of the family or community. For example, while gay and lesbian couples are increasingly open within the family context, our society continues to perpetuate a deep negativity toward homosexuality, and our laws do not validate homosexual marriages. Thus a general invisibility is forced on gay and lesbian couples, and that makes their couplehood more difficult. They are often forced to keep their relationships secret. Families may not celebrate their lifecycle transitions, or they may be excluded from all family participation.

Everyone in the family and in the society pays for such secrecy and disqualification. Family relationships tend to become distorted because the overt connections of the family do not match the private ties. It is important to do whatever you can to see that the overt connections of your family match with the underlying connections as well. Exploring the relationships that are at the boundary of what society allows will teach you a good deal about how your family deals with social conventions, independence, and difference. Explore each family member's life for the ways he or she has broken with convention or been constricted by it. Those whose lives are at the cutting edge of the family may tell most about the family's strengths and vulnerabilities.

To understand your family, you need to track the marital patterns over time. Look especially at periods of high marital tension, periods when partners became involved in affairs, periods of intense triangling with a child, a mother-in-law, or other outsiders. See whether you can find any correlations between other family stresses and marital patterns in your family. Note also the messages that have been passed down in your family about marriage.

In the remarkable Blackwell family *(Genogram 8.1)*, several unmarried aunts had a major role in raising a number of extraordinary children and apparently warned them repeatedly against marriage. In the grandparents' generation one grandfather was a quarrelsome ne'er-do-well who was said to have "crushed the life out of his wife." The other disgraced the family, first with his promiscuity and then with his arrest and deportation for forgery. In the next generation the father died relatively young, leaving his wife and nine children unprovided for, as had his father and father-in-law. The family stories in the wake of such experiences may create powerful messages about the role and meaning of marriage. They do not, of course, doom the next generation to repeat the pattern. On the contrary, such marriages may become signals to the next generation for creativity in their life choices.

This was certainly the case for the Blackwells. All five of the Blackwell daughters chose to remain unmarried, though four of them

The Blackwell Family

Genogram 8.1

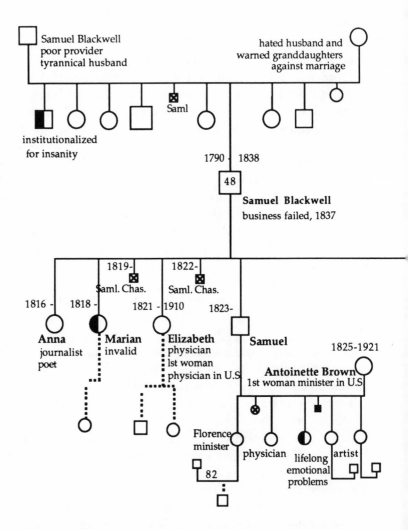

adopted children. One, Elizabeth, became the first woman physician in the United States; another, Emily, followed her soon after; a third, Anna, became a journalist, and a fourth, Ellen, an artist. The fifth was an invalid, though she, like three of her sisters, adopted children to raise. The three sons were also amazing men in what they did with the family messages about marriage. Henry Blackwell fell in love with

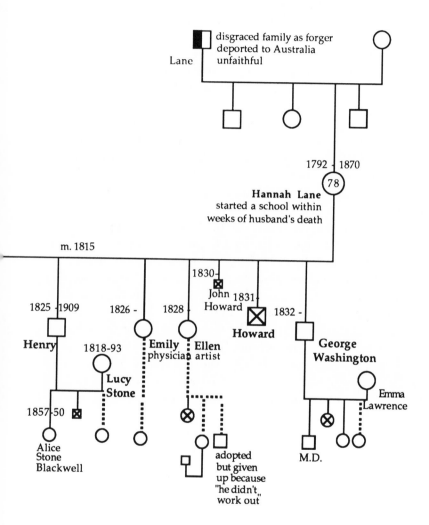

the famous suffragist Lucy Stone. He was attracted by her fiery speeches on the abolition of slavery and the rights of women. Indeed, her speeches were impassioned pleas against traditional marriage.

Henry Blackwell and Lucy Stone wrote their own marriage vows, which deliberately omitted the promise for the wife to obey, followed by an eloquent protest Henry had prepared against a woman's legal subservience to her husband in marriage. "I wish, as a husband, to renounce all the privileges which the law confers upon me, which are not strictly mutual,"[4] he said. Henry's protest became the model for generations of couples who wanted to transcend the traditional gender inequality of marriage. The couple kept separate names and bank accounts, and he encouraged her wholeheartedly in her career as in everything else.

Lucy's family had also given her negative messages and stories about marriage. She had grown up anguishing over her mother's "bondage" and self-denial in relation to her father's abuse and dominance. Her father was "ugly" to his wife about money, and Lucy felt pained by the lack of freedom of her mother and all other women in marriage. She wrote a friend: "It will take more than my lifetime for the obstacles to be removed which are in the way of a married woman having any being of her own."

In fact, she had grown up determined never to marry and changed her mind with great reluctance, becoming severely symptomatic with migraines and a near breakdown at the prospect. Her symptoms were so severe that the marriage to Henry Blackwell had to be postponed several times. Shortly before she "succumbed" she joked to her closest friend and future sister-in-law Antoinette Brown, who soon after married Henry's brother Samuel: "If the ceremony is in New York, we want you to harden your heart enough to help in so cruel an operation as putting Lucy Stone to death. But it will be all according to law, so you need fear no punishment. I expect, however, to go to Cincinnati to have the ruin complete there." Henry himself wrote with similar humor to one of his good friends: "I have just entangled myself beyond the possibility of release. . . . I lose no time in conveying information of the frightful casualty." Despite Lucy's fears, the marriage was a long and happy one for both of them.

Soon after Henry and Lucy's marriage, Henry's older brother Samuel Blackwell, met and wooed Antoinette Brown, the first woman minister in the United States, overcoming her early reservations about marriage, as Henry had done with Lucy.

In the long marriage that ensued, Samuel was extraordinary for the untraditional caring role he played within his family. He readily shared in the work of the home and was viewed as a saint by the entire Blackwell family. Antoinette was also remarkable in her far-sighted views about women's roles. She believed we needed to go farther than just give women more rights in a man's world. She made the revolutionary step of asserting that human knowledge would be enriched by adding to the traditions of logic and scientific inquiry the traditional "female" ways of knowing: intuition and personal experience. Antoinette and Lucy Stone had met years before at Oberlin College, where they formed a deep attachment and vowed never to marry. Both believed that marriage would be a severe hindrance to their work. Antoinette took the radical step of advocating that men's obligations should extend to family and home, a view that took other feminists a full century to espouse. No other writer publicly proposed that men should share child care and homemaking as well as the work for pay.

Supported by Samuel, who lived out his wife's ideas wholeheartedly, Antoinette had a full life as a minister, a speaker, and the author of poems, novels, and philosophical tracts until her death at age ninety-six. She lived long enough to vote and receive an honorary Doctorate of Divinity from Oberlin, which had in her youth refused to grant her a ministerial degree, even after she had completed her studies there.

Of the marriages in the next generation, Antoinette said: "All of the sons-in-law are good men and the marriages are more than usually satisfactory."[5] Samuel and Antoinette had five daughters, four successful and one an invalid, just as there had been five daughters in the previous generation (also four successful and one invalid). And as in the previous generation, there were five unmarried aunts who played a critical formative role in the development of the children. It is interesting that at least one of these daughters, Florence, rebelled against the prescription for women to have an independent career. She married a storekeeper, to the family's great disapproval, though everyone eventually realized that he was an excellent choice for a husband, much in the model of Samuel. Moreover, Flo herself later followed in her mother's footsteps, becoming a lay minister.

Although couples rarely notice the connection, it is surprising how often people meet their spouses or make the decision to marry shortly after a critical family event. Antoinette Brown (*Genogram 8.2*): for example, had lost five siblings in the years before she met Samuel Blackwell. She was perhaps impelled toward Oberlin and the ministry out of a need to come to terms with the early deaths of four of her siblings. The death of a fifth sister, Augusta, who had followed Antoinette to Oberlin and succumbed after a five-year struggle to tuberculosis, appears to have symbolized for Antoinette the end of her family. This seemed to prepare the context in which, unpon meeting Samuel the very next year, she reversed her decision never to marry.

The connections between extended family events and marital deci-

The Antoinette Brown Family
Genogram 8.2

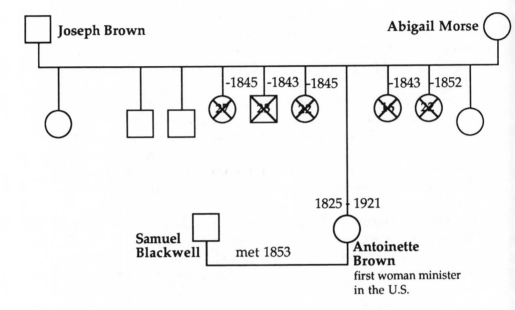

Joseph Brown

Abigail Morse

-1845 -1843 -1845 -1843 -1852

1825 1921

Samuel
Blackwell

met 1853

Antoinette
Brown
first woman minister
in the U.S.

sions, as occurred in the Brown family, are often obscured. Families tell many stories about the reasons for marriage: love at first sight, the need for security, prospects of money and prestige, anxiety about growing old alone, or the wish to have and raise children. A systems thinker might see Romeo and Juliet as falling in love with each other to deal with their anxiety about conflicts within their warring families. It is worth exploring behind family stories of love and marriage for family events, particularly losses, that may have influenced decisions to marry (as well as decisions to divorce).

There are, of course, sex differences in the way couples experience their relationships since women have traditionally been expected to give themselves up in a relationship and men have been raised to see intimacy as a threat to their autonomy. Thus men more often maintain pseudo independent stances in marriage ("I am totally self-sufficient"), implicitly depending on their wives to take care of them, while denying their dependence and admitting no needs, doubts, or mistakes. Women, on the other hand, are generally expected to maintain pseudo intimacies ("I want to do whatever you want to").

Men's fear of admitting dependence and women's adaptiveness

often work together to inhibit an intimate marital relationship that would permit differences. Generally speaking, we have socialized men so that they tend to remain on the periphery of the family emotionally, while women are constrained when they try to be anywhere else. In particular we have promoted the myth that marriage is like Cinderella's being found by Prince Charming and then sacrificing her identity to his. As you think about the marriages in your family, explore how different family members have responded to this conundrum. You may then expand your view of your "spinster" aunt Mamie. You may get a new appreciation of your granduncle, who, though he never made "a success" in the business world, was the beloved nurturer of his children and grandchildren. You may see hidden strengths in his having overcome so many of society's rules for men in being the kind of affectionate stay-at-home man he was.

A COMPLEX MARRIAGE: GUSTAV AND ALMA MAHLER

In 1902 in Vienna, Austria, Gustav Mahler, one of the most gifted composers of the century, married Alma Schindler, also a musical talent, who eventually married three of the major artistic geniuses of her time and had love relationships with at least three others. Gustav and Alma Mahler's marriage *(Genogram 8.3)* illustrates many of the complexities of marriage with traditional gender roles and some of the typical triangles that couples get into with work and affairs. Gustav Mahler had met Alma four months earlier. He was a forty-two-year-old famous, difficult Jewish composer and conductor who had converted to Christianity and been baptized in order to cope with the anti-Semitism of his times; she was a beautiful, partially deaf twenty-three-year-old-Austrian Catholic musician and composer, already engaged to another older musician, who was teaching her composition.

Until then Gustav seems to have avoided marriage, perhaps because his parents' marriage was so unhappy. The mother, Maria, had suffered from unrequited love for someone else and married Gustav's father, Bernard, without loving him. She was a sweet, frail, quietly affectionate woman, who was born lame. Gustav's irascible father brutalized his wife, beat his children, and ran after every servant. Gustav's love for his mother was as intense as was his dislike for his

The Mahler and Schindler Families

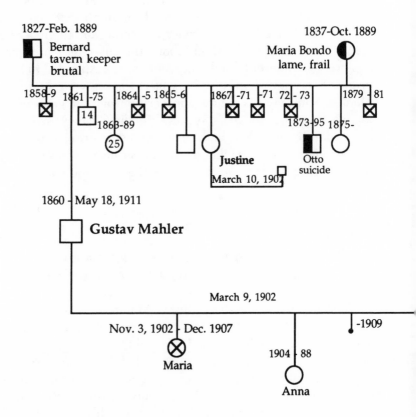

father. Maria bore fourteen children in twenty-one years, losing eight sons in childhood. Gustav, the oldest surviving child, who had nursed one younger brother unceasingly until he died at fourteen, became the caretaker for the others. Until his marriage he lived with his sister Justine, who served as his housekeeper, companion, and hostess for two decades. At thirty-three Justine had begun to think she was doomed to the fate of tending to her brother and would never have a life of her own. She loved him but felt like his servant. She was in love with Arnold Rose, the first violinist at the Vienna Opera, which Gustav conducted. Not surprisingly, perhaps, she married Rose the very day after her brother married Alma.

Gustav's attraction for Alma was immediate. She was beautiful, strong-minded, creative, and full of youth. The romance flourished

Genogram 8.3

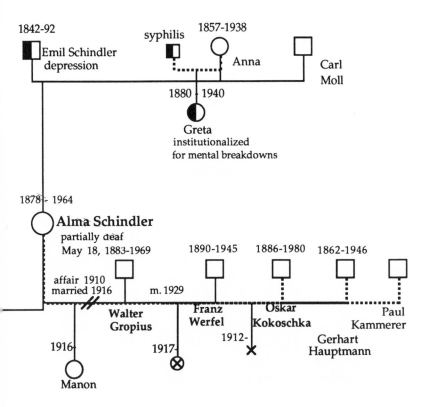

rapidly, but soon there were storm clouds. Alma apparently stated her continuing ambitions to be a musician and composer. Gustav responded harshly, calling her arrogant and reminding her of his view of a wife: "You must become what I need, if we are to be happy together. . . . The roles . . . must be correctly assigned. The role of 'composer' falls to me—yours is that of loving companion and understanding partner. . . . You must give yourself to me unconditionally, shape your future life in every detail entirely in accordance with my needs and desire nothing in return save my love."[6] Alma was shocked. He was asking her to give up her work and her self and requiring her instead to dedicate herself to him and his music, which she didn't even like. Alma had grown up devoted to her father, who had died when she was fourteen. When Alma showed Gustav's letter to her mother, for whom she had always felt resentment, her mother urged her to end the relationship. Alma chose to do the opposite and soon paid heavily for the acquiescence!

As plans for the wedding proceeded, the tension between the couple continued. Gustav's friends found Alma rude and unappreciative of his work. His sister Justine was jealous. In addition, as Alma soon realized, Gustav was completely neglectful of his finances and heavily in debt. It would take her five years to remedy the situation. And while he showed some greater flexibility during their brief courtship, as soon as they were married, he reverted to his rigid obsession with his work and acted more like her teacher than her lover.

Alma's assignment was, in addition to copying his work for him, to keep everything running smoothly. She had become pregnant even before they married, and as the pregnancy developed, she felt her freedom disappearing. "Nothing has reached fruition for me, neither my beauty, nor my spirit, nor my talent. . . . I am living what only appears to be a life. I hold so much inside of me. I am not free—I suffer, but I don't know why or what for." Like so many women, she was mystified by her problem, which was denied by her husband, who, when he found her crying one day, concluded she was unhappy because she didn't love him enough. In her diary she wrote: "I don't know how to begin, there is such a silent struggle going on inside me! And such a dreadful longing for someone who thinks about ME—that helps me find MYSELF! I am drowning beneath the altar of family life. . . . It came over me that I had crossed that bridge once and for all—someone had taken me roughly by the arm and led me far away from my own self."[7]

Even when she did try to find words for her frustration, complaining to him the next year about his lack of interest in what went on inside her and lack of acknowledgment of her work, his response was to blame her unhappiness on her: "Just because your budding dreams have not been fulfilled . . . that's entirely up to you." Over the next few years the couple grew farther apart. Gustav was preoccupied with his work. Alma was depressed and frustrated. Their first daughter, Maria, named for Gustav's beloved but frail mother, died in 1907, at the age of five. In his grief Mahler withdrew further into himself.

Mahler was diagnosed with a life-threatening heart condition, and Alma was often physically ill as well as depressed. Neither parent had much energy left over for their second daughter, Anna, born in 1904, who, left to her own devices, blamed herself for years afterward for her sister's death, though it occurred when she was only three. Gustav became preoccupied with anxieties that he himself would die.

Having written eight symphonies, he feared that like Schubert, Beethoven, and Bruckner, he would not live past a ninth. He therefore chose to call his next work not his ninth symphony but *The Song of the Earth,* convincing himself that he was thus not tempting fate.[8]

During this stormy period Alma became emotionally involved with one of Mahler's devotees, a common triangling pattern in situations of loss or threatened loss. Mahler was also preoccupied with his career struggles with the Vienna Opera and with anti-Semitism, a major factor in the sociopolitical atmosphere of the era, which limited his opportunities. For a time they came to the United States, where he was appreciated much more, but where Alma was all the more isolated and cut off. In addition, in 1909 she had a miscarriage, which revived the pain of the death of their first child.

In May 1910 Alma consulted a physician for what she called the "wear and tear of being driven on without respite by a spirit so intense as [Gustav's]."[9] She feared she was on the brink of collapse. The doctor recommended a long rest cure, and she left for a spa. Not surprising in this context, she became involved in a new romance, this time with Walter Gropius, a handsome, imaginative, talented German architect five years younger than she. Shortly afterward, Gropius wrote to Mahler, as if he were Alma's father, asking permission to marry her. Gustav went into a tailspin and became obsessed with losing her. He vowed to change, and sought consultation with Freud.

Freud's intervention is interesting from a family systems perspective. He zeroed in on the unresolved issues the couple had with their own parents, which had drawn Gustav and Alma to each other in the first place. He posed the challenge: "How dared a man in your state ask a young woman to be tied to him? . . . I know your wife. She loved her father and she can only choose and love a man of his sort. Your age, of which you are so much afraid, is precisely what attracts her. You need not be anxious. You loved your mother and you looked for her in every woman. She was careworn and ailing, and unconsciously you wish your wife to be the same." Gustave began writing love letters to Alma, saying he must sound like a "schoolboy in love," but not hiding his feelings: "Freud is quite right—you were always for me the light and the central point! That inner light, I mean, which rose over all."

Here is the paradoxical aspect of so many marriages: Though men may have controlled and inhibited their wives' personal development, their own unarticulated dependence on their wives may be very intense. This may leave a woman in a paradoxical situation:

Alma Schindler (Mahler) at twelve, with her mother and sister, Grete, age ten. Alma, at least in this picture, is clearly the favorite. Grete was apparently the result of her mother's brief affair while the father was in deep depression. (Below), Alma Mahler at twenty-seven in 1905, with her two daughters. The older girl was to die while still in childhood.
Bildarchiv der Österreichischen Nationalbibliothek, Wien

While she is seen as vulnerable and emotionally dependent on her husband, she may be expected to survive with almost no emotional support, validation, or understanding from him.

In this case, spurred by the crisis, Gustav began for the first time to play the songs Alma had written years before, wanting her to return to the composing he had forced her to give up nine years earlier. Instead of feeling supported, Alma now felt he was invading her privacy. She never gained the courage to return to her composing, though gradually their marriage mellowed. Gustav became more gentle. Heretofore he had ignored her birthday and other holidays; he had never even given her a wedding present. Now he bought her a diamond ring and made elaborate preparations for a Christmas celebration. He also became more expressive to his daughter Anna. Then, shortly after Christmas in 1911, Gustav contracted influenza and within a few months was dead. Alma was thirty-two.

Alma went on to marry twice more and had relationships with a number of other men, including the dramatist Gerhart Hauptmann, a brilliant and controversial biologist, Paul Kammerer, and the artist Oskar Kokoschka, whose demands were similar to those of Mahler: "Love, you must force yourself to give up every thought of every production from your past and of every advisor prior to me. . . . I want you very much when you find your own being, your peace, and your freedom in my existence. . . . I warn you to decide whether you want to be free from me or in me." He actually took to signing his letters "Alma Oskar Kokoschka," as if to fuse their two identities. Though deeply drawn to Kokoschka, Alma had the wisdom, perhaps from hard experience, to resist his demands for fusion. She was deeply disturbed by the relationship, though she came to feel she could never be free of it: "I would like to break free from Oskar. . . . He makes me lose my momentum. . . . But now I know I will sing only in death. Then I'll be a slave to no man, because I will tend to my own well-being and to myself."

In an attempt to get away, she looked up Gropius again and convinced him within two weeks that they were in love with each other. It was not inconsequential to her that Gropius's birthday fell on May 18, Gustav's death day. She connected him with her loss in another way as well. Remembering her first meeting with him, she wrote: "I believe that I was old and hateful . . . and suddenly there came a man into my life who was new to me and immediately taken by me. When he first told me that he loved me, I was happy as I had not been in years. This happened right after I had lost my beautiful child. I was destroyed and suffering." Since this relationship was built on her previous losses, it is perhaps not surprising that she wanted to end the relationship soon after she and Gropius married and had a daughter in 1916. She tried to keep him from getting close to their daughter, Manon, and turned her attention to the poet Franz Werfel, eleven years her junior. Soon she became pregnant by him. Gropius was led to believe the child was his, but when he realized it was not, he let Anna go in a most dignified way and without reproach. The baby, born prematurely, died after a few months.

Over the next few years Alma struggled with herself about how to arrange her life. She could not marry Werfel, and she could not leave him. Several times a year the couple parted to do their own work, and then they reunited. Eventually, in 1929, they did marry. Their relationship was never really happy. Shortly before Werfel died in 1944, he wrote Alma a poem:

> *How very much I love you,*
> *I had not known . . .*
> *Why do we realize things*
> *Only after they have been taken from us?* . . .

In Alma's last years Oskar Kokoschka turned up in New York, where she was living, and asked to visit her. They had corresponded over the years in fits and starts, in letters full of dreams of reuniting and unfulfilled possibilities. In the end Alma refused to see him. Perhaps she preferred to hold on to her dream of love than to confront once again its complex reality.

MARITAL COMPLEMENTARITY

The saw that opposites attract is not entirely true, since people generally choose partners who are similar to them in most important ways. Yet couples do tend to fall into reciprocal, complementary, and opposite roles in their relationships. It is almost as if partners chose each other to express a hidden side of themselves.

Marriage involves so many levels of interdependence that outsiders may never really know the quid pro quo that binds a couple together. And while differentness or complementarity may form the basis for the initial attraction, as things go along, these same differences can become the problem. For example, a wife who is one of eight children in a voluble working-class Italian family from Brooklyn may be extremely attracted to an upper-class midwestern WASP who is an only child. Seeing him as the embodiment of the "American dream," she admires his quiet, stable strength, ambition, and ability to stay calm and rational, no matter how provoked. He finds her fun-loving, warm, and vivacious. He loves her family's spontaneity and open affection, not to mention the delicious rich food and joy in continuous celebration.

Everything is fine until they settle in after the wedding. At that point she begins to view his industriousness as "workaholism" and resents his stoic calm. Her liveliness and charm now seem full of histrionics and hysteria, and he calls her "careless," not "easygoing." Her family, instead of being "fun-loving and colorful," is "boisterous, intrusive, and smothering." His family has gone from being "quietly charming and gracious" to "boring, vanilla, and uptight."

In your own family maybe your mother played the martyr and stifled her own identity, while your father played the bully. Or maybe couple relationships in your family were characterized by power struggles, in which neither partner could give in and fighting resulted in a stalemate. Perhaps wives ran the show, while their husbands sat quietly smoking and reading newspapers in the corner. Whatever the patterns, you need to identify them and explore their meaning before you can be sure what your own role is and what you want it to be.

Exploring the patterns of complementarity in your family, particularly in marital relationships, will give you insights about patterns that are being passed down that you may want to change. As George Bernard Shaw's wife wrote, "The conflict of temperaments is nature's way of avenging the race. Nature thrusts men and women into the arms of their opposites. . . . Ordinary, commonplace people are attracted by unlikeness: the strong by the weak, the passionate by the calm, the dark by the fair . . . marriage causes untold unhappiness . . . brought about by the clash. . . . We constantly blame only one, and probably the wrong one. For the troubles of my youth my mother seemed entirely to blame, but on mature reflection I see that this is a wrong view."[10]

At the age of forty-two George Bernard Shaw married Charlotte Payne-Townshend, who was then forty-one *(Genogram 8.4)*. Until that year Charlotte had been determined never to marry and had turned down many proposals. Shaw was cynical about marriage, opposing it partly on political grounds, as a bourgeois institution, and partly because of his childhood experience of his parents' miserable marriage. When Shaw was twelve, his mother replaced his father

The Shaw and Payne-Townshend Families
Genogram 8.4

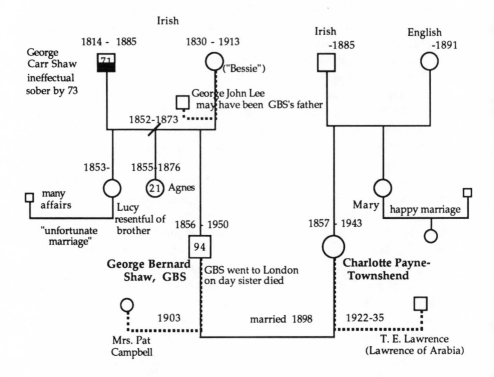

with a lover, who moved into their home together with the father. (It is even possible that the mother's lover was GBS's father.)

Shaw's pattern of distancing himself from women who pursued him was long-standing. One such admirer said of him: "The sight of a woman deeply in love with him annoyed him."[11] His view of this woman was that "I give her nothing; and I do not even take . . . anything, which makes her most miserable. When I tell her so, it only mortifies and tantalises and attracts her and makes her worse."

This is the typical pattern of the pursuer-distancer relationship. The pursuer's pursuit distances the distancer, and his distancing attracts the pursuer more. What is most interesting about the pattern is that when either one changes role, the other seems to change as well. When Charlotte stopped pursuing, Shaw began to pursue her, and when he pursued her, she tended to distance herself. Though Charlotte was in general the emotional pursuer, she also had the money and liked to travel. This enabled her to distance herself physically from Shaw and gave her a certain power over him.

She was the older of two sisters and had perceived her parents' marriage as a disaster. Her mother, who was English, hated Ireland and everything Irish. Charlotte's father, who was Irish, adored Ireland and was like a fish out of water anywhere else. Charlotte adored her sweet Irish father, whose gentleness provoked his wife to rage. Charlotte's mother longed for him to assert himself. Instead he tried to deafen himself to his wife and make himself invisible. He was a dreamer who hummed mildly under his breath and drummed his fingers on the arms of chairs. As Charlotte saw it, her mother extinguished his dreams and finally squeezed all the life out of him. Later Charlotte wondered whether her own hatred of her mother had killed her, as she thought her mother's hatred had killed her father.

Charlotte's mother pushed her relentlessly to marry, and Charlotte just as vehemently resisted. It wasn't until the mother died that Charlotte let herself fall in love for the first time. When this love ended in rejection, Charlotte wandered about for several years, trying to establish a meaning for her life. A friend who soon introduced her to Shaw described her thus: "She found herself . . . alone in the world, without ties, without any definite creed, and with a large income. For . . . years she . . . drifted about—in India, in Italy, in Egypt, in London, seeking occupation and fellow spirits. . . . By temperament she is an anarchist—feeling any regulation or rule intolerable. . . . She is by nature a rebel. She has no snobbishness and no convention."[12] Then she met Shaw. He was forty; she was thirty-nine. They had a remarkable amount in common, not least their loathing of marriage. They were both rebels, radicals, and nonconformists who valued their independence. Shaw wrote of their early relationship: "She also being Irish does not succumb to my arts . . . but we get on together all the better, repairing bicycles, talking philosophy and religion . . . or, when we are in a mischievous or sentimental hour, philandering shamelessly and outrageously. . . . She knows the value of her unencumbered independence, having suffered a good deal from family bonds and conventionality. . . . The idea of tying herself up again by a marriage . . . seems to her intellect to be unbearably foolish. Her theory is that she won't do it."[13] This makes their personalities sound ideally suited for each other. But, like most couples, they fell into complementary roles as their relationship evolved.

Charlotte began seeking more connection, and when she did, Shaw retreated, warning, "From the moment that you can't do with-

*George Bernard Shaw and his wife, Charlotte Payne-Townshend, in 1900,
two years after their marriage. She was oldest among her siblings, he the
youngest. The families of both were characterized by chaotic marriages.*
The Hulton Deutsch Collection

out me, you're lost." When she took his advice and tried to resist him
by suddenly leaving for Ireland, he was nonplussed and complained:
"Why do you choose this time of all others to desert me—just now
when you are most wanted?" He tried to distance himself into other
relationships, but the greater distance she kept, the more he found
himself falling in love with her, though it petrified him. He wrote to
her on the day before her return from Ireland: "I will contrive to see
you somehow, at all hazards. I must, and that 'must' which 'rather
alarms' you, terrifies me. . . . If it were possible to run away—if it
would do any good—I'd do it; so mortally afraid am I that my trifling
and lying and ingrained treachery and levity with women are going
to make you miserable, when my whole sane desire is to make you
hap—I mean strong and self possessed and tranquil. . . . For there is
something between us aside and apart from all my villainy." He
couldn't even admit that he cared enough to want to make her happy.
That would imply too much dependence. Before seeing her, he
instructed her on how she must keep her distance when they were
alone together. But over the next few months their lives became
more entwined. He ended his various relationships with other

women, and she gradually made herself indispensable to him, becoming his secretary and caretaker as well as his companion. Shaw believed the status of marriage was almost essential for a woman's greatest possible freedom—but, of course, eschewed it for himself! When Charlotte finally tried to take his advice and proposed to him, he apparently responded "with shuddering horror & wildly asked the fare to Australia."

The couple were soon reconciled, but Charlotte was, as usual, in the position of emotional pursuer. When Shaw rebuffed her, she backed off again: "I am in the rather unusual position of being perfectly free. . . . The personal happiness, which everyone puts first and which I had within my grasp was lost to me . . . and my life is a wreck; so I am free from the ordinary individual hopes, fears and despairs, which are so apt to become chains."[14] In her absence Shaw began to realize how much he missed her: "It is so damnably inconvenient to have you out of my reach." He now began having accidents and physical symptoms. First he fell off his bicycle. Dramatist that he was, he played up his black eye and cut face to the hilt. But when Charlotte soon after invited him to go on a trip, he responded with sarcasm and avoidance: "No use in looking for human sympathy from me. I have turned the switch and am your very good friend, but as hard as nails."

When she went off without him, his sarcastic humor intensified:

> What do you mean by this inconceivable conduct? Do you forsake all your duties—even those of secretary? Is it not enough that I have returned without a complaint to my stark and joyless life? . . . Are there no stamps? . . . Go then, ungrateful wretch: have your heart's desire: find a Master—one who will spend your money and rule your house. . . . Protect yourself for ever from freedom, independence, love, unfettered communion with the choice spirits of your day, a lofty path on which to go your own way and keep your own counsel, and all the other blessings which 999 women cry for and the thousandth cries to get away from.

The longer Charlotte was away, the more unstable he grew. Finally he wrote, describing himself as "detestably deserted," and pleading, "Oh Charlotte, Charlotte: is this a time to be gadding about in Rome?"[15] Soon both of them were becoming symptomatic, he with headaches, toothaches, accidents, and finally gout, she with neuralgia, restlessness, and depression. As much as he missed her, he also feared her: "But then I think of the other Charlotte, the terrible Charlotte, the lier-in-wait, the soul hypochondriac, always watching and dragging me into bondage, always planning nice, sensible, comfortable, selfish destruction for me, wincing at every accent of freedom in my voice, so that at last I get the trick of hiding myself from her, hating me and longing for me with the absorbing passion of the spider for the fly."

By the time she returned from Rome, he was desperate for her and in a disastrous situation, almost an invalid by virtue of an infected foot. Charlotte was appalled when she saw the circumstances in which he was living: filthy, wretched, malnourished, uncared for. His mother, with whom he lived, did nothing for him if she even noticed his condition at all. Charlotte could never forgive her for her neglect of her son, though from the time of their marriage Charlotte provided an annuity for her. In fact, both families had a lasting antagonism to the couple. Charlotte's sister never even wanted to meet Shaw, and his sister, who resented him in the first place, had even more resentment for Charlotte.

Exactly how the couple came to their final decision to marry will never be known. Charlotte never spoke of private things, and Shaw always hid the deeply emotional events of his life in clownish descriptions. Something was changing with him. He had written: "I had always, from my boyhood had the impression that 38 to 40 was a dangerous age for men of genius and that I should possibly die like Mozart, Schiller, and Mendelssohn at that crisis." He was at the time in constant pain and in need of a serious operation, which Charlotte finally arranged. His situation was somehow changed "by a change in my own consciousness. I found that my own objection to my own marriage had ceased with my objection to my own death,"[16] said Shaw. "Death did not come; but something which I had always objected to far worse: to wit, Marriage did."[17]

GBS later told the story that he married because being a wretch on crutches, stifled by chloroform, and determined to die, "I proposed to make her my widow."[18] Even years later Shaw insisted that he had made the decision from the point of view of a dying man and said Charlotte had predicted he would otherwise become a permanent invalid. In fact, he wrote his own humorous announcement of the wedding for the newspapers, describing it as a totally chance event: "As a lady and gentleman were out driving in . . . Covent Garden yesterday, a heavy shower drove them to take shelter in the office of the . . . Registrar there, and in the confusion of the moment married them. The lady was . . . Miss Payne Townshend and the gentleman was George Bernard Shaw. . . . Startling as was the liberty undertaken by the . . . official, it turns out well. Miss Payne Townshend is an Irish lady with an income many times the volume of that which

'Corno di Bassetto' used to earn, but to that happy man, being a vegetarian, the circumstance is of no moment."[19]

In ways the two "chance" partners were very different people. Like many oldests, Charlotte was responsible, accustomed to dominating and being the caretaker. Shaw, on the other hand, was the younger brother of two sisters. Like many younger brothers of older sisters, he was irreverent, creative, and irresponsible and used to having others take care of him. Charlotte may have married Shaw because she enjoyed his unpredictability and creative genius. Also, he was someone who seemed to need a caretaker. Though Shaw had finally achieved economic stability through the success of one of his plays a few months before he married, his decision may have been facilitated by Charlotte's wealth, which enabled him to provide for his mother, with whom he had lived until his marriage.

As is often the case, the complementary differences that brought them together were not enough to make a successful marriage. Although the marriage did last for forty-five years and Shaw insisted to the end of his life that he could not have married anyone else, the two grew less intimate as the years went by. Charlotte loved to travel; he hated it. She, like her father, loved to be in Ireland, while Shaw was ambivalent about ever returning to his homeland. Most important, Shaw came to believe that his wife was not a worthy discussant on one topic after another—religion, politics, and so forth—and he closed her out. Charlotte did handle Shaw's one major affair, with Mrs. Patrick Campbell, with great skill, continuing to socialize with him and refusing to be put off by the rumors of the affair. She was meanwhile preoccupied with her own spiritual search, which she did not share with her husband. From about 1922 she developed an intimate friendship with T. E. Lawrence (Lawrence of Arabia), twenty years her junior, certainly one of the geniuses of the era, sharing with him the personal thoughts she could not share with her husband. This relationship lasted until Lawrence's death in 1935.

It was not until Charlotte's death in 1943 that Shaw, then in his eighties, read her correspondence with Lawrence and realized how he had misjudged her. He saw that he had missed out on the intellectual and emotional richness that she obviously had to share. He wrote: "From a diary I discovered lately and some letters which she wrote to T. E. Lawrence, I realize that there were many parts of her character that even I did not know, for she poured out her soul to Lawrence. . . . I lived with Charlotte for forty years and I see now that there was a great deal about her that I didn't know. It has been a shock." Shaw had expected someone to take care of him, not someone to be his intellectual companion. Unable to move beyond the expectations of his own unhappy family, he had not seen his wife for who she was. One might hypothesize that sibling complementarity (he a youngest, she an oldest) enabled them to remain married for forty-five years, but the family legacy of marital unhappiness, along with our society's constrants on gender roles, seems to have influenced their own expectations of marriage, such that they were unable to be really intimate with each other.

COUPLE TRIANGLES

When couples cannot resolve issues themselves, there are a number of common triangles that develop. They may come together around a mischievous or sick child and thus distract themselves from their problems with each other. Or they may focus on their in-laws as the source of the problem: "If it weren't for your mother's intrusiveness, we'd be all right." Men have traditionally moved outside the family when they have had marital problems, concentrating on their work, seeking an affair outside the marriage, or focusing their energies on "male" activities: socializing with buddies at the pub, playing golf, etc. Addictions are surely the most destructive of the common male responses to marital tension. Women, on the other hand, may turn their marital frustrations into anxiety, depression, social withdrawal, rigid housekeeping, or overinvestment in their children. Recently women are also turning more to addictions and affairs.

It has been said that the twenty-first century will be about the invention of the marriage-divorce cycle as the normal pattern of life for families, since this has become such a common process in family life. But generally families do not handle the breakdown of a marriage very well, and the unresolved relationships come back to haunt them later. Divorce most often leaves a legacy of dangling ends—the bric-a-brac of a lifetime, along with bitterness and cutoff that have to be gotten past. One young man summed up his resentment toward his father's second wife by saying, "There she was redecorating my past with all her fake antiques."

When there are new or missing marital partners in your family brought on by separation, divorce, or early death, bridging the cutoffs in your family will open up for you another set of connections to people who are also yours, people with an investment in your past as well as your future. Getting to know about every branch of your family may involve getting past some intense reactions of other family members and holding yourself steady in pursuit of the missing information on your family tree.

QUESTIONS ABOUT MARRIAGE

- What are the stories told in your family about how couples got together? What attracted spouses to each other? What made them decide to marry? What were the underlying dreams about marriage and the underlying fears? What messages got passed from one generation to another about it?
- Are there coincidences in timing between marriage decisions (when partners met, fell in love, decided to marry, or began to have marital problems) and other family events, particularly loss (deaths, moves, family traumas, or other life cycle transitions)?
- What unresolved issues from their families of origin did members of your family bring into their marriages?
- How did people's characterizations of each other change from the time of courtship through the marriage?
- What are the typical patterns of marriage in your family? Are there certain typical patterns of symmetry or complementarity: The tyrant-battleax and the doormat-mouse? Fiery foes? Mutt and Jeff? Tweedledum and Tweedledee? The hand and the glove? The caretaker and the patient? The obsessive and the hysteric? The silent clam and the babbler?
- Did couples get into power struggles? Were they conflict avoiders? Ships passing in the night?
- Are there typical triangling patterns in the marriages in your family: with a child? With an "affair?" With sports/TV/work/Mah-Jongg/the telephone? A mother-in-law?
- Are there typical gender patterns in the marriages in your family: The men leave? The women are long-suffering? The women are frustrated impresarios? The men are silent, distant, impulsive, or frightening?
- Are there patterns of divorce? Remarriage? Late marriage? Non-marriage? Long marriage? Happy marriage?
- Are there any family messages or rules about marriage, such as:

Men are dangerous? Women are dangerous? Marriage takes away
your freedom? You can never be happy unless you're married?

■ Have family weddings in your family typically been traumatic
affairs or happy gatherings? Large and lavish? Elopements? Plain-
clothes affairs with a justice of the peace? Did anyone not go to a
wedding who "should have"? Have any cutoffs occurred around a
wedding?

■ Do marital partners tend to fight over money? Sex? Children?
Leisure activities? Food? Religion? Politics? Mothers-in-law?

■ Do spouses tend to be from the same ethnic or class background?
If not, do they have issues about moving "up" in class?

■ How did couples in your family negotiate the use of space, time,
and money, where to go on vacation, which family traditions and rituals to retain from each family of origin and which ones to develop
anew, relationships with parents, siblings, friends, extended family,
and coworkers?

■ Are parts of your family tree missing or blurry because of
divorce, early death of a parent, or in-law triangles? Can you see ways
to gain access to the missing information? Who would be most upset
if you connected with these sources? Can you gain the courage to deal
with the loyalty conflicts, jealousy, or sense of betrayal others may
feel in order to reclaim your whole family?

■ What are the norms in your family for marriage, and are they
different from the dominant norms? Are there patterns of late marriage? Not marrying? Divorce and remarriage? Living together in
unmarriage or in unconventional groupings? Are there lesbian or gay
couples? May–December marriages? Marriages with an "extra"
adult?

CLASS, CULTURE, AND FAMILY RELATIONSHIPS

If the heart of Africa still remained illusive, my search for it had brought me closer to understanding myself and other human beings. The ache for home lives in all of us, the safe place where we can go as we are and not be questioned. It impels mighty ambitions and dangerous capers. . . . Hoping that by doing these things home will find us acceptable or, failing that, that we all forget our awful yearning for it.

—Maya Angelou

Chinese Americans, when you try to understand what things in you are Chinese, how do you separate what is peculiar to childhood, to poverty, insanities, one family, your mother who marked your growing up with stories, from what is Chinese? What is Chinese tradition and what is the movies?

—Maxine Hong Kingston

Probably all of us are more a hodgepodge of identities, cultural and otherwise, than anything else. Our identities are made up of the complexities of our heritage, our judgments about what is possible or preferable to mention in a given context, and other people's projections onto us. The narrator, Vivian Twostar, offers a brilliant expression of this complexity in Louise Erdrich and Michael Dorris's *The Crown of Columbus*, which, with different details, might be the story of any one of us:

I belong to the lost tribe of mixed bloods, that hodgepodge amalgam of hue and cry that defies easy placement. When the DNA of my various ancestors— Irish and Coeur d'Alene and Spanish and Navajo and God knows what else— combined to form me, the result was not some genteel indecipherable puree that comes from a Cuisinart. . . . There are times when I control who I'll be, and times when I let other people decide. I'm not all anything, but I'm a little

more often than others, it's because they need it more. . . . I've read anthropological papers written about people like me. We're called marginal, as if we
exist anywhere but on the center of the page. We're parked in the bleachers
looking into the arena, never the main players, but there are bonuses to
peripheral vision. Out beyond the normal bounds, you at least know where
you're not. You escape the claustrophobia of belonging, and what you lack in
security you gain by realizing—as those insiders never do—that security is an
illusion. . . . "Caught between two worlds," is the way we're often characterized, but I'd put it differently. We are the catch.[1]

When you think about yourself and your family, consider the ambi-
guities that surround belonging and group identifications for each
person. Consider as well what those who "belong" have to learn from
those who are marginalized. It will help you in getting a fundamental
grasp of thinking of your family as a system, each person playing a role
in relation to one another. A complex web of connections cushions us
as we move through life: family, community, culture. And even
though we may be moving toward becoming a larger, global community, we are still very much embedded in our local context. Families
do not develop their rules, beliefs, and rituals in a vacuum. What you
think, how you act, even your language are all transmitted through
the family from the wider cultural context. This context includes the
culture in which you now live and that of your ancestors. It is influenced by your family's class, religion, and geographic background, as
well as by its ethnicity and cultural experiences. And culture itself is
not a monologue but a dialogue.[2] No matter what your background
is, in effect it is multicultural. In the same vein, all marriage is to a
degree an intermarriage. No two families share the exact same cultural roots. Thus the family into which you were born is made up of
many cultural strands from many cultural roots. Understanding your
cultural roots is essential to understanding your family and yourself.

Cultural groups have varying attitudes toward life, death, sex,
food, men, women, children, the elderly, birth, and death. The
strength of your ethnic identity will be influenced by your family's
particular pattern of migration, religion, socioeconomic status, education, type of work, and geographic location, by your ethnic group's
place in the larger society, and by your particular family's experience
as part of this group. If you are at home with your ethnic identity,
as with your family identity, you are likely to lead a healthier and
happier life.

Understanding your family's cultural background is one sure way
of making sense of its behavior because there are few universal meanings to behavior. For example, when close family members fail to

attend a funeral, it makes a difference if the family is of British ancestry, where services at a death may not be considered the most important life cycle ritual, as they are in families of Irish or African American ancestry.

RITUALS

The longer your family has lived in the United States and the less embedded it is in a cultural enclave, the more it has probably moved away from its cultural traditions. Exceptions are likely to occur at times of transition, however, or during rituals that reflect the importance of the group: at holidays, marriages, funerals, reunions. At those times families tend to rely on their inner resources, harking back to values that seemed lost at other times.

For this reason the times when family rituals surface are excellent opportunities for exploring your family beliefs and values. If you listen carefully, you will hear many stories and have the chance to observe the alliances and cutoffs at work in the family. Rituals are prime occasions to bridge cutoffs, to open up closed issues. They are a perfect opportunity to bring about healing in your family.

Think about some of the general characteristics of the cultural group to which your family belongs. How much has it conformed to what is expected of men, of women in that group? The amount of closeness, for example, that is expected or desired between family members varies in different groups. Italians tend to be close and enmeshed, sharing everything with one another and spending all holidays and much free time together. The Italian belief is that if you lose your family, you might as well be dead. Scandinavian families generally maintain a greater distance and are less likely to demonstrate anger or affection, even among close family members.

Every culture has its strengths and vulnerabilities. In your own family you will need to recognize these without becoming too reactive. There is a joke that addresses such differences in several European ethic groups.

> Heaven is a place where the police are British, the cooks are French, the mechanics are German, the lovers are Italian, and it is all organized by the Swiss.
> Hell is a place where the chefs are British, the mechanics are French, the lovers are Swiss, the police are German, and it is all organized by the Italians.

In understanding your family, you will want to see how much its values fit with those of the groups to which it belongs. If family members had strong reactions against acknowledging their cultural background, it may be because of earlier immigrant experiences of prejudice or of feeling they were "outsiders." If they are extremely nationalistic, they may have felt oppressed as a minority within the larger community. Sometimes there is an attempt to hold on tightly to cultural traditions, even if this means being closed to new experiences. Seeing its attitudes toward culture from a systemic perspective can help you understand your family's origins and what led it to hold on to certain beliefs or shift to different beliefs. Under pressure from the dominant society, family members may try to "pass," renouncing their heritage, or they may cling to it unduly.

An important "critical event" to explore in your family is its migration experience. For many Americans, especially those brought over as slaves from Africa, this history is probably lost. However, even if the specifics of your family's history are lost, you can educate yourself enough about your culture's general history to allow you to speculate about how it played out in your particular family.

When you do have access to details of family history, it makes a great difference why the family came, what it was leaving behind, and what dreams or fears it brought with it. The ages of children at the time of migration can influence family patterns profoundly. It is also important to study the remigrations once the family came to the United States. If children in your family learned English before parents, that undoubtedly influenced family relationships, triangles, coalitions, alliances, and cutoffs which perhaps developed later. If parents lost their status in the process of immigration or if, on the other hand, they increased their status by coming and succeeding in ways they had hardly dreamed of when they came, these patterns will influence family relationships for generations to come.

Ethnic patterns are not fixed but constantly in flux and in many ways hard to define. Ethnicity encompasses more than religion or country of origin. Someone might, for example, have a strong sense of Jewish identity without being particularly religious or even believing in God. And of course, even without a single country of origin or a common language, Jews often have a profound sense of shared cultural values and shared history. Ethnic patterns are retained much longer than we consciously realize, even though they are modified by complex socioeconomic forces, ethnic intermarriage, geographic mobility, and the rapidly changing patterns of the family life cycle in our times. At the same time everyone's values reflect cultural influences, and culture is a major force to reckon with if you want to understand your family.

The patterns I am referring to are much more complex than the few examples offered here, but I hope these few suggestions will give you a clue about the many possible questions you can ask to learn about your cultural history. What are your family's values in relation to the ethnic groups from which you come? Does your family fit into the patterns of its group? If not, was it attempting to move away from its cultural roots?

To illustrate with a brief example, consider your family's attitude toward communication. Do family members believe everything must get talked out? Do they dance around issues that might cause conflict, while talking a lot about politics or daily activities? Does one person do the talking for the whole family? Do family members express themselves in body language, music, food, or gifts rather than talk?

In Jewish culture, for instance, talk—articulating the meaning of experience—may be even more important than the experience itself. Verbal communication—sharing one's ideas and perceptions—is deeply valued as a way of finding meaning in life. Among those of Anglo-Saxon background, on the other hand, words seem valued primarily for their utilitarian, pragmatic function. As the son says in the movie *Ordinary People* about his brother's death, "What's the point of talking about it. It doesn't change anything." In Chinese culture, families may communicate about important issues through food rather than through words. Italians use both food and words—but words are used primarily for drama—to convey the emotional intensity of an experience. The Irish, who are perhaps the greatest poets in the world, often use words to buffer experience. They call on poetry or the humor of language to make reality somehow more tolerable; it has been suggested that the Irish use words more to cover up or embellish the truth than to express it. A different attitude is found in Sioux culture where speech is actually proscribed in certain family relationships! I have a colleague married for years to a Sioux man who has never exchanged a word with her father-in-law, yet as she has told me, she feels a deep intimacy with him. Such a relationship is almost inconceivable in our digital, pragmatic world. My colleague states that the reduced emphasis on verbal expression seems to free up Native American families for other kinds of experience: of each other, of nature, of the spiritual world.

Groups also differ on this dimension of spirituality. Anglo-Saxons and Jews tend to be more "reality"-oriented than other cultures do. Even to call the physical world "reality" expresses the dominant society's devaluing of other "realities," such as spirituality, imagination, and dreams. Hispanics, for instance, are more likely to think of reality as a fluid continuum between dreams and the physical world. In contrast with the British, who value work, reason, truth, and, above all, individuality, the Irish have always preferred their dreams to the truth. A character in a recent Irish novel, when accused of being an inveterate liar, explains: "It's the poet's way of reaching for truth."[3] George Bernard Shaw has a character lay it all out: "Oh the dreaming! The dreaming! the torturing, heartscalding, never satisfying dreaming. . . . An Irishman's imagination never lets him alone, never convinces him, never satisfies him; but it makes him that he can't face reality nor deal with it nor handle it nor conquer it; he can only sneer at them that do . . . and imagination's such a torture that you can't bear it without whiskey . . . you nag and squabble at home because your wife isn't an angel, and she despises you because you're not a hero."[4]

Paradoxically, the dream serves as protection against reality. James O'Neill said of his own dream to become an actor: "What's an Irish lad without his dream? And so I carried mine along with me cherishing it."[5]

> EDMUND: Yes, facts don't mean a thing, do they? What you want to believe, that's the only truth! Shakespeare was an Irish Catholic, for example.
>
> JAMES: So he was. The proof is in his plays.
>
> EDMUNDS: . . . To hell with sense! . . . Who wants to see life as it is, if they can help it?[6]

Ways of relating to illness are also culturally influenced. In Jewish families illness tends to be dealt with very actively and assertively. Family members are generally knowledgeable about medicine and assertive in seeking doctors and treatments. For others, such as the Irish, more reticence is usual, and for some, nothing could be more embarrassing than talking about their bodies with anyone. There is a tendency among the Irish to believe that what goes wrong is a result of your sins, so if you become ill, it may be viewed as God's punishment. Medical science thus becomes almost irrelevant.

Some groups live primarily in the present, others pay more attention to the past, while still others think mostly of the future. Indeed, in terms of the valuing of "time," the dominant cultural group in our society (Anglo-Saxon) generally values the present and the near future over either the past or the long-range future, so the values espoused in this book regarding attention to both our history and the legacies we leave for our children's children are not mainstream ideas. For some cultural groups, however, this is a most natural way of looking at things.

If yours is a family of mixed cultural background, you will want to explore how the values of *each* culture complemented or clashed with the other. Cultural patterns in a family come into particular focus when two spouses of different ethnic backgrounds intermarry. Eugene O'Neill's third wife, Carlotta Monterey, who was a child of intermarriage,[7] once responded to a friend's description of her as "a girl of strong emotions" by saying, after listing her scrambled parentage: "I have often wondered if the mixed blood of those different nationalities had much to do with it. It seems that I am always vacillating between extremes, and never choose a compromising and restful middle course. There are times when I feel within me a calling for the primitive, the wild and the elemental in nature and in art. . . . Then at times I crave the very reverse, the exquisite and the ultra-refined. . . . It is not pleasant to be like a living pendulum swinging between two natures. . . . Please do not think me morbid or abnormal. . . . I enjoy too thoroughly to fight for my place in the world."

Couples from different cultural groups may be drawn together by the very differences between them. Even physically similar groups, such as those of English and Irish heritage, differ on many dimensions, and these differences are compounded if the WASP is of the upper class and the Irish of working-class background, as has been the most common social arrangement historically. They differ in emotional expression, the WASP preferring restraint, decorum, logic, and stoicism in all situations, the Irish more erratic, less predictable, less interested in logic. Dorothy Parker once said of Katharine Hepburn, a product of a stoic Protestant family of Scottish and English ancestry: "She runs the gamut of emotion all the way from A to B!"[8] Spencer Tracy, on the other hand, would go from violent drunken rages to merry times to sullen withdrawal in roller-coaster fashion. With him there was a lot less clarity. "With Spencer it was virtually impossible to know when he was pretending and when on the level." While she is careful, thorough, methodical, analytical, he was an instinctive, intuitive player, who thought you went stale by overrehearsing and preferred to trust his intuition. Hepburn's values of propriety, cleanliness, frugality, hard work, and rugged individualism are legendary. She "has created, with diligence and intention, a world of her own, and she lives in it happily ever after." Tracy, on the other hand, saw fun in everything, except his religion, but was full of unpredictable highs and lows. A full-scale hell raiser from his youth, he announced to his astonished family in adolescence that he wanted to become a priest but changed his mind soon after and went into the military instead. The cultural and class differences between Hepburn and Tracy are most apparent in these comments from Garson Kanin, who knew them both. Regarding Hepburn, he says:

> When you enter her world you are expected to observe its strictness and you do without question. You eat a cooked fruit with every meat dish; you arrive on time and leave as early as possible (say, on her third yawn); you do not gossip; you agree with every one of her many opinions and approve each of her numerous plans; you do not get drunk no matter how much you drink . . . you do not complain (you may, however, rail); you say nothing that may not be repeated; you refrain from lies, dissemblances, and exaggerations, you omit discussion of your physical state, symptoms, or ailments (unless preparatory to asking her advice); you take her advice; you do not use obscene, coarse, or lewd expressions.

This is as well the essence of Hepburn's approach to work, which she never viewed as a chore, but always a challenge. She never says, "That will do." She does not settle for less. "She takes endless showers, she says. Sometimes as many as seven or eight in the course of a day. Aside from her belief that cleanliness is next to Godliness, she uses cold baths as a hairshirt sort of self-discipline, to strengthen character and intention and drive."

Spencer Tracy, a loner who flitted in and out of relationships from his youth, could shift from charming merriment to weeklong alcoholic binges, becoming more cantankerous than usual, unshaven, not changing his smelly clothes for weeks, holing up in the dark in a heavy overcoat he wore even in summer.[9] Always a fighter and a rebel, he felt most comfortable in working-class contexts, dropping out of many schools, even before he dropped out of college, whereas Hepburn, whose roots were upper-class WASP, was one to set herself very clear goals and work extremely hard to achieve them.

Often those who marry out of their groups do so in rebellion or for adventure, but then the very differences that have attracted them to other groups can become "the rub," once they have settled into the marriages. For example, it has been common for Italians and Irish to intermarry. The two groups share the same religion but are otherwise almost total opposites in style and values. To begin with basic items, food and drink, Italians use drink to accompany good food, while the Irish fear that food may spoil good drink. For Italians, eating is an essential and sensuous experience. They eat to celebrate, to share, to get better if they are sick or depressed. For the Irish, drinking serves these functions. On the other hand, the Irish have been known to be inhibited or even embarrassed about displaying too much enjoyment over food.

Secondly, Italians are often highly expressive, with a tendency toward intense, passionate relationships. The Irish are more conflicted about expressing their emotions, particularly those related to anger or sexual feelings (even though they are, in general, highly articulate talkers, poets, jokesters, and storytellers). While they are among the world's greatest fighters, when in a justifiable battle for a morally just cause, particularly involving politics or religion, leaving the scene is the primary response to family situations when they are upset—to cool off, regain composure, and avoid saying or doing something that might be regretted later. Italians, on the other hand, are generally comfortable with any emotional expression, so long as the partner does *not* leave the scene; thus in a marital argument an Italian wife might make outrageous dramatic accusations or threats in order to convey the depth of her passion on a certain issue. An Irish husband might leave or be immobilized into stony silence by this outpouring, unable to formulate a response to the wife's "attack." The Italian wife would surely feel devastated, certain her husband didn't love her. For him such a response would merely be a way to stay sane and in control. Her "ranting" would be a sign of loss of control, what he fears most.

Usually in such intermarriages the spouses personalize their differences and then try harder to do whatever they are accustomed to do to cope with the problem. They may blame the other: "You don't love me. If you loved me, you would never behave that way." Or they may blame themselves. (Italian wife: "If only I try harder to make him understand how upset I am, he will stop." Irish husband: "If only I try harder to keep quiet and under control, this will blow over, and she will stop acting so hysterical.") Such solutions naturally intensify the problem.

A family's sense of "otherness" may also play a profound role in their behavior with each other and with outsiders. We have already considered some of Gustav Mahler's rigidities in relation to the expectations he had for his wife. However, his attitudes of entitlement or arrogance may come into a different perspective when we think of him in the cultural context of his own society, where he felt an outsider. He once wrote: "I am thrice without a country, a Bohemian among Austrians, an Austrian among Germans, and a Jew among the peoples of the world."[10]

CLASS

We tend to operate on the myth that the United States is a classless society, but it is not. While we cannot change our gender, our cultural background, or the facts of our history, most families have moved from one class to another over the past generation or two. And we are, many of us, trying to change class all the time.

Changes involving class are among the most profound social changes we can experience and generally cannot be talked about within a family, though they are constantly played out in conflicts and alliances between siblings and in-laws or parents and children. Through marriage siblings may end up in different classes, especially sisters who "marry up." Remember that Dear Abby and Ann Landers had to separate for the first time because one didn't have enough money to continue the honeymoon. Such money differences are often the beginning of class differences between siblings that play out for years or generations without being acknowledged or resolved. This kind of experience plays out over and over again in families as intermarriage introduces spouses of different incomes, education, social status, and cultural background. Brothers can also experience class differences, according to profession, education, or income. Parents and children may have class differences if the children are upwardly mobile or, conversely, if the children have less education than their parents. Note the class shifts and cultural distance in your own family, especially parent-child relationships in adult life and the marriage and sibling patterns. Pressure on a member of a different class or one who married into a very different cultural group may have been intense. It is interesting to ask yourself what circumstances in your family influence members to move toward a different class or cultural group. Have these shifts been influenced by sibling position, temperament, talent, disability, a family legacy, a secret, or some other factor, which then impacted on the future structure and relationships in the family?

Class differences created in a family when a child is the first to have a college or professional education may also create a chasm because the loss created by the resulting social distance cannot generally be acknowledged. The same is true for the class distance created in a family by a child who is downwardly mobile through disability—retardation, schizophrenia, or other dysfunction. Families often feel shamed by their children's consequent loss of class status, especially because our society does not allow families to deal directly with issues of class. You will want to explore family responses to class change, whether brought about by education, financial success or failure, dysfunction of a family member, or a person's shifting social position through work or marriage.

Family cutoffs often get played out in stereotypes about class difference: "They've gotten above themselves," "They've got no manners," etc. The inability to talk about the class distance makes it worse. In addition, people may feel obliged in social situations to hide their origins—whether because of financial straits or because they were privileged—for fear of alienating others. And family members who are ashamed of their class or cultural background may cut off from the family out of shame or embarrassment.

Class is about power. Though the American myth is that we are a classless society, families are extremely conscious of class in their interactions, especially in relation to outsiders. As a child you probably sized up your family in relation to the friends you brought home and vice versa. Were you embarrassed because your parents didn't speak "correctly"? If your class experience was privileged, did your family seem snobbish or intimidating when introduced to your school friends? Generally speaking, we subconsciously measure ourselves in every interaction. We also tend to measure our families on this dimension, in relation to the rest of the community at large. Couple choices are much influenced by class aspirations, and in most families the acceptability of a marriage partner is probably determined more by class issues than by the new spouse's character. It may take years for a family to revise its initial perceptions of a spouse who marries in—if ever. As has been seen, both the families of Beethoven's parents thought their children were marrying down—a common experience and a common source of conflict and triangles in marital relationships ("Your family looks down on my family; therefore you don't love me").

At times a family's prejudice against a spouse on the basis of either culture or class borders on what family therapist Edwin Friedman calls "cultural camouflage," hiding personal fears and emotionally charged issues behind excuses that the fiancé or fiancée is unacceptable because he or she comes from a different background.[11] It is true, of course, that when children choose marriage partners from radically different cultural or class backgrounds, families do have to work hard to bridge the distances the alliance creates.

Class is primarily determined by birth and marriage. A woman's class is still generally dependent on that of her husband. Education is another determinant of class, and in this country it is the most secure way we have of changing class. We seem to operate according to the notion that anyone can become anything through education, but in fact, we still have a remarkably stratified system of access to education, as well as of judging class along school lines: from the Seven Sisters colleges and the Ivy League to state universities to community colleges, and so forth. Occupation or profession is another indicator of class. Certain professions, such as the clergy, acting, or politics, may elevate a person beyond his or her class niche. Finally there is money. This factor is extremely dangerous to other values. As Tom Wolfe says, if the "money nexus" becomes the primary determinant of class, as appears to be happening in our society, then all other ties and values, like kith and kin, are out the window. And the money nexus does seem to be taking over, as the distance between the haves and the have-nots becomes wider year by year.

Symbols of class tend to show up in family rituals, especially weddings. For example, the upper class and working class may go all out for a wedding. The upper middle class may see such display as "gauche." But class values permeate all sorts of everyday activities, such as what car you drive (or even feel comfortable driving) or what music you listen to. Opera, for example, generally defines your class, unless you're Italian, as does a penchant for country and western music. Your leisure activities also reflect class attitudes: Golf or tennis tend to signify one thing; bowling, something different.

It is also important to appreciate that various cultural groups view class differently: WASPs tend to take class stratification as a given, revealed in your first words and defining all social interactions. Puerto Ricans have also taken class stratification for granted. They are less likely to assume that people change class. On the other hand, Jewish families tend to encourage their children to rise in class, if at all possible. Others, notably Italian families, may feel ambivalent about their children's rising in class, fearing the child will leave the family. The Irish traditionally had a more or less one-class society. In the United States the terms "shanty Irish" and "lace curtain Irish" came to indicate class difference, but even the latter carried a negative undertone because the Irish have a strong sense of "not getting above yourself." African Americans have tended to believe that education offers the greatest likelihood of "making it," but they too have concerns about "getting above yourself" or "putting on airs." Polish families also have important historical reasons for their intense ambivalence about rising in class, since traditionally the upper classes were identified with foreigners (especially the French). For them, remaining "salt of the earth" has been a strong value.

MONEY

Families are full of myths and slogans about money and its role in human affairs. The misquote from the Bible that "Money is the root of all evil" reflects a common perception of money as dangerous and dirty. The correct quote is that "the love of money is the root of all evil."

We all recognize the different values about money in various cultural groups and the caricatures that have developed of the Scot who hoards his money, the Jewish wife who constantly shops, the Irishman who squanders money, the Indian ascetic who eschews money. My own friends and relatives have often recited to me the Irish saying "The fool and his [her] money are soon parted" because of my careless attitudes about spending. However, there is a second part to the saying, which is my typical retort: "But there are no pockets in shrouds."

If you want to understand your own family, a specific exploration of its relationship to money is worthwhile, as a symbolic clue to some of its most deeply held views about the meaning of life. Money may represent love, security, happiness, success, power, shame, pride, fear, and many other things. Conflicts between the "tightwad" and the "spendthrift" may dominate family interactions, causing children to be in collusion with one parent against the other and disrupting or distorting family relationships. Nor are attitudes toward money necessarily based in "reality." Millionaire family members may be unable to enjoy a meal for fear of the expense, while others who don't have two nickels to rub together feel quite secure that they will always have enough—and indeed, they always seem to manage.

RELIGION AND SPIRITUAL VALUES

Your family's spiritual values are also part of the bedrock of understanding them. In adolescence and young adulthood especially, family members may be in conflict with the spiritual beliefs of their parents, rebelling against traditional practices and customs and seeking to coalesce their own religious and spiritual beliefs. This may create deep strains within the family as parents feel threatened at a personal level and for the whole continuity of the family. In your journey to understand your family you will need to push past the polemics of family arguments over religion and politics to understand the roots of each member's most cherished beliefs. Why has Uncle Joe become an atheist? Why does your mother hold so tightly to saying the rosary every day? Why did your grandparents sit shiva for their son when he married a *shiksa?* Unless you can imagine your way into the mind-set of each family member, you will not really understand your family.

You can also learn a great deal by asking family members what kind of education they had in spiritual matters. Family secrets about your aunt's years in the convent or your father's aspirations to become a rabbi or minister may surface. Such dreams and ambitions may be critical to understanding later life choices. Your family's relation to organized religion as well as its informal beliefs in what is sacred—music, art, good works, spending time in nature—will be essential to an understanding of what makes your family tick. A particularly interesting question involves beliefs about an afterlife since the answers give such an indication of what family members value about life itself.

Without doubt, your family's religious beliefs influence their assumptions about sexuality, marriage, death, and illness, relationships with other cultural and religious groups, personal needs versus group needs and many other fundamental attitudes. In approaching your family, you will need to appreciate both the context in which their religious beliefs have evolved and what they mean to your particular family. If your family believes that homosexuality is sinful and that is your sexual preference, you can respect the possible fears and pain of your parents without sharing their beliefs. If your family threatens to disown you for marrying outside of your religion, you will need to discover why this is an issue, possibly by exploring the fear of outsiders to which it is connected.

QUESTIONS

■ What are the ethnic backgrounds of members of your family? Do they fit into the stereotypes of those ethnic groups? If not, can you think of reasons why they might not? Were they proud of their heritage? Were there aspects of it they were ashamed of? Did you grow up with ethnic stories, religious practices, foods, music, holiday rituals? Are you carrying these on with your own children?

■ What is your family's migration history? Where did family members come from? Why did they come? How many came together? What were their ages when they came, and how did that influence family patterns? What was their experience as new immigrants, and how did that influence your family's mythology—hopes, dreams, beliefs? Did they dream of returning to the country of origin? Did they try to leave their history behind? How did they deal with language differences? Religious customs? The loss of those left behind?

■ What were your family's rules about class? How were they transmitted? Have family members changed class over the generations? Were there family members who changed class by "marrying up" or "marrying down"? How about within the same sibling group? How did this affect sibling relationships? Have class changes occurred through education? Financial success or failure? Marriage into another cultural group? Professional status? Disability? How did this affect sibling patterns? Family holidays, get-togethers, and rituals?

■ What were the attitudes in your family toward money? That it is the root of all evil? That you should always pay cash? That you should save for a rainy day? That you should always spend as if you had enough even if you don't? What roles have family members played around money: the gambler, the tightwad, the compulsive shopper, the bargain hunter, the miser, the spendthrift, the hoarder? What are your family's beliefs about the legitimate uses of money—for education, real estate, jewelry, to save in a bank? Can money be discussed openly, or is it kept secret within or outside the family? How do family members believe money shoud be shared or distributed to various family members before or after death?

TEN

RECONNECTING

Shall I turn out to be the hero of my own life?
—Charles Dickens, *David Copperfield*

If you have a family gathering and a distant cousin comes who has been kept out of the family for a long time, it's a little uncomfortable. Let's bear the discomfort. It's worth it.
—Paul Robeson, Jr.

Composing a life involves a continual reimagining of the future and reinterpretation of the past to give meaning to the present. . . . Storytelling is fundamental to the human search for meaning. . . . Each [of us] is involved in inventing a new kind of story.
—Mary Catherine Bateson, *Composing a Life*

We would all like to be ourselves with our families, to have them accept us for who we really are. But we may lose sight of the prerequisite: that we accept *them* for who they really are, getting past the anger, resentments, and regrets of not being a family like the Brady Bunch. On our visits home even those of us who are highly successful in careers and other relationships may revert to childish responses. A daughter tenses up within a few minutes in reaction to her mother's implied criticism of her clothes, her haircut, or her boyfriend. A son returns for Thanksgiving with the image of those other families who have happy get-togethers—convivial, delicious, and full of good family feeling—while he experiences the subtle bitterness of his parents' ongoing war.

A part of us always longs to go back to the family—but to have it be different. This time, you tell yourself, you'll hold on to your adult perspective and not become defensive. You won't get caught up in your parents' battles or in competing with your siblings for attention.

Maturity, objectivity, humor, and serenity will carry the day, if only you can keep your distance.

Sometimes you can even manage to hold on to your sense of self for a little while. But then something seemingly trivial happens. Perhaps your father makes a sarcastic joke at your mother's expense, and she goes silent. This little scene may have occurred a hundred times in the past. In a second you fall into the role you played in childhood, jabbing back, moving in to protect your mother. In your frustration you gossip with your siblings about how impossible your parents are, and you wonder how you managed to survive all the underlying hostility in your family for so long.

But if you want to reconnect with your family, you will need to develop a kind of empathy which recognizes that you and your family belong to each other. This requires an acceptance of our fundamental human connectedness as people that is almost mystical. It means accepting that whatever terrible things another person could do, that person is human and you could be in his or her shoes. It means accepting our parents with all their imperfections, which is not the same thing as accepting their imperfections themselves. It means, for example, acknowledging your father without needing to even the score for his emotional neglect or physical abuse or for his irrational demands and attempts at intimidation, which is not the same thing as accepting the abuse or not holding him accountable for what he did. It is a matter of acknowledging that your relationship is about more than the abuse alone. The grown-up child who truly has an individual identity can be generous to a critical, distant father without becoming defensive, even when that father continues to be critical.

You need an approach that allows you to see the world from the perspective of each person in your family, to accept that the other person did not always meet your needs or understand your feelings. Too often people try to change their families as a way of changing themselves rather than change themselves as a way of changing family patterns. There is a story of an old Hasidic rabbi who said: "When I was young, I set out to change the world. When I grew a little older, I perceived that this was too ambitious, so I set out to change my state. This too, I realized as I grew older, was too ambitious, so I set out to change my town. When I realized I could not even do this, I tried to change my family. Now as an old man, I know that I should have started by changing myself. If I had started with myself, maybe then I would have succeeded in changing my family, the town, or even the state—and who knows, maybe even the world!"

You need to give up focusing on whether family members might have been different or have met your needs, understood your feelings, and always made you proud. This means arriving at a new perspective from which you can evaluate your own personal worth for yourself. It also means risking family disapproval, rejection, or inattention, without your becoming disapproving, rejecting, or inattentive in return.

The fundamental guideline for going home again is: Don't attack and don't defend. Going home again means finding a way to be yourself and stay connected to your family without defending yourself or attacking others. The typical dysfunctional roles people get into in their families—in which one becomes the caretaker and the other the caretakee or one always pursues and the other distances—develop because family members have not evolved sufficient sense of self to function for themselves. One plays wounded daughter to the arrogant and uncaring father or dutiful brother to a prodigal sibling.

Defining your actual responsibility toward family members is a very personal matter. Only you can know what obligations you have to be generous, loving, or thoughtful toward them, no matter what hurt they have caused you. The experience of many adult children of alcoholics stands as an example. If your father chooses to be a depressed and withdrawn alcoholic, you may decide to treat him with compassion and to do what you can to change his self-destructive behavior, realizing also that his destiny is beyond your control. At the same time you must learn to appreciate your own limitations. The Alcoholics Anonymous serenity prayer can be very helpful to anyone facing difficult family circumstances: "May I have the serenity to accept the things I cannot change, the courage to change the things I can, and the wisdom to know the difference."

An important place to reconnect with your family is at the celebrations that mark family holidays and transitions: weddings, funerals, and reunions. Family rituals are important family experiences, incorporating familiar and often symbolic meanings. Such occasions frequently involve intentional repetition of words, music, food, drink, smells, sights, ceremony, and behavior that suggests continuity. While this can be stifling if the rituals are hollow, it can be healing and enriching if you make the rituals meaningful for yourself. Family gatherings also offer a good opportunity to hear family stories, to observe family relationships in action, and to practice changing your own part in the family drama.

Consider what family stories might be like from the angle of a different participant, the so-called villains, for example. Imagine what Cinderella's stepmother's perspective might be on that spoiled step-daughter to whom everything came naturally and whom everyone adored for her "sweetness"; her Goody Two-shoes behavior could drive you to drink. Consider also the dilemma her stepsisters were in because they happened not to conform to the culture's requirements of a woman: that she be small, beautiful, gentle, long-suffering, and unassertive!

You can also think about what would happen if you changed your own part in family relationships. If you always lock horns with your father, you could change your tune and begin to say, "You've got a point there, Dad." If you have had a poor relationship with a parent for a long time, it is important to proceed slowly. Don't expect too much too soon. You can't force a relationship.

Letters can be useful in your reconnecting efforts. They can be a very effective method of reconnecting with an estranged or difficult parent, for example. In letters you can prepare exactly what you want to say and say it in just the way you want, without accusation or defense. Most important, letters allow you to convey your whole mes-sage before having to respond to the other person's reactions. With luck, the letter will be a first step, leading to further, more personal communications.

And don't forget the use of pictures to trigger memories or help family members feel they are receiving, even as they share difficult memories. By enlarging old family photographs and distributing them to the family, you can convey new messages about continuity and about the value of the lessons and experience of those who came before you.

There are few pure saints or sinners in real families. While you need to protect yourself from a relative who might actually hurt you—an active alcoholic or drug addict, for example—it is important not to write these people off as family members. You never know when they might change their ways, even after a lifetime of destructive behav-ior. Various events, especially aging and loss, can trigger transfor-mation.

Mary Catherine Bateson, the only daughter of two world-re-nowned anthropologists, Margaret Mead and Gregory Bateson (*Gen-ogram 10.1*), has written two inspiring and touching memoirs that detail in a remarkable way the process of coming to terms with her parents. She started from "a disgruntled reflection" on her own life as an improvisation and came to appreciate that the stories we often

The Bateson and Mead Families
Genogram 10.1

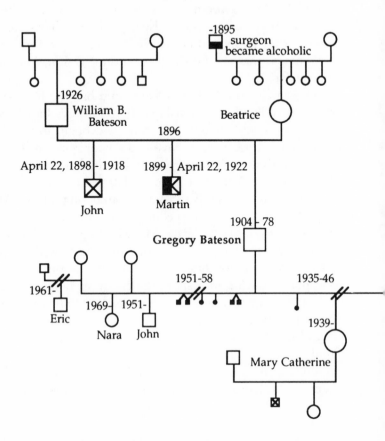

create about our lives give them an illusory sense of purpose rather than convey the complex way we reinvent ourselves again and again as we go along in life, responding to new circumstances.

Her childhood was not an easy one. The relationship between her parents was not harmonious. Her father left her mother when she was seven, and they divorced when she was eleven. Her mother often left her with other caretakers for long periods. Her parents were often preoccupied with their own concerns and attended to her needs only partially and intermittently. As an infant she was mostly cared for by a nurse. After her parents separated, she periodically visited her father, who soon remarried and fathered another child, a son. On at least two occasions her father made inappropriate sexual advances to

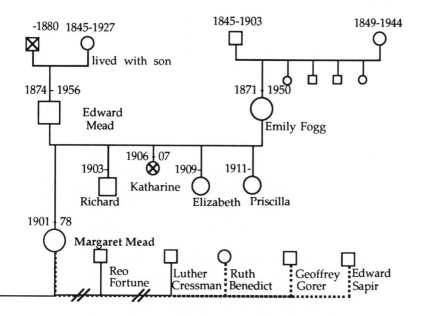

her. However, she was able to maintain emotionally important, if sometimes physically distant, relationships with both her parents. She provides a stirring example of a child who as an adult was able to go home again.

Catherine was surprised when her mother, in her autobiographical writings, described herself and Gregory Bateson as nurturing personalities. Where her parents felt she was a perfectly contented child, Bateson admits she never complained because she had to be the non-whining "good girl," so that her parents would want to be with her as much as possible. If she was unpleasant to be with, she would lose them to other activities.

Throughout her memoir Bateson shows an astute perception of the need to remain her own self—not a replica of her parents: "I have not read or reread all the published works of Mead and Bateson, neither of which I know completely, for to do so would be to remake myself as an expert instead of a daughter."[1]

Her story is one of acceptance of her parents as they were—with their faults and limitations—and of looking for the value in her relationship with each of them: "The voices of my parents are still very much with me, for I hear their echo in so much that I see and encounter. . . . Their voices are blended now into the complex skein. It was difficult for me sometimes, as a child, to decode the differences and similarities and to pitch my own voice in harmony but yet distinct."

Finally, Bateson remembered more what she got than what she did not get from her parents. She believed that she got a sense of basic trust, self-confidence, faith, strength, and resiliency from her mother. As a professional anthropologist and mother herself Bateson came to appreciate how well organized and masterful Mead had been to have kept her always well cared for in the "extended family" of professional colleagues she had created. Catherine made, as she described it, her own synthesis from the models offered by her parents and others around her. Like her mother, Catherine had to combine multiple commitments and to adapt and improvise in a culture in which she could only partly be at home. As for her father, although she spent less time with him, she was grateful for their long walks and talks in which he taught her about nature and science and answered her difficult questions about the way the world works.

Having struggled greatly with her parents' separation and divorce, Catherine came to fear she would follow in her parents' footsteps of numerous failed marriages. She spent a lot of time trying to understand her parents' marriages and their differences.

Bateson's memoirs demonstrate in a most touching way her effort to see her parents from many perspectives: as children in their own families, as lovers and marital partners, as siblings, as professionals. In many ways Mead and Bateson were opposites. She was American, practical, effusive, poetic. He was British, impractical, detached, scientific. Margaret thought that problems usually have a solution, whereas Gregory thought that most people's efforts to improve things usually made them worse. Margaret appreciated the various conventions and rules of different societies, while Gregory lived his life as unconventionally as possible. She loved religious ritual; he was an atheist. She loved people; he preferred animals. Her moral concerns focused on the development of societies; his focused on ecology or the world as a whole. She loved to be the organizer; he eventually came to see her organizing abilities as controlling. He was more abstract, more interested in finding the patterns of life than in controlling the particulars. She paid attention to the details: "In the marriage she was the one who set the patterns, for Gregory lacked this fascination with pervasive elaboration. . . . His life was full of loose ends and unstitched edges, while for Margaret each thread became an occasion for embroidery."

Catherine was forced to wonder how two such different people ever married. She speculated that her mother had been most attracted to Bateson's cultural differentness and noted that she herself had also married a man from a different culture (Iran).

In trying to understand her parents' differences for herself, she noted their different sibling positions and roles in their families, Margaret the eldest of five, all but one girls, Gregory the youngest of three—all boys. She said of her parents' differing approaches to solving problems: "Margaret's approach must have been based on early success in dealing with problems, perhaps related to the experience of being an older child and amplified by years of successfully organizing the younger ones. Gregory's experience was that of a younger child with relatively little capacity for changing what went on around him. Instead, he would seek understanding."

She speculated further on the influence of early family events on her father's approach to life: "It may be that the suicide of his brother Martin in 1922, which followed on heavy-handed parental attempts at guidance and led to a period of increasing efforts to shape Gregory's choices as well, was an ingredient in his anxiety about problem solving and indeed about any effort to act in the world."

Gregory Bateson was the youngest of three sons of a famous British geneticist. He was considered the least promising of the three sons, sickly in childhood and not an outstanding student. The eldest son, John, was supposed to be the leader. He and the middle brother, Martin, two years apart in age, were extremely close. Gregory was four years younger and grew up somewhat separately. When John was twenty, he was killed in World War I. A few days later his mother wrote to Martin: "You and Gregory are left to me still and you must help me back to some of the braveness that John has taken away."[2]

Following John's death a rift developed between Martin and his father, whose mother had coincidentally died two months before John. The father, perhaps now doubly bereft, began to pressure his second son, Martin, who was a poet, to become a zoologist. Relations between father and son deteriorated. When, in addition, Martin felt rebuffed by a young woman he admired, he took a gun and shot himself in Trafalgar Square on his brother John's birthday, April 22, 1922, in what was described as "probably the most dramatic and deliberate suicide ever witnessed in London."

This was the legacy for Gregory, "the runt," as he called himself. All the family's expectations that their eldest son would become a great scientist, following in the father's footsteps, now came down upon him. Gregory's solution was to study anthropology, a science different from his father's field, biology, which also allowed him to escape from the family pressure by way of fieldwork. All his life Gregory resisted the expectations of others. The shift in Gregory's sibling position in early adult life may indeed have contributed to the incompatibility between him and Margaret, even though their birth positions were complementary.

There is also some similarity between Gregory, whose role in his family as the only surviving child intensified to the point of toxicity his relationship with his mother, and Margaret Mead's father, who was an only child doted on by his mother after his father's death, when he was only six. While Bateson cut off his mother to avoid the pressure of the legacy, his future father-in-law, Edward Mead, had brought his widowed mother with him into his marriage, and she lived in the Mead household for the rest of her life. Catherine traced her father's relationship with his parents to the eventual difficulties between her parents: "Gregory felt that to move ahead with his own life he would have to leave Margaret, bringing into his conflicts with her a store of hoarded hostility to his mother. . . . It was Gregory, more than anyone else, who lashed back at her for trying to manage his life . . . . [He] began with his rebellion against Margaret, a rebellion shot through with resentment against his family and especially against his mother."[3]

When we trace back marital relationships in the Bateson family, we can observe problematic issues even in the previous generation. Gregory's parents had a prolonged courtship, which would lead one to suspect possible difficulties in the family relationships. The fact is that his maternal grandmother called off her daughter Beatrice's engagement to William Bateson because he got drunk. The maternal grandfather had been an alcoholic, and his wife was trying to protect her daughter from the same fate. However, Beatrice recontacted William through an ad shortly after her father died and married him soon afterward.

In the next generation Gregory happened to meet and fall in love with Margaret just after becoming estranged from his mother, Beatrice. Margaret and her second husband were doing anthropological work in a remote area of the world at that time. One might speculate that the children in this family tended to connect to their spouses by disconnecting, through death or cutoff, from a parent.

Catherine made an enormous effort to understand her parents through an exploration of their lives. She worked to see them as people with their own sets of problems. Most important, she tried see them as children in the multigenerational context of the family, struggling to come to terms with their parents, in much the same way as she struggled to come to terms with them. She was able to accept their differences without blaming either of them. Although it was her father who left her mother, she tried not to judge him, only to understand him. Throughout their lives she maintained connections with both parents. Gregory always sought to interest his daughter in what *he* considered "important matters" but never paid attention to hers. She did not reject her father for not validating her interests. Nor did she try to change him. When, toward the end of his life, he became interested in ecology, he elicited and got her help in organizing his project.

Catherine maintained both personal and professional contact with her mother as well. They did presentations together. They planned a conference on rituals together. Particularly important, Catherine was able to appreciate her mother's efforts not to dominate her life. She says of her: "The thing she was most afraid of as a parent was that her capacity to think herself into the lives of others, imagining possible futures, would lead her to guide me in a way I would later repudiate. In any quarrel between us, the thing that would have hurt her most, because it had been said to her so many times, would have been to accuse her of dominating me or interfering with my life." We can see here that Margaret herself was concerned about differentiation in the sense of not intruding on her daughter's personhood, which probably was important modeling for Catherine. It may also reflect a WASP sensibility to privacy and not intruding on anyone else's space, which might be viewed very differently in other cultures. Mother and daughter both worked at their separateness:

> This was a point of vulnerability so deep that we conspired to protect the relationship, she by refraining from advice and indeed by trying to restrain her imagination about me, I by carefully monitoring the kinds of indecision or uncertainty I shared with her. I learned to show my imagined futures to her only when they already had a degree of vividness that I could continue to acknowledge as my own, unable to say, this is your plan I have been living, your fantasy projected onto me. She had the capacity to live many lives, participating richly, reaching out in complex empathy, grasping hold of possibilities

that had so far eluded the imagination of others, and so she had to monitor the dreams she dreamed for others.

Through these efforts not to have a parent-child relationship of control, they were able to avoid the power struggle that so plagued the parents' marriage.

One of the most touching issues Bateson explores is the impact of her mother's secret and what the secrecy cost both of them. Margaret's sexual liaisons and particularly her bisexuality were discovered by her daughter only after her death in 1978, when a close family friend gave her a letter that Margaret had written many years earlier, intended for those she loved in the event of her sudden death. The letter, expressed Mead's concern that details of her life might be revealed under circumstances of scandal or notoriety without her being able to provide explanation or reassurance. Margaret apparently became increasingly grieved that many aspects of her life could not be shared and troubled about the pain that the revelation of her secret might cause to others:

> I have become increasingly conscious of the extent to which my life is becoming segmented, each piece shared with a separate person, even where within the time and space of that segment I feel that I am being myself, and my whole self in that particular relationship. . . . It has not been my choice of concealment that any one of you have been left in ignorance of some part of my life which would seem, I know, of great importance. Nor has it been from lack of trust—in any person—on my part, but only from the exigencies of the mid-twentieth century when each one of us—at least those of us who are my age—seems fated for a life which is no longer sharable.

Catherine, who was only fifteen when her mother wrote this letter, was one of the ones to whom it would have been sent. She says:

> I knew little until after her death of the pattern of relationships to male and female lovers that she had developed, so that trying to look back on who she was as a person and as my mother has been complicated by the need to revise my picture of her in important ways and by the need to deal with the fact of concealment. I have been at times angered at the sense of being deliberately deceived and at having been without doubt a collaborator in my own deception, limiting my perceptions to the images she was willing to have me see. I have sometimes felt myself doubly bereaved as well, having radically to reconsider my convictions about who she was and therefore, in relationship to her, about who I was and am, surprised at last by the sense of continuing recognition.

Margaret's concern about the possible negative impact of the secrets in her life is impressive, as is her effort to counteract their negative potential by her letter. But what is most impressive about Catherine's commentary is her recognition of the part she played in her mother's secrecy and her willingness to explore her own complicity.

In the end, Catherine Bateson was able to accept both her mother and her father in herself. Margaret and Gregory were far from perfect as parents, but their daughter's ability to take what they had to offer her and transform it into a significant part of her own self is most impressive. She used this acceptance to deal with their deaths: "The contained world of early childhood no longer exists, but my concerns remain similar to theirs and the analogies that bridge from the microcosm to the wider world continue. . . . I have wanted to write a small book. . . . I have tried to weave my own ambivalence into this book, letting love and grief, longing and anger, lie close to the surface, and making it clear that there is no perfection to enshrine and no orthodoxy to defend, but much to use and much of value."

Bateson says she started with a view of her life as a sort of desperate improvisation in which she was constantly trying to make some coherence from conflicting elements to fit rapidly changing settings:

> When we speak to our children about our own lives, we tend to reshape our pasts to give them an illusory look of purpose. But our children are unlikely to be able to define their goals and then live happily ever after. Instead, they will need to reinvent themselves again and again in response to changing environment. . . . Life [is] an improvisatory art, about the ways we combine familiar and unfamiliar components in response to new situations. . . . I believe that [we have] overfocused on the stubborn struggle toward a single goal rather than on the fluid, the protean. . . . Women have always lived discontinuous and contingent lives, but men today are newly vulnerable, which turns women's traditional adaptations into a resource.[4]

We and our families are always struggling to reinvent ourselves and transform our difficult and painful experiences into something creative and positive. As Bateson says:

> Part of the task of composing a life is the artist's need to find a way to take what is simply ugly and instead of trying to deny it, to use it in the broader design. There is a famous story about a Chinese master painting a landscape. Just as he is nearly finished, a drop of ink falls on the white scroll, and the disciples standing around him gasp, believing the scroll is ruined. Without

hesitating, the master takes the finest of hair brushes and, using the tiny glob of ink already fallen, paints a fly hovering in the foreground of the landscape. . . . The purpose here is to discover grace and meaning in a picture larger still.

The idea of reconnecting with your family is so that "hope and history will rhyme"—that is, so that your connections to your history will open up your future. This requires creating a sense of family and "home," in which no one's experience has to be outside history, whether because of race, class, gender, shame, or secrecy, a place where the complex and ambiguous connections that entwine your family can be validated.

The work of understanding and reconnecting is a lifetime project. To create something new you will have to struggle against the definitions you are given so that you can define connectedness in ways that you find meaningful. As Edwin Markham once wrote:

> *He drew a circle that shut me out—*
> *Heretic, rebel, a thing to flout.*
> *But Love and I had the wit to win.*
> *We drew a circle that drew him in.*

Best of luck with this project of going home again, even though it is never the place you left. May you find yourself as you find your family.

NOTES

CHAPTER 1: WHY GO HOME AGAIN?

1. Stephen B. Oates, *With Malice toward None: The Life of Abraham Lincoln* (New York: New American Library, 1977).

2. Pat Conroy, *The Prince of Tides* (Boston: Houghton Mifflin, 1988).

3. Ernest Jones, ed., *Letters of Sigmund Freud* (London: Cambridge University Press, 1975).

4. Cecil Woodham-Smith, *Queen Victoria*. (New York: Donald Fine, Inc., 1972).

5. Stanley Weintraub, *Victoria* (New York: E. P. Dutton, 1987).

6. E. F. Benson, *Queen Victoria* (London: Chatto & Windus, 1987).

7. Lytton Strachey, *Queen Victoria* (New York: Harcourt Brace Jovanovich, 1921).

8. Louis Auchincloss, *Persons of Consequence: Queen Victoria and Her Circle* (New York: Random House, 1979).

CHAPTER 2: YOUR FAMILY TREE: THE PAST AS PROLOGUE

1. Carl Van Doren, *Benjamin Franklin* (New York: Viking Press, 1958).

2. Catherine Drinker Bowen, *The Most Dangerous Man in America: Scenes from the Life of Benjamin Franklin* (Boston: Little, Brown, 1974).

3. D. H. Lawrence, *Studies in Classic American Literature* (New York: Viking Press, 1951).

4. Mark Twain, "The Late Benjamin Franklin," *Writings of Mark Twain*, vol. 19 (Hartford: American Publishing Co., 1907).

5. Herman Melville, *Israel Potter* (London: Constable, 1923).

6. William Cobbett, *Porcupine's Works*, cited in Esmond Wright, *Franklin of Philadelphia* (Cambridge, Mass.: Harvard University Press, 1986).

7. Willard Randall, *A Little Revenge: Benjamin Franklin and His Son* (Boston: Little, Brown, 1984).

8. Benjamin Franklin, *The Autobiography of Benjamin Franklin* (New York: Lancer, 1968).

9. Claude-Anne Lopez and Eugenia W. Herbert, *The Private Franklin: The Man and His Family* (New York: W. W. Norton, 1975).

10. Esmond Wright, *Benjamin Franklin: His Life as He Wrote It* (Cambridge, Mass.: Harvard University Press, 1990).

11. Maya Angelou, *Poems: Maya Angelou* (New York: Bantam Books, 1986).

CHAPTER 3: FAMILY STORIES, MYTHS, AND SECRETS

1. John Kotre and Elizabeth Hall, *Seasons of Life* (Boston: Little, Brown, 1990).

2. Rebecca Frazer, *The Brontës: Charlotte Brontë and Her Family* (New York: Crown, 1988). The following quotes are from the same source.

3. Paul C. Nagel, *Descent from Glory* (New York: Oxford University Press, 1983). The following references are from the same source.

4. Jack Shepherd, *The Adams Chronicles: Four Generations of Greatness* (Boston: Little, Brown, 1975).

5. James Truslow Adams, *The Adams Family* (New York: Signet Books, 1976).

6. Nagel, op. cit.

7. David Musto, "The Adams Family," *Proceedings of the Massachusetts Historical Society* (1981). The following quotations are from the same source.

8. Paul C. Nagel, *The Adams Women* (New York: Oxford University Press, 1987).

9. Nagel, *Descent from Glory*. The following quotes are from the same source.

10. Shepard, op. cit.

11. Musto, op. cit.

12. Nagel, *The Adams Women*.

13. Alex Witchel, "Laughter, Tears," *New York Times Magazine* (November 12, 1989).

14. Maxine Hong Kingston, *The Woman Warrior* (New York: Vintage, 1989).

15 Philip Young, *Hawthorne's Secret: An Untold Tale* (Boston: David R. Godine, 1984).

CHAPTER 4: FAMILY TIES AND BINDS

1. Elizabeth A. Carter, "The Transgenerational Scripts and Nuclear Family Stress: Theory and Clinical Implications," *Georgetown Family Symposium*, ed. R. R. Sager, vol. 3 (1975–76). (Washington, D.C.: Georgetown University, 1978).

2. Nathan Miller, *Theodore Roosevelt* (New York: William Morrow & Co., 1992).

3. Howard Teichman, *Alice: The Life and Times of Alice Roosevelt* (Englewood Cliffs, N.J.: Prentice-Hall, 1979).

4. Carol Felsenthal, *Alice Roosevelt Longworth* (New York: G. P. Putnam's Sons, 1988).

5. Kay Stables, *The Marx Bros.* (Greenwich, Conn.: Brompton Books, 1992).

6. Joe Adamson, *Groucho, Harpo, Chico, and Sometimes Zeppo* (New York: Simon & Schuster, 1973).

7. Groucho Marx, *Groucho and Me* (New York: Simon & Schuster, 1959).

8. Maxine Marx, *Growing Up with Chico* (New York: Limelight Editions, 1986).

9. Groucho Marx, op. cit. The following quotes are from the same source.

10. Harpo Marx, with Rowland Barber, *Harpo Speaks* (New York: Limelight Editions, 1985).

11. Maxine Marx, op. cit. The following quotes are from the same source.

12. James Baldwin, "Sonny's Blues," in Minnesota Humanities Commission, ed., *Braided Lives: An Anthology of Multicultural American Writing* (St. Paul: Viking Press, 1957).

13. Tom D. Crouch, *The Bishop's Boys: A Life of Wilbur and Orville Wright* (New York: W. W. Norton, 1989).

14. John Evangelist Walsh, *One Day at Kitty Hawk: The Untold Story of the Wright Brothers and the Airplane* (New York: Crowell, 1975).

15. Fred Howard, *Wilbur and Orville: A Biography of the Wright Brothers* (New York: Alfred A. Knopf, 1987).

16. Crouch, op. cit.

17. Doris Kearns Goodwin, *The Fitzgeralds and the Kennedys* (New York: Simon & Schuster, 1987).

18. Louis Sheaffer, *O'Neill: Son and Playwright* (Boston: Little, Brown, 1968).

19. Arthur Gelb and Barbara Gelb, *O'Neill* (New York: Harper & Row, 1987).

20. Molly Haskell, *Love and Other Infectious Diseases* (New York: W. W. Norton, 1990).

21. For Brentano the involvement with Beethoven seems also to have been part of a complex web of triangular relationships that began in childhood with her deep attachment to a father she rarely saw. When she did fall in love, her father instead arranged for her to marry a wealthy, older German businessman and emigrate from Austria to Germany, which she experienced as an exile. She returned to Vienna eleven years later, when her adored father died. It was during this nostalgic and

painful return to her homeland that she met Beethoven, who was apparently the one person who could draw her out of depression. Having procrastinated as long as she could about returning to Germany, she at last made the desperate proposal to Beethoven that she would give up her family for him. Was Beethoven a replacement for her father or her early love and thus a part of the interlocking triangles in her family? It seems likely.

22. Maynard Solomon, *Beethoven* (New York: Schirmer, 1977).

23. Elliot Forbes, ed., *Thayer's Life of Beethoven* (Princeton: Princeton University Press, 1969).

CHAPTER 5: LOSS: THE PIVOTAL HUMAN EXPERIENCE

1. Robert Anderson, *I Never Sang for My Father* (New York: Random House, 1968).

2. Joan Laird, "Women and Stories: Restorying Women's Self-constructions," *Women in Families*, ed., Monica McGoldrick, Carol Anderson, and Froma Walsh (New York: W. W. Norton, 1989).

3. H. S. Schiff, *The Bereaved Parent* (New York: Penguin, 1970).

4. L. Videcka-Sherman, "Coping with the Death of a Child: A Study over Time," *American Journal of Orthopsychiatry*, Vol. 52 (1982).

5. Kearns Goodwin, op. cit.

6. Edward J. Dunne, John L. McIntosh, and Karen Dunne-Maxim, eds., *Suicide and Its Aftermath* (New York: W. W. Norton, 19487); Iris Bolton, *My Son . . . My Son . . .: A Guide to Healing after Death, Loss, or Suicide* (Atlanta: Bolton Press, 1983); Steve Gutstein, "Adolescent Suicide: The Loss of Reconciliation," *Living beyond Loss*, ed. Froma Walsh and Monica McGoldrick (New York: W. W. Norton, 1991).

7. Pauline Boss, "Ambiguous Loss," *Living beyond Loss*, loc. cit.

8. Peter Collier and David Horowitz, *The Kennedys* (New York: Summit Books, 1984). The following quotes are from the same source.

9. Christopher Anderson, *Young Kate* (New York: Henry Holt, 1988).

10. Katharine Hepburn, *Me* (New York: Alfred A. Knopf, 1991).

11. Christopher Anderson, op. cit. The following quote is from the same source.

12. Vivienne Browning, *My Browning Family Album* (London: Springwood, 1979).

13. Jeanette Marks, *The Family of the Barrett* (New York: Macmillan, 1938).

14. The father's other relationships included one black and one Jewish woman. It is interesting that one of the reasons for Edward's later disapproval of his daughter's relationship with Robert Browning was apparently the suggestion that Browning had African and Jewish blood in his heritage, which he did not.

15. Marks, op. cit.

16. David Karlin, *The Courtship of Robert Browning and Elizabeth Barrett* (New York: Oxford University Press, 1987).

17. "Browning Society Notes," vol. 3 (December 1973), in Browning, op. cit.

18. Karlin, op. cit. The following quote is from the same source.

19. Marks, op. cit.

20. Lawrence Leamer, *The Kennedy Women* (New York: Villard Books, 1994).

21. Goodwin, op. cit.

22. Collier and Horowitz, op. cit.

23. Rose Kennedy, *Times to Remember* (New York: Bantam Books, 1975).

24. John H. Davis, *The Kennedys: Dynasty and Disaster* (New York: McGraw-Hill, 1984).

25. Kennedy, op. cit.

26. Lynne McTaggart, *Kathleen Kennedy: Her Life and Times* (New York: Dial Press, 1983).

27. Goodwin, op. cit.

28. Kennedy, op. cit.

29. Marianne Krull, *Freud and His Father* (New York: W. W. Norton, 1986).

30. Peter Gay, "Six Names in Search of an Interpretation," *Reading Freud* (New Haven: Yale University Press, 1990).

31. Jeffrey Masson, ed., *The Complete Letters of Sigmund Freud to Wilhelm Fliess: 1887–1904* (Cambridge, Mass.: Belknap Press, 1985).

32. Peter Swales, "Freud, Minna Bernays, and the Conquest of Rome: New Light on the Origins of Psychoanalysis," *New American Review*, vol. 1, no. 2/3 (1982); "Freud, His Origins and Family History," Presentation at UMDNJ-Robert Wood Johnson Medical School, November 15, 1986; "What Freud Didn't Say," Presentation at UMDNJ-Robert Wood Johnson Medical School, May 15, 1987.

33. Norman Paul and Betty Paul, *A Marital Puzzle* (New York: W. W. Norton, 1975).

34. Sophie Freud, *My Three Mothers and Other Passions* (New York: New York University Press, 1988).

35. Ernest Jones, *The Life and Work of Sigmund Freud*, vol. 1 (New York: Basic Books, 1953).

36. Masson, op. cit., letter of November 2, 1896.

37. Jones, op. cit., vol. 3.

38. Masson, op. cit.

39. Ronald W. Clark, *Freud: The Man and the Cause* (New York: Random House, 1980).

CHAPTER 6: WHERE DO WE COME FROM? PARENTS AND CHILDREN

1. Maya Angelou, *All God's Children Need Traveling Shoes* (New York: Vintage, 1986).

2. Robert Anderson, op. cit.

3. Pam Kleiner, *Good Mother, Good Daughter* (forthcoming).

4. Joseph P. Lash, *Eleanor and Franklin* (New York: W. W. Norton, 1976).

5. Eleanor Roosevelt, *The Autobiography of Eleanor Roosevelt* (Boston: G. K. Hall, 1984). The following quotes are from the same source.

6. Bernard Asbell, *Mother and Daughter: The Letters of Eleanor and Anna Roosevelt* (New York: Coward, McCann & Geoghegan, 1982).

7. James Roosevelt, *My Parents: A Differing View* (Chicago: Playboy Press, 1976).

8. Asbell, op. cit. The following quote is from the same source.

9. Franz Kafka, *Letter to His Father* (New York: Schocken Books, 1953).

10. Phyllis Rose, *Parallel Lives: Five Victorian Marriages* (New York: Vintage, 1984). The following quotes are from the same source.

11. Gladys Storey, *Dickens and Daughter* (London: Frederick Muller Ltd., 1939).

12. Norman and Jeanne Mackenzie, *Dickens: A Life* (New York: Oxford University Press, 1979). The following quote is from the same source.

13. Rose, op. cit. The following quote is from the same source.

14. Mary Catherine Bateson, *Composing a Life* (New York: Atlantic Monthly Press, 1990).

15. Carolyn Heilbrun, *Writing a Woman's Life* (New York: W. W. Norton, 1988).

16. Louise Smoluchowski, *Lev and Sonya: The Story of the Tolstoy Marriage* (New York: G. P. Putnam's, 1987). The following quote is from the same source.

17. Simone de Beauvoir, *A Very Easy Death* (New York: Warner, 1973). The following quotes are from the same source.

CHAPTER 7: SISTERS AND BROTHERS

1. Hepburn, op. cit.

2. George Valliant, *Adaptation to Life* (Boston: Little, Brown, 1977).

3. David Robinson, *Chaplin: His Life and Art* (New York: McGraw-Hill, 1985).

4. Charles Chaplin, *My Autobiography* (New York: Simon & Schuster, 1964).

5. Robinson, op. cit.

6. Crouch, op. cit.

7. Louise Berkinow, *Among Women* (New York: Harper & Row, 1980).

8. Jackie Robinson, *I Never Had It Made* (New York: G. P. Putnam's Sons, 1972).

9. Paulette Hines, Nydia Garcia Preto, Monica McGoldrick, Evelyn Lee, and Susan Weltman, "Intergenerational Relationships in Different Cultures," *International Family Therapy* (1992).

10. Monica McGoldrick, "Sisters," *Women in Families*, loc. cit.

11. Margaret Mead, *Blackberry Winter, My Earlier Years* (New York: Simon & Schuster, 1972). The following quote is from the same source.

12. Kurt R. Eissler, *Sigmund Freud: His Life in Pictures and Words* (New York: Harcourt Brace Jovanovich, 1978).

13. Jones, op. cit., vol. 1.

14. Like Freud, Washington had two very much older half brothers, who were educated abroad and whom he did not get to know until adolescence, when the older of them, Lawrence, fourteen years his senior, became his guardian upon their father's death.

15. M. A. Bourne, *First Family: George Washington and His Intimate Relations* (New York: W. W. Norton, 1982).

16. Carl Van Doren, *Benjamin Franklin* (New York: Viking Press, 1938).

17. Rosalynd Pflaum, *Grand Obsession: Madame Curie and Her World* (New York: Doubleday, 1989). The following quote is from the same source.

18. Eve Curie, *Marie Curie: A Biography* (New York: Doubleday, 1939).

19. Paul Robeson, *Here I Stand* (Boston: Beacon Press, 1988). The following quote is from the same source.

20. Phillip Hayes Dean, "Paul Robeson," in *Black Heroes: Severn Plays,* ed. Errol Hill (New York: Applause Theatre Book Publishers, 1989).

21. Patricia O'Toole, *The Five of Hearts: An Intimate Portrait of Henry Adams and His Friends* (New York: Ballantine, 1990).

22. Elizabeth Fishel, *Sisters: Love and Rivalry inside the Family and Beyond* (New York: William Morrow and Co., 1979).

23. Jean H. Baker, *Mary Todd Lincoln: A Biography* (New York: W. W. Norton, 1987).

24. Jean Paul Sartre, *The Word* (Greenwich, Conn.: Fawcett, 1964).

25. A. Cohen-Solal, *Sartre, a Life* (New York: Pantheon Books, 1987).

26. This contract which Sara negotiated for Franklin and Eleanor is the only document in the Roosevelt archives that is unavailable to the public.

27. Asbell, op. cit.

28. De Beauvoir, op. cit.

CHAPTER 8: COUPLE RELATIONSHIPS

1. Gelb, op. cit.

2. Janet Dunbar, *Mrs. G.B.S.: A Portrait* (New York, Harper & Row, 1963).

3. Groucho Marx, op. cit.

4. Leslie Wheeler, *Loving Warriers: Selected Letters of Lucy Stone and Henry B. Blackwell, 1853 to 1893* (New York: Dial Press, 1961). The following references are to the same source.

5. Elizabeth Cazden, *Antoinette Brown Blackwell: A Biography* (Old Westbury, N.Y.: Feminist Press, 1983).

6. Karen Monson, *Alma Mahler: Muse to Genius* (Boston: Houghton Mifflin, 1983). The following quote is from the same source.

7. Susanne Keegan, *The Bride of the Wind: The Life of Alma Mahler* (New York: Viking Press, 1992). The following quote is from the same source.

8. He did later complete a ninth symphony, but he never lived to complete his tenth.

9. Monson, op. cit. The following references are to the same source.

10. Dunbar, op. cit.

11. Michael Holroyd, *The Search for Love*, vol. 1, *Bernard Shaw* (New York: Random House, 1988). The following quotes are from the same reference.

12. Dunbar, op. cit.

13. Holroyd, op. cit. the following quotes are from the same reference.

14. Dunbar, op. cit. The following quotes are from the same reference.

15. Holroyd, op. cit. The following quotes are from the same reference.

16. Dunbar, op. cit.

17. Holyroyd, op. cit. The following quotes are from the same reference.

18. Whether or not this humorous method was the one Shaw actually used, it is a remarkably Irish proposal, the joke being that the Irish ask women to marry by saying, "How'd you like to be buried with my folk?" For details see *Living beyond Loss*, loc. cit.

19. Dunbar, op. cit.

CHAPTER 9: CLASS, CULTURE, AND FAMILY RELATIONSHIPS

1. Louise Erdrich and Michael Dorris, *The Crown of Columbus* (New York: Harper & Row, 1991).

2. Paul Robeson, Jr. Keynote speech, Piscataway High School, Piscataway, N.J., January 18, 1992.

3. Thomas Flanagan, *The Year of the French* (New York: Holt, Rinehart & Winston, 1979).

4. George Barnard Shaw, 1975.

5. Gelb and Gelb, op. cit.

6. Eugene O'Neill, *Long Day's Journey into Night* (New Haven: Yale University Press, 1955).

7. Her father was Danish; her mother, who grew up in California, was of mixed German, Dutch, and Swiss background. See Louis Shaeffer, *O'Neill: Son and Artist* (Boston: Little, Brown, 1973). The following quote is from the same source.

8. Garson Kanin, *Tracy and Hepburn: An Intimate Memoir* (New York: Donald I. Fine, 1988). The following quotes are from the same source.

9. Bill Davidson, *Spencer Tracy: Tragic Idol* (New York: Dutton, 1987).

10. Keegan, op. cit.

11. Edwin Friedman, "The Myth of the Shiksa," *Ethnicity and Family Therapy*, ed. Monica McGoldrick, John K. Pearce, and Joseph Giordano. (New York: Guilford, 1982).

CHAPTER 10: RECONNECTING

1. Mary Catherine Bateson, *With a Daughter's Eye* (New York: William Morrow & Co., 1984). The following quotes are from the same source.

2. David Lipset, *Gregory Bateson: The Legacy of a Scientist* (Englewood Cliffs, N.J.: Prentice Hall, 1980). The following quote is from the same source.

3. Bateson, op. cit. The following quotes are from the same source.

4. Bateson, *Composing a Life*, loc. cit. The following quotes are from the same source.

BIBLIOGRAPHY

Anderson, Carol; Susan Stewart; and Sona Dimidjian. *Flying Solo*. New York: W. W. Norton, 1994.

Anderson, Robert. *I Never Sang for My Father*. New York: Random House, 1968.

Bagarozzi, D. A., and S. A. Anderson. *Personal, Marital and Family Myths*. New York: W. W. Norton, 1989.

Baldwin, James. "Sonny's Blues." In *Braided Lives: An Anthology of Multicultural American Writing*, ed. Minnesota Humanities Commission. St. Paul: Viking Press, 1991.

Barth, Joan. *It Runs in My Family*. New York: Bruner/Mazel, 1993.

Bernikow, Louise. *Among Women*. New York: Harper & Row, 1980.

Boller, Paul F., Jr. *Presidential Wives*. New York: Oxford University Press, 1988.

Bolton, Iris. *My Son . . . My Son . . .: Helping Families after Death, Loss, or Suicide*, Atlanta: Bolton Press, 1983.

Boose, Lynda E., and Betty S. Flowers, eds. *Fathers and Daughters*. Baltimore: Johns Hopkins University Press, 1989.

Boss, Pauline. "Ambiguous Loss." In *Living beyond Loss*, ed. Froma Walsh and Monica McGoldrick. New York: W. W. Norton, 1991.

Bowen, Murray. *Family Therapy in Clinical Practice*. New York: Jason Aronson, 1978.

Brodzki, Bella, and Celeste Schenck, eds. *Life/Lines, Theorizing Women's Autobiography*. Ithaca and London: Cornell University Press, 1988.

Butler, R., and M. Lewis, *Aging and Mental Health,* St. Louis: C. V. Mosby, 1983.

Caroli, Betty Boyd. *First Ladies*. New York: Oxford University Press, 1987.

Carter, Elizabeth A. "The Transgenerational Scripts and Nuclear Family Stress: Theory and Clinical Implications." In *Georgetown Family Symposium*, vol. 3, (1975–76). Washington, D.C.: Georgetown University, 1978.

Carter, Betty, and Monica McGoldrick. "Overview: The Changing Family Life Cycle: A Framework for Family Therapy." In *The Changing Family Life Cycle.*, ed. Betty Carter and Monica McGoldrick. Boston: Allyn & Bacon, 1988.

Cath, Stanley; Alan Gurwitt; and Linda Gunsberg. *Fathers and Their Families*. Hillsdale, N.J.: Analytic Press, 1989.

Cicirelli, V. G. "Sibling Relationships throughout the Life Cycle." In *The Handbook of Family Psychology and Therapy*, ed. L. L'Abate. Homewood, Ill: Dorsey Press, 1985.

Conroy, Pat. *The Prince of Tides*. New York: Houghton Mifflin, 1988.

Dardis, Tom. *The Thirsty Muse: Alcohol and the American Writer*. New York: Ticknor & Fields, 1989.

DeFrain, J.; J. Taylor; and L. Ernst. *Coping with Sudden Infant Death*. Lexington, Mass.: D. C. Heath, 1982.

Diagram Group. *Mothers: 100 Mothers of the Famous and the Infamous*. New York: Paddington Press, 1976.

Downing, C. *Psyche's Sisters: Reimagining the Meaning of Sisterhood*. San Francisco: Harper & Row, 1988.

Dunne, Edward J.; John L. McIntosh; and Karen Dunne-Maxim, eds. *Suicide and Its Aftermath*. New York: W. W. Norton, 1987.

Eisler, Riane. *The Chalice and the Blade: Our History, Our Future*. New York: Harper & Row, 1987.

Fishel, Elizabeth. *Sisters: Love and Rivalry inside the Family and Beyond*. New York: William Morrow & Co., 1979.

Fishel, Elizabeth. "The Special Language of Sisters." *Radcliffe Quarterly* (March 1990).

Flanagan, Thomas. *The Year of the French*. New York: Holt, Rinehart & Winston, 1979.

Forbes, Malcolm. *They Went That-a-way: How the Famous, the Infamous, and the Great Died*. New York: Ballantine, 1988.

———. *What Happened to Their Kids? Children of the Rich and Famous*. New York: Simon & Schuster, 1990.

Giamatti, A. Bartlett. *Take Time for Paradise: Americans and Their Games*. New York: Summit, 1989.

Goodwin, Donald W. *Alcohol and the Writer*. New York: Penguin, 1990.

Greenblatt, Robert B. *Sex and Circumstance*. Tallahassee, Fla.: Loiry Publishing House, 1987.

Griffin, Susan. *A Chorus of Stones.* New York: Doubleday, 1992.

Gutstein, Steven. *Adolescent Suicide: The Loss of Reconciliation.* In *Living beyond Loss,* ed. Froma Walsh and Monica McGoldrick. New York: W. W. Norton, 1991.

Hadley, T.; T. Jacob; J. Miliones; J. Caplan; and D. Spitz. "The Relationship between Family Development Crisis and the Appearance of Symptoms in a Family Member." *Family Process,* vol. 13 (1974).

Haley, Alex. *Roots: The Saga of an American Family.* New York: Doubleday, 1974.

Haskell, Molly. *Love and Other Infectious Diseases.* New York: William Morrow and Co., 1990.

Healy, Diana Dixon. *America's First Ladies: Private Lives of the Presidential Wives.* New York: Atheneum, 1988.

Heilbrun, Carolyn G. *Writing a Woman's Life.* New York: W. W. Norton, 1988.

———. *Hamlet's Mother and Other Women.* New York: Columbia University Press, 1990.

Hochschild, Arlie. *The Second Shift, Working Parents and the Revolution at Home.* New York: Viking Press, 1989.

Holmes, T., and T. H. Rahe. "The Social Adjustment Rating Scale." *Journal of Psychosomatic Research,* vol. 11 (1967).

Holt, Georgia, and Phyllis Quinn, with Sue Russell. *Star Mothers.* New York: St. Martin's Press, 1989.

Huygen, F. J. A.; H. J. M. van den Hoogen; J. T. M. van Eijk; and A. J. A. Smits. "Death and Dying: A Longitudinal Study of Their Medical Impact on the Family." *Family Systems Medicine,* vol. 7 (1989).

Imber Black, Evan. *Rituals of our Time.* New York: Harper & Row, 1993.

———. *Secrets in Families and Family Therapy.* New York: W. W. Norton, 1993.

Kingston, Maxine Hong. *The Woman Warrior.* New York: Vintage, 1989.

Kleiner, Pam. *Good Mother; Good Daughter.* Forthcoming.

Kotre, John, and Elizabeth Hall. *Seasons of Life.* Boston: Little, Brown, 1990.

Laird, J. "Women and Stories: Restorying Women's Self-constructions." In *Women in Families,* ed. Monica McGoldrick, Carol M. Anderson, and Froma Walsh. New York: W. W. Norton, 1989.

Leman, K. *The Birth Order Book: Why You Are the Way You Are.* Old Tappan, N.J.: Fleming H. Revell Co., 1984.

Lerner, Harriet. *The Dance of Anger.* New York: Harper & Row, 1988.

———. *The Dance of Deception.* New York: Harper & Row, 1990.

———. *The Dance of Intimacy.* New York: Harper & Row, 1993.

Lerner, Max. *Wrestling with the Angel.* New York: W. W. Norton, 1990.

Liebowitz, Herbert. *Fabricating Lives: Explorations in American Autobiography.* New York: Alfred A. Knopf, 1989.

Lindemann, E. "Symptomatology and Management of Acute Grief." *American Journal of Psychiatry* (1944).

Luepnitz, Debra. *The Family Interpreted.* New York: Basic Books, 1988.

Mallon, Thomas. *A Book of One's Own: People and Their Diaries.* Harrisburg, Va.: R. R. Donnelley & Sons Co., 1984.

Maloney, M. L., and A. Maloney. *The Hand that Rocks the Cradle: Mothers, Sons and Leadership.* Englewood Cliffs, N.J.: Prentice Hall, 1985.

McGoldrick, Monica. "Sisters." In *Women in Families,* ed. Monica McGoldrick, Carol Anderson, and Froma Walsh. New York: W. W. Norton, 1988.

———. "Women through the Family Life Cycle." In *Women in Families,* ed. Monica McGoldrick, Carol Anderson, and Froma Walsh. New York: W. W. Norton, 1988.

———. "Echoes from the Past: Helping Families Mourn their Losses." In *Living beyond Loss,* ed. Froma Walsh and Monica McGoldrick. New York: W. W. Norton, 1991.

———. "The Legacy of Loss." In *Living beyond Loss,* ed. Froma Walsh and Monica McGoldrick. New York: W. W. Norton, 1991.

———, John K. Pearce, and Joseph Giordano. *Ethnicity and Family Therapy.* New York: Guilford, 1982.

———, and Nydia Garcia-Preto. "Ethnic Intermarriage: Implications for Therapy." *Family Process,* vol. 23, no. 3 (1984).

———, and Randy Gerson. "Genograms and the Family Life Cycle." In *The Changing Family Life Cycle,* ed. Betty Carter and Monica McGoldrick. New York: W. W. Norton, 1988.

———, Nydia Garcia-Preto, Paulette Moore Hines, and Evelyn Lee. "Ethnicity and Women." In *Women in Families,* ed. Monica McGoldrick, Carol Anderson, and Froma Walsh. New York: W. W. Norton, 1988.

———, Rhea Almeida, Paulette Moore Hines, Nydia Garcia Preto, Elliott Rosen, and Evelyn Lee. "Mourning in Different Cultures." In *Living beyond Loss.,* ed. Froma Walsh and Monica McGoldrick. New York: W. W. Norton, 1991.

———, and Froma Walsh. "Death and the Family Life Cycle." In *Living beyond Loss,* ed. Froma Walsh and Monica McGoldrick. New York: W. W. Norton, 1991.

McNaron, T. A. H. *The Sister Bond: A Feminist View of a Timeless Connection.* New York: Pergamon Press, 1985. Includes Jane Austen, Virginia Woolf, Emily Dickinson.

Michael, Princess of Kent. *Crowned in a Far Country: Portraits of Eight Royal Brides.* New York: Weidenfeld & Nicolson, 1986.

Osterweis, M.; F. Solomon; and M. Green, eds. *Bereavement: Reactions, Consequences, and Care.* Washington, D.C.: National Academy Press/Solomon & Green, 1984.

Parkes, C. Murray. *Bereavement: Studies of Grief in Adult Life.* New York: International Universities Press, 1972.

Paul, N., and G. Grosser. "Operational Mourning and Its Role in Conjoint Family Therapy." *Community Mental Health Journal,* vol. 1 (1965).

———, and Betty Paul. *A Marital Puzzle.* New York: W. W. Norton, 1975.

———, and B. B. Paul. "Death and Changes in Sexual Behavior." In *Normal Family Processes.,* ed. Froma Walsh. New York: Guilford, 1982.

Purnell, D. *Exploring Your Family Story.* Melbourne, Australia: Joint Board of Christian Education, 1983.

Rilke, Rainer Maria. *Letters to a Young Poet.* Translated by M. D. Heath. New York: W. W. Norton, 1954.

Rose, Phyllis. *Parallel Lives: Five Victorian Marriages.* New York: Vintage, 1984.

Robe, Lucy Barry. *Co-starring Famous Women and Alcohol.* Minneapolis: Comp-Care Publications, 1986.

Scarf, Maggie. *Intimate Partners: Patterns in Love & Marrriage.* New York: Random House, 1987.

Schiff, H. S. *The Bereaved Parent.* New York: Penguin, 1970.

Simpson, Eileen. *Orphans: Real and Imaginary.* New York: Weidenfeld & Nicolson, 1987.

Stone, Elizabeth. *Black Sheep & Kissing Cousins: How Our Family Stories Shape Us.* New York: Times Books, 1988.

Thomas, E. H. Gwynne. *The Presidential Families.* New York: Hippocrene Books, 1989.

Valliant, G. E. *Adaption to Life.* Boston: Little, Brown, 1977.

Vidal, Gore; V. S. Pritchett; David Caute; Bruce Chatwin; Peter Conrad; and Edward Jay Epstein. *Great American Families.* New York: W. W. Norton, 1975.

Videcka-Sherman, L. "Coping with the Death of a Child: A Study over Time." *American Journal of Orthopsychiatry,* vol. 52 (1982).

Wallace, Irving; Amy Wallace; David Wallechinsky; and Sylvia Wallace. *The Intimate Sex Lives of Famous People.* New York: Dell, 1982.

Walsh, Froma, and Monica McGoldrick, eds. *Living beyond Loss: A Systemic Perspective.* New York: W. W. Norton, 1991.

———. "Loss and the family: A Systemic Perspective." In *Living beyond Loss,* ed. Froma Walsh and Monica McGoldrick. New York: W. W. Norton, 1991.

Watzlawick, Paul; Janet Helmich Beavin; and Don D. Jackson. *Pragmatics of Human Communication.* New York: W. W. Norton, 1967.

Wolin, Steven J.; Linda A. Bennett; and Jane S. Jacobs. "Assessing Family Rituals in Alcoholic Families." In *Rituals in Families and Family Therapy,* ed. Evan Imber-Black, Janine Roberts, and Richard Whiting. New York: Guilford, 1988.

Wortman, C., and R. Silver. "The Myths of Coping with Loss." *Journal of Counseling and Clinical Psychology,* vol. 57 (1989).

ADAMS SOURCES

Adams, Abigail, and Adams, John. *The Book of Abigail and John: Selected Letters of the Adams Family: 1762–1784,* ed. L. H. Butterfield, Mark Friedlaender, and Mary-Jo Kline. Cambridge: Harvard University Press, 1975.

Adams, James Truslow. *The Adams Family.* New York: Signet, 1976.

Conroy, Sarah Booth. *Refinements of Love: A Novel about Clover and Henry Adams.* New York: Pantheon Books, 1993.

Homans, Abigail Adams. *Education by Uncles.* Boston: Houghton Mifflin, 1966.

Levin, Phyllis Lee. *Abigail Adams: A Biography.* New York: St. Martin's Press, 1987.

Musto, David. "The Adams Family." *Proceedings of the Massachusetts Historical Society* (1981).

Nagel, Paul C. *Descent from Glory.* New York: Oxford University Press, 1983.

———. *The Adams Women.* New York: Oxford University Press, 1987.

O'Toole, Patricia. *The Five of Hearts: An Intimate Portrait of Henry Adams and His Friends 1880–1918.* New York: Ballantine, 1990.

Richards, Leonard L. *The Life and Times of Congressman John Quincy Adams.* New York: Oxford University Press, 1986.

Shaw, Peter. *The Character of John Adams.* New York: W. W. Norton, 1976.

Shepherd, Jack. *The Adams Chronicles: Four Generations of Greatness.* Boston: Little, Brown, 1975.

Withey, Lynne. *Dearest Friend: A Life of Abigail Adams.* New York: Free Press, 1981.

ANGELOU SOURCES

Angelou, Maya. *I Know Why the Caged Bird Sings.* New York: Random House, 1970.

———. *Gather Together in My Name,* New York: Bantam Books, 1974.

———. *The Heart of a Woman.* New York: Bantam Books, 1981.

———. *Poems: Maya Angelou.* New York: Bantam Books, 1986.

———. *All God's Children Need Traveling Shoes.* New York: Vintage, 1986.

———. *Wouldn't Take Nothing for My Journey Now.* New York: Random House, 1993.

Elliot, Jeffrey, M., ed. *Conversations with Maya Angelou.* Jackson: University Press of Mississippi, 1989.

McPherson, Dolly A. *Order out of Chaos: The Autobiographical Works of Maya Angelou.* New York: Peter Lang, 1990.

O'Neale, Sondra. "Rconstruction of the Composite Self: New Images of Black Women in Maya Angelou's Continuing Autobiography." In *Black Women Writers: 1950–1980,* ed. Mari Evans. New York: Doubleday, 1984.

Shuker, Nancy. *Maya Angelou.* Englewood Cliffs, N.J.: Silver Burdett Press, 1990.

BARRETT AND BROWNING SOURCES

Browning, Robert, and Elizabeth Barrett Browning. *The Letters of Robert Browning and Elizabeth Barrett Browning, 1845–1846.* New York: Harper and Brothers, 1902.

Browning, Vivienne. *My Browning Family Album.* London: Springwood, 1979.

Forster, Margaret. *Elizabeth Barrett Browning: A Biography.* New York: Doubleday, 1988.

Hewlett, Dorothy. *Elizabeth Barrett Browning.* New York: Cassell, 1953.

Honan, Park, and William Irvine. *The Book, the Ring and the Poet: A Biography of Robert Browning.* New York: Bodley Head, 1974.

Karlin, Daniel. *The Courtship of Robert Browning and Elizabeth Barrett.* New York: Oxford University Press, 1987.

Leighton, Angela. *Elizabeth Barrett Browning.* New York: Harvester Press, 1986.

Mander, R. *Mrs. Browning: The Story of Elizabeth Barrett.* London: Weidenfeld & Nicolson, 1980.

Marks, Jeannette. *The Family of the Barrett.* New York: Macmillan, 1938.

Mason, Cyrus. *The Poet Robert Browning and His Kinsfolk by His Cousin Cyrus Mason,* ed. with Afterword by W. C. Turner. Waco, Texas: Baylor University Press, 1983.

Maynard, John. *Browning's Youth.* Cambridge: Harvard University Press, 1977.

Miller, Betty. *Robert Browning: A Portrait.* New York: Scribner, 1973.

Orr, S. *Life and Letters of Robert Browning,* new ed., rev. and in part rewritten by F. G. Kenyon. New York: John Murray, 1908.

Robinson, J. "Mrs. Barrett Browning's Parentage." *Athenaeum,* vol. 3486 (August 18, 1894).

Ryals, Clyde de L. *The Life of Robert Browning.* Cambridge, Mass.: Blackwell, 1993.

Taplin, Gardner B. *The Life of Elizabeth Barrett Browning.* New York: John Murray, 1957.

Thomas, D. *Robert Browning: A Life within a Life.* London: Weidenfeld & Nicolson, 1982.

Ward, Maisie. *The Tragi-Comedy of Pen Browning.* New York: Sheed & Ward Browning Institute, 1972.

Ward, Maisie. *Robert Browning and His World: The Private Face (1812–61).* New York: Holt, Rinehart & Winston, 1955.

BATESON AND MEAD SOURCES

Bateson, Mary Catherine. *With a Daughter's Eye.* New York: William Morrow & Co., 1984.

———. *Composing a Life.* New York: Atlantic Monthly Press, 1990.

———. *Peripheral Visions.* New York: Harper Collins, 1994.

Cassidy, Robert. *Margaret Mead, a Voice for the Century.* New York: Universe Books, 1982.

Grosskurth, Phyllis. *Margaret Mead, Life of Controversy.* London: Penguin Books, 1988.

Howard, Jane. *Margaret Mead, Life.* New York: Ballantine Books, 1984.

Lipset, David. *Gregory Bateson, Legacy of a Scientist.* Englewood Cliffs, N.J.: Prentice-Hall, 1980.

Mead, Margaret. *Blackberry Winter, My Earlier Years.* New York: Simon & Schuster, 1972.

Rice, Edward. *Margaret Mead, Portrait.* New York: Harper & Row, 1979.

De BEAUVOIR SOURCES

Appignanesi, Lisa. *Simone de Beauvoir*. New York: Viking Penguin, 1988.

Ascher, Carol. *Simone de Beauvoir: A Life of Freedom*. Boston: Beacon, 1981.

Bair, Deirdre. *Simone de Beauvoir: A Biography*. New York: Summit, 1990.

Beauvoir, Simone de. *Memoirs of a Dutiful Daughter*. New York: Harper & Row, 1959.

———. *A Very Easy Death*. New York: Warner Paperback Library, 1973.

———. *The Second Sex*. New York: Vintage Books, 1974.

Francis, Claude, and Fernande Gontier. *Simone de Beauvoir: A Life a Love Story*. New York: St. Martin's Press, 1987.

BEETHOVEN SOURCES

Ciardello, Jean A. "Beethoven: Modern Analytic View of the Man and His Music," *Psychoanalytic Review*, vol. 72, no. 1 (1985).

Cooper, Martin. *Beethoven: The Last Decade: 1817–1827*. New York: Oxford University Press, 1985.

Editore, Arnoldo Mondadori. *Beethoven: Portraits of Greatness*. New York: Curtis, 1967.

Forbes, Elliot, ed. *Thayer's Life of Beethoven*. Princeton: Princeton University Press, 1969.

Hamburger, Michael, ed. *Beethoven: Letters, Journals and Conversations*. New York: Thames & Hudson, 1951.

James, R. M. *Beethoven*. New York: St. Martin's Press, 1983.

Kerst, Friedrich, and Henry Edward Krehbiel, eds. *Beethoven: The Man and Artist as Revealed in His Own Words*. New York: Dover, 1964.

MacArdle, Donald W. "The Family van Beethoven." *Musical Quarterly*, vol. xxv, no. 4 (1949).

Marek, George R. *Beethoven: Biography of a Genius*. New York: Thomas Y. Crowell, 1969.

Matthews, Denis. *Beethoven*. New York: Vintage, 1988.

Rodman, Selden, and James Kearns. *The Heart of Beethoven*. New York: Shorewood, 1962.

Solomon, Maynard. *Beethoven*. New York: Schirmer, 1977.

———. *Beethoven Essays*. Cambridge: Harvard University Press, 1988.

Sterbe, E., and R. Sterbe. *Beethoven and His Nephew*. New York: Pantheon Books, 1954.

Sullivan, J. W. N. *Beethoven: His Spiritual Development*. New York: Vintage, 1960.

BLACKWELL, STONE, AND BROWN SOURCES

Cazden, Elizabeth. *Antoinette Brown Blackwell: A Biography*. Old Westbury, N.Y.: Feminist Press, 1983.

Hays, Elinor Rice. *Those Extraordinary Blackwells.* New York: Harcourt Brace, 1967.

Horn, Margo. *"Family Ties: The Blackwells, a Study of the Dynamics of Family Life in Nineteenth Century America."* Ph.D. dissertation, Tufts University, 1980.

————. "Sisters Worthy of Respect: Family Dynamics and Women's Roles in the Blackwell Family." *Journal of Family History,* vol. 8, no. 4 (1983).

Wheeler, Leslie, ed. *Loving Warriers: Selected Letters of Lucy Stone and Henry B. Blackwell, 1853 to 1893.* New York: Dial Press, 1981.

BRONTË SOURCES

Barker, Juliet. *The Brontës.* London: Weidenfeld & Nicolson, 1994.

Bentley, Phyllis. *The Brontës and Their World.* New York: Viking, 1969.

Cannon, John. *The Road to Haworth: The story of the Brontës' Irish Ancestry.* London: Weidenfeld & Nicolson, 1980.

Chadwick, E. H. *In the Footsteps of the Brontës.* London: Sir Isaac Pitman & Sons, 1914.

Chitham, Edward. *The Brontës' Irish Background.* New York: St. Martin's Press, 1986.

————. *A Life of Emily Brontë.* New York: Basil Blackwell, 1988.

————, and T. Winnifrith. *Brontë Facts and Brontë Problems.* London: Macmillan, 1983.

Du Maurier, Daphne. *The Infernal World of Branwell Brontë.* Garden City, N.Y.: Doubleday, 1961.

Frazer, Rebecca. *The Brontës: Charlotte Brontë and Her Family.* New York: Crown, 1988.

Gaskell, Elizabeth. *The Life of Charlotte Brontë.* London: Penguin, 1975.

Gerin, Winifred. *Branwell Brontë.* London: Thomas Nelson & Sons, 1961.

————. *Emily Brontë: A Biography.* London: Oxford University Press, 1971.

Hannah, Barbara. *Striving toward Wholeness.* Boston: Signpress, 1988.

Hanson, L., and E. Hanson, *The Four Brontës.* New York: Archon Press, 1967.

Hardwick, Elizabeth. "The Brontës." In *Seduction and Betrayal: Women and Literature.* New York: Vintage, 1975.

Hinkley, L. L. *The Brontës: Charlotte and Emily.* New York: Hastings House, 1945.

Hopkins, A. B. *The Father of the Brontës.* Baltimore: Johns Hopkins University Press, 1958.

Lane, Margaret. *The Brontë Story.* London: Fontana, 1969.

Lock, J., and W. T. Dixon. *A Man of Sorrow: The Life, Letters, and Times of Reverend Patrick Brontë.* Westport, Conn.: Meckler Books, 1965.

Mackay, A. M. *The Brontës: Fact and Fiction.* New York: Dodd, Mead, 1897.

Maurat, C. *The Brontës' Secret,* tr. M. Meldrum. New York: Barnes & Noble, 1970.

Moglen, Helene. *Charlotte Brontë: The Self Conceived.* Madison: University of Wisconsin Press, 1984.

Morrison, N. B. *Haworth Harvest: The Story of the Brontës.* New York: Vanguard, 1969.

Peters, Margot. *An Enigma of Brontës.* New York: St. Martin's Press, 1974.

————. *Unquiet Soul: A Biography of Charlotte Brontë.* New York: Atheneum, 1975.

Ratchford, F. W. *The Brontës' Web of Childhood.* New York: Russell & Russell, 1954.

Raymond, E. *In the Steps of the Brontës.* London: Rich & Cowan, 1948.

Spark, Muriel, and Derek Stanford. *Emily Brontë: Her Life and Work.* London: Arrow Books, 1960.

White, W. B. *The Miracle of Haworth: A Brontë Story.* New York: E. P. Dutton, 1939.

Wilks, Brian. *The Brontës: An Illustrated Biography.* New York: Peter Bedrick Books, 1986 (paper).

————. *The Illustrated Brontës of Haworth.* New York: Facts on File Publications, 1986.

Winnifith, T. Z. *The Brontës and their Background: Romance and Reality.* New York: Collier, 1977.

Wright, William. *The Brontës in Ireland.* New York: D. Appleton & Company, 1893.

CHAPLIN SOURCES

Bessy, Maurice. *Charlie Chaplin.* New York: Harper & Row, 1983.

Chaplin, Charles. *My Autobiography.* New York: Simon & Schuster, 1964.

Chaplin, Charles, Jr., with N. and M. Rau. *My Father, Charlie Chaplin.* New York: Random House, 1960.

Chaplin, Lita Grey, with Morton Cooper. *My Life with Chaplin: An Intimate Memoir.* Brattleboro, Vt.: Book Press, 1966.

Epstein, Jerry. *Remembering Charlie.* New York: Doubleday, 1989.

Haining, Peter, ed. *The Legend of Charlie Chaplin.* London: W. H. Allen, 1982.

Karney, Robyn, and Robin Cross. *The Life and Times of Charlie Chaplin.* London: Green Wood Publishing, 1992.

Maland, Charles. *Chaplin and American Culture: The Evolution of a Star Image.* Princeton: Princeton University Press, 1989.

McCabe, John. *Charlie Chaplin.* New York: Doubleday, 1978.

Robinson, David. *Chaplin: The Mirror of Opinion.* Bloomington: Indiana University Press, 1983.

————. *Chaplin: His Life and Art.* New York: McGraw-Hill, 1985.

Smith, Julian. *Chaplin.* Boston: Twayne Publishers, 1984.

CURIE SOURCES

Curie, Eve. *Marie Curie: A Biography.* New York: Doubleday, 1939.

Giroud, Francoise. *Marie Curie: A Life.* New York: Holmes & Meier, 1986.

Pflaum, Rosalynd. *Grand Obsession: Madame Curie and Her World.* New York: Doubleday, 1989.

Reid, Robert. *Marie Curie.* New York: E. P. Dutton, 1974.

Steinke, Ann E. *Marie Curie.* New York: Barrons, 1987.

DICKENS SOURCES

Johnson, Edgar. *Charles Dickens: His Tragedy and Triumph*. New York: Penguin, 1980.

Kaplan, Fred. *Dickens: A Biography*. New York: William Morrow & Co., 1988.

Mackenzie, Norman and Jeanne. *Dickens: A Life*. New York: Oxford, 1979.

Storey, Gladys. *Dickens and Daughter*. London: Frederick Muller Ltd., 1939.

Tomalin, Claire. *The Invisible Woman: The Story of Nelly Ternan and Charles Dickens*. New York: Alfred A. Knopf, 1991.

EDISON SOURCES

Conot, Robert. *Thomas A. Edison: A Streak of Luck*. New York: Plenum, 1979.

Frost, L. A. *The Edison Album: A Pictorial Biography of Thomas Alva Edison*. Mattituck, N.Y.: Amereon House, 1984.

Josephson, Matthew. *Edison: A Biography*. New York: McGraw-Hill, 1959.

Venable, John D. *Mina Miller Edison: Daughter, Wife and Mother of Inventors*. East Orange, N.J.: Charles Edison Fund, 1961.

Wachhorst, Wynn. *Thomas Alva Edison: An American Myth*. Cambridge: MIT Press, 1984.

FONDA SOURCES

Guiles, F. L. *Jane Fonda: The Actress in Her Time*. New York: Pinnacle, 1981.

Hayward, Brooks. *Haywire*. New York: Alfred A. Knopf, 1977.

Kiernan, T. *Jane: An Intimate Biography of Jane Fonda*. New York: G. P. Putnam's Sons, 1973.

Sheed, Wilfred. *Clare Boothe Luce*. New York: E. P. Dutton, 1982.

Springer, J. *The Fondas*. Secaucus, N.J.: Citadel, 1970.

Teichman, Howard. *Fonda: My Life*. New York: New American Library, 1981.

FRANKLIN SOURCES

Bowen, Catherine Drinker. *The Most Dangerous Man in America: Scenes from the Life of Benjamin Franklin*. Boston: Little, Brown, 1974.

Clark, Ronald W. *Benjamin Franklin: A Biography*. New York: Random House, 1983.

Fay, Bernard. *The Two Franklins: Fathers of American Democracy*. New York: AMS Press, 1969.

Franklin, Benjamin. *The Autobiography of Benjamin Franklin*. New York: Lancer, 1968.

Hall, Max. *Benjamin Franklin and Polly Baker*. Chapel Hill: University of North Carolina Press, 1960.

Labaree, Leonard W.; Ralph L. Ketcham; Helen C. Boarfield; and Helen H. Fine-
    man, eds. *The Autobiography of Benjamin Franklin*. New Haven: Yale Univer-
    sity Press, 1964.
Lopez, Claude-Anne, and Eugenia W. Herbert. *The Private Franklin: The Man and
    His Family*. New York: W. W. Norton, 1975.
National Center for Constitutional Studies. *The Real Benjamin Franklin: The True
    Story of America's Greatest Diplomat*. Washington, D.C.:, 1987.
Osborne, Mary Pope. *The Many Lives of Benjamin Franklin*. New York: Dial,
    1990.
Randall, Willard. *A Little Revenge: Benjamin Franklin and His Son*. Boston: Little,
    Brown, 1984.
Seavey, Ormond. *Becoming Benjamin Franklin: The Autobiography and the Life*.
    University Park: Pennsylvania State University Press, 1988.
Skemp, Sheila L. *William Franklin, Son of a Patriot, Servant of a King*. New York:
    Oxford University Press, 1990.
Van Doren, Carl. *Benjamin Franklin*. New York: Viking Press, 1938.
Wright, Esmond. *Franklin of Philadelphia*. Cambridge: Harvard University Press,
    1986.
————. *Benjamin Franklin: His Life as He Wrote it*. Cambridge: Harvard University
    Press, 1990.

FREUD SOURCES

Anzieu, Didier. *Freud's Self Analysis*. Madison, Conn.: International Universities
    Press, 1986.
Carotenuto, Also. *A Secret Symmetry: Sabina Spielrein between Jung and Freud*.
    New York: Pantheon Books, 1982.
Clark, Ronald W. *Freud: The Man and the Cause*. New York: Random House, 1980.
Eissler, Kurt R. *Sigmund Freud: His Life in Pictures and Words*. New York: Helen
    & Kurt Wolff Books/Harcourt Brace Jovanovich, 1978.
Freeman, Lucy, and Herbert S. Strean. *Freud and Women*. New York: Frederick
    Ungar Publishing Co., 1981.
Freud, Martin. *Sigmund Freud: Man and Father*. New York: Jason Aronson, 1982.
Freud, Sophie. *My Three Mothers and Other Passions*. New York: New York Uni-
    versity Press, 1988.
Gay, Peter. *Freud: A Life for Our Time*. New York: W. W. Norton, 1988.
————. *Reading Freud*. New Haven: Yale University Press, 1990.
Gerson, Randy, and Monica McGoldrick. "Constructing and Interpreting Geno-
    grams: The Example of Sigmund Freud's Family." In *Innovations in Clinical
    Practice: A Source Book*, vol. 5, 1986.
Glickhorn, Rose. "The Freiberg Period of the Freud Family." *Journal of the History
    of Medicine*, vol. 24 (1979).
Jones, Ernest. *The Life and Work of Sigmund Freud*. New York: Basic Books, 1953–
    55. 3 vols.
————, ed. *Letters of Sigmund Freud 1873–1939*. London: Cambridge University
    Press, 1975.

Kerr, John. *A Most Dangerous Method: The Story of Jung, Freud, and Sabina Spielrein*. New York: Alfred A. Knopf, 1993.

Krull, Marianne. *Freud and His Father*. New York: W. W. Norton, 1986.

Mannoni, O. *Freud*. New York: Vintage, 1974.

Masson, Jeffrey. *The Assault on Truth: Freud's Suppression of the Seduction Theory*. New York: HarperCollins, 1984.

———, ed. *The Complete Letters of Sigmund Freud to Wilhelm Fliess: 1887–1904*. Cambridge, Mass.: Belknap Press, 1985.

McGoldrick, Monica, and Randy Gerson. *Genograms in Family Assessment*. New York: W. W. Norton, 1985.

McGoldrick, Monica, and Randy Gerson. "Genograms and the Family Life Cycle." In *The Changing Family Life Cycle*, ed. Betty Carter and Monica McGoldrick. Boston: Allyn & Bacon, 1988.

Nelken, Michael. "Freud's Heroic Struggle with His Mother." Manuscript in preparation.

Peters, Uwe Henrik. *Anna Freud: A Life Dedicated to Children*. New York: Schocken Book's, 1985.

Roazen, Paul. *Meeting Freud's Family*. Amherst: University of Massachusetts Press, 1993.

Schur, Max. *Freud: Living and Dying*. New York: International Universities Press, 1972.

Swales, Peter. "Freud, Minna Bernays, and the Conquest of Rome: New Light on the Origins of Psychoanalysis." *New American Review*, vol. 1, no. 2/3 (1982).

———. "Freud, his Origins and Family History." UMDNJ-Robert Wood Johnson Medical School. November 15, 1986.

———. "What Freud didn't say." UMDNJ Robert Wood Johnson Medical School, May 15, 1987.

Young-Bruehl, Elizabeth. *Anna Freud: A Biography*. New York: Summit Books, 1988.

GURNEY SOURCE

Witchel, Alex. "Laughter, Tears." *New York Times Magazine* (November 12, 1989).

HAWTHORNE SOURCES

Bassan, Maurice. *Hawthorne's Son: The Life and Literary Career of Julian Hawthorne*. Columbus: Ohio State University Press, 1970.

Carton, Evan. "A Daughter of the Puritans and Her Old Master: Hawthorne, Una, and the Sexuality of Romance." *Daughters and Fathers*, ed. Lynda E. Boose and Betty S. Flowers. Baltimore: Johns Hopkins University Press, 1989.

Cowley, Malcolm, ed. *The Hawthorne Reader*. New York: Viking, 1983.

Hawthorne, Julian. *Nathaniel Hawthorne and His Wife: A Biography*. Grosse Pointe, Mich.: Scholarly Press, 1968. 2 vols.

Maynard, Theodore. *A Fire Was Lighted: The Life of Rose Hawthorne Lathrop*. Milwaukee: Bruce Publishing Co., 1948.

Mellow, James R. *Nathaniel Hawthorne in His Times*. Boston: Houghton Mifflin, 1980.

Wagenknecht, Edward. *Nathaniel Hawthorne: Man and Writer*. New York: Oxford University Press, 1961.

Waggoner, Hyatt. "Article on Alice Doane's Appeal." *University of Kansas City Review* (1950).

Young, Philip. *Hawthorne's Secret: An Untold Tale*. Boston: David R. Godine, 1984.

HEPBURN AND TRACY SOURCES

Anderson, Christopher. *Young Kate*. New York: Henry Holt, 1988.

Carey, Gary. *Katharine Hepburn: A Hollywood Yankee*. New York: Dell, 1983.

Davidson, Bill. *Spencer Tracy: Tragic Idol*. New York: E. P. Dutton, 1987.

Edwards, Anne. *A Remarkable Woman: A Biography of Katharine Hepburn*. New York: Simon & Schuster, 1985.

Hepburn, Katharine. *Me*. New York: Alfred A. Knopf, 1991.

Higham, Charles. *Kate: The Life of Katharine Hepburn*. New York: Signet, 1981.

Kanin, Garson. *Tracy and Hepburn: An Intimate Memoir*. New York: Donald I. Fine, 1988.

Leaming, Barbara. *Katharine Hepburn*. New York: Crown, 1995.

Morley, Sheridan. *Katharine Hepburn*. London: Pavilion Books, 1984.

KAFKA SOURCES

Citati, Pietro. *Kafka*. New York: Alfred A. Knopf, 1989.

Gray, R., ed. *Kafka: A Collection of Critical Essays*. Englewood Cliffs, N.J.: Prentice Hall, 1962.

Glazer, N. N. *The Loves of Franz Kafka*. New York: Schocken Books, 1986.

Heller, E. *Franz Kafka*. Princeton: Princeton University Press, 1974.

Kafka, Franz. *Letter to His Father*. New York: Schocken Books, 1953.

———. *Letters to Ottla and the Family*. 1982.

Pawel, E. *The Nightmare of Reason: A Life of Franz Kafka*. New York: Vintage, 1984.

Robert, M. *As Lonely as Franz Kafka: A Psychological Biography*. New York: Schocken Books, 1986.

Wagenbach, K. *Franz Kafka: Pictures of a Life*. New York: Random House, 1984.

KENNEDY SOURCES

Collier, Peter, and David Horowitz. *The Kennedys*. New York: Summit Books, 1984.

Davis, John H. *The Kennedys: Dynasty and Disaster*. New York: McGraw-Hill, 1984.

Goodwin, Doris Kearns. *The Fitzgeralds and the Kennedys.* New York: Simon & Schuster, 1987.

Hamilton, Nigel. *JFK Reckless Youth.* New York: Random House, 1992.

Heymann, C. David. *A Woman Named Jackie.* New York: New American Library, 1989.

James, Ann. *The Kennedy Scandals and Tragedies.* Lincolnwood, Ill.: Publication International, 1991.

Kennedy, Rose. *Times to Remember:* New York: Bantam Books, 1975.

Latham, Caroline, and Jeannie Sakol. *Kennedy Encyclopedia.* New York: New American Library, 1989.

Leamer, Lawrence. *The Kennedy Women.* New York: Villard Books, 1994.

McTaggart, Lynne. *Kathleen Kennedy: Her Life and Times.* New York: Dial, 1983.

Rachlin, Harvey. *The Kennedys: A Chronological History 1823–Present.* New York: World Almanac, 1986.

Rainie, Harrison, and John Quinn. *Growing Up Kennedy: The Third Wave Comes of Age.* New York: G. P. Putnam's Sons, 1983.

Saunders, Frank. *Torn Lace Curtain: Life with the Kennedys.* New York: Pinnacle Books, 1982.

Wills, Garry. *The Kennedy Imprisonment: A Mediation on Power.* New York: Little, Brown, 1981.

ANN LANDERS AND DEAR ABBY SOURCES

Pottker, Jan, and Bob Speziale. *Dear Ann, Dear Abby: The Unauthorized Biography of Ann Landers and Abigail Van Buren.* New York: Dodd, Mead & Company, 1987.

LINCOLN AND TODD SOURCES

Baker, Jean. *Mary Todd Lincoln: A Biography.* New York: W. W. Norton, 1987.

Eliot, Alexander. *Abraham Lincoln: An Illustrated Biography.* New York: W. H. Smith, 1985.

Neely, Mark E., and R. Gerald McMurtry. *The Insanity File: The Case of Mary Todd Lincoln.* Carbondale: Southern Illinois University Press, 1986.

Oates, Stephen B. *With Malice toward None: The Life of Abraham Lincoln.* New York: New American Library, 1977.

———. *Abraham Lincoln: The Man behind the Myths.* New York: Harper & Row, 1984.

Sandburg, Carl. *Abraham Lincoln: The Prairie Years,* vol. I and II. New York: Harcourt, Brace & Company.

Schreiner, Samuel A. *The Trials of Mrs. Lincoln.* New York: Donald I. Fine, 1987.

MAHLER SOURCES

Blaukopf, Kurt. *Gustav Mahler.* New York: Limelight Editions, 1985.

Keegan, Susanne. *The Bride of the Wind: The Life of Alma Mahler.* New York: Viking Press, 1992.

La Grange, Henry-Louis de. *Mahler*. London: Victor Gollancz Ltd., 1976.

Mahler, Alma. *Gustav Mahler: Memories and Letters*. Seattle: University of Washington Press, 1971.

Martner, Knud, ed. *Selected Letters of Gustav Mahler*. New York: Farrar, Straus, Giroux, 1979.

Monson, Karen. *Alma Mahler: Muse to Genius*. Boston: Houghton Mifflin, 1983.

Secherson, Edward. *Mahler*. New York: Omnibus Press, 1982.

MARX BROTHERS SOURCES

Adamson, Joe. *Groucho, Harpo, Chico, and Sometimes Zeppo*. New York: Simon & Schuster, 1973.

Arce, Hector. *Groucho*. New York: G. P. Putnam's Sons, 1979.

Bergan, Ronald. *The Life and Times of the Marx Brothers*. London: Green Wood Publishing, 1992.

Chandler, Charlotte. *Hello, I Must Be Going: Groucho and His Friends*. Garden City, N.Y.: Doubleday, 1978.

Crichton, Kyle. *The Marx Brothers*. Garden City, N.Y.: Doubleday, 1950.

Marx, Arthur. *Son of Groucho*. New York: David McKay Co., 1972.

———. *My Life with Groucho*. Fort Lee, N.J.: Barricade Books, 1988.

Marx, Groucho. *Groucho and Me*. New York: Simon & Schuster, 1959.

———. *Memoirs of a ? Lover*. New York: Simon & Schuster, 1963.

———. *The Groucho Letters*. New York: Simon & Schuster, 1967.

Marx, Harpo. "My Brother Groucho." *Coronet* (February 1951).

———, with Rowland Barber. *Harpo Speaks*. New York: Limelight Editions, 1985.

Marx, Maxine. *Growing Up with Chico*. New York: Limelight Editions, 1986.

Stables, Kate. *The Marx Bros*. Greenwich, Conn.: Brompton Books, 1992.

O'NEILL SOURCES

Bowen, Croswell. *The Curse of the Misbegotten*. New York: McGraw-Hill, 1959.

Gelb, Arthur, and Barbara Gelb. *O'Neill*. New York: Harper & Row, 1987.

O'Neill, Eugene. *Long Day's Journey into Night*. New Haven: Yale University Press, 1955.

Sheaffer, Louis. *O'Neill: Son and Playwright*. Boston: Little, Brown, 1968.

———. *O'Neill: Son and Artist*. Boston: Little, Brown, 1973.

ROBESON SOURCES

Dean, Phillip Hayes. "Paul Robeson." In *Black Heroes: Seven Plays*, ed. Errol Hill. New York: Applause Theatre Book Publishers, 1989.

Duberman, Martin Bauml. *Paul Robeson*. New York: Alfred A. Knopf, 1988.

Ehrlich, Scott. *Paul Robeson: Singer and Actor*. New York: Chelsea House, 1988.

Larsen, Rebecca. *Paul Robeson: Hero before His Time*. New York: Franklin Watts, 1989.

Ramdin, Ron. *Paul Robeson: The Man and His Mission*. London: Peter Owen, 1987.

Robeson, Paul. *Here I Stand*. Boston: Beacon Press, 1988.

Robeson, Susan. *The Whole World in His Hands: A Pictorial Biography of Paul Robeson*. New York: Carol Publishing Group, 1981.

ROBINSON SOURCES

Alvarez, Mark. *The Official Baseball Hall of Fame Story of Jackie Robinson*. New York: Simon & Schuster, 1990.

Robinson, Jackie. *I Never Had It Made*. New York: G. P. Putnam's Sons, 1972.

ROOSEVELT SOURCES

Asbell, Bernard, ed. *Mother and Daughter: The Letters of Eleanor and Anna Roosevelt*. New York: Coward, McCann & Geoghegan, 1982.

Bishop, Joseph B., ed. *Theodore Roosevelt's Letters to His Children*. New York: Charles Scribner's Sons, 1919.

Brough, James. *Princess Alice: A Biography of Alice Roosevelt Longworth*. Boston: Little, Brown, 1975.

Collier, Peter with David Horowitz. *The Roosevelts*. New York: Simon and Schuster, 1994.

Cook, Blanche Wiesen. *Eleanor Roosevelt 1884–1933: A Life: Mysteries of the Heart* Vol. 1, New York: Viking Penguin, 1992.

Felsenthal, Carol. *Alice Roosevelt Longworth*. New York: G. P. Putnam's Sons, 1988.

Fritz, Jean. *Bully for You, Teddy Roosevelt*. New York: G. P. Putnam's Sons, 1991.

Hagedorn, Hermann. *The Roosevelt Family of Sagamore Hill*. New York: Macmillan, 1954.

Lash, Joseph P. *Eleanor and Franklin*. New York: W. W. Norton, 1971.

McCullough, David. *Mornings on Horseback*. New York: Simon & Schuster, 1981.

Miller, Nathan. *Theodore Roosevelt*. New York: William Morrow & Co., 1992.

Morgan, Ted. *FDR: A Biography*. New York: Simon & Schuster, 1985.

Morris, Edmund. *The Rise of Theodore Roosevelt*. New York: Ballantine, 1979.

Pringle, Henry F. *Theodore Roosevelt*. New York: Harcourt, Brace & World, 1931.

Roosevelt, Eleanor. *The Autobiography of Eleanor Roosevelt*. Boston: G. K. Hall, 1984.

Roosevelt, James. *My Parents: A Differing View*. Chicago: Playboy Press, 1976.

Roosevelt, Theodore. *An Autobiography*. New York: Charles Scribner's Sons, 1925.

Teichman, Howard. *Alice: The Life and Times of Alice Roosevelt*. Englewood Cliffs, N.J.: Prentice Hall, 1979.

SARTRE SOURCES

Cohen-Solal, A. *Sartre, a Life*. New York: Pantheon Books, 1987.

Sartre, Jean Paul. *The Words*. Greenwich, Conn.: Fawcett, 1964.

SHAW AND PAYNE-TOWNSHEND SOURCES

Colbourne, M. *The Real Bernard Shaw*. New York: Philosophical Library, 1949.

Dervin, D. *Bernard Shaw: A Psychological Study*. Lewisburg, Penn.: Bucknell University Press, 1975.

Dunbar, Janet. *Mrs. G.B.S.: A Portrait*. New York: Harper & Row, 1963.

Holroyd, Michael. *Bernard Shaw*, vol. I, *The Search for Love, 1856–1898*. New York: Random House, 1988.

———. *Bernard Shaw*, vol. II, *The Pursuit of Power, 1989–1918*. New York: Random House, 1989.

———. *Bernard Shaw*, vol. III, *The Lure of Fantasy, 1918–1951*. New York: Random House, 1991.

Shaw, Bernard. *Complete Plays*, vol. III. New York: Dodd, Mead, 1968.

Smith, J. P. *The Unrepentant Pilgrim: A Study of the Development of Bernard Shaw*. Boston: Houghton Mifflin, 1965.

TOLSTOY SOURCES

Citati, Pietro. *Tolstoy*. New York: Schocken Books, 1986.

Courcel, Martine de. *Tolstoy: The Ultimate Reconciliation*. New York: Charles Scribner's Sons, 1980.

Edwards, Anne. *Sonya: The Life of Countess Tolstoy*. New York: Simon & Schuster, 1981.

Maude, Aylmer. *The Life of Tolstoy*, vols. I and II. New York: Oxford University Press, 1987.

Simmons, Ernest J. *Leo Tolstoy*, vols. I and II. New York: Vintage, 1960.

Smoluchowski, Louise. *Lev & Sonya: The Story of the Tolstoy Marriage*. New York: G. P. Putnam's Sons, 1987.

Stilman, Leon, ed. *Leo Tolstoy: Last Diaries*. New York: G. P. Putnam's Sons, 1960.

Tolstoy, Leo. *Childhood, Boyhood, Youth*. Baltimore: Penguin, 1964.

Tolstoy, Nikolai. *The Tolstoys: Twenty-four Generations of Russian History*. New York: William Morrow & Co., 1983.

Troyat, Henri. *Tolstoy*. New York: Dell, 1967.

Howard, Fred. *Wilbur and Orville: A Biography of the Wright Brothers*. New York: Alfred A. Knopf, 1987.

Kelly, Fred C. *The Wright Brothers: A Biography*. New York: Dover, 1989.

Kinnane, Adrian. "The Crucible of Flight." Unpublished manuscript. George Washington University, Meyer Treatment Center.

————. "A House United: Morality and Invention in the Wright Brothers' Home." *Psychohistory Review* (1988).

McMahon, John R. *The Wright Brothers: Fathers of Flight.* Boston: Little, Brown, 1930.

Miller, Ivonnette Wright. *Wright Reminiscences.* Dayton, Ohio: Privately printed, 1978.

Renstrom, Arthur G. *Wilbur and Orville Wright: A Chronology Commemorating the One Hundredth Anniversary of the Birth of Orville Wright.* Washington, D.C.: Library of Congress, 1975.

Reynolds, Quenton. *The Wright Brothers.* New York: Random House, 1950.

Walsh, John Evangelist. *One Day at Kitty Hawk: The Untold Story of the Wright Brothers and the Airplane.* New York: Crowell, 1975.

Wilson, A. N. *Tolstoy.* New York: W. W. Norton, 1988.

QUEEN VICTORIA SOURCES

Auchincloss, Louis. *Persons of Consqeunce: Queen Victoria and Her Circle.* New York: Random House, 1979.

Benson, E. F. *Queen Victoria.* London: Chatto & Windus, 1987.

Charlot, Monica. *Victoria: The Young Queen.* Oxford: Blackwell, 1991.

Hibbert, Christopher. *Queen Victoria in Her Letters and Journals.* New York: Viking, 1985.

James, Robert Rhodes. *Prince Albert.* New York: Alfred A. Knopf, 1984.

Stoney, Benita. *Victoria and Albert, a Family Life at Osborne House.* New York: Prentice Hall, 1991.

Strachey, Lytton. *Queen Victoria.* New York: Harcourt, Brace, Jovanovich, 1921.

Thompson, Dorothy. *Queen Victoria: The Woman, the Monarchy, and the People.* New York: Pantheon Books, 1990.

Weintraub, Stanley. *Victoria.* New York: E. P. Dutton, 1987.

Wilson, E. *Eminent Victorians.* New York: W. W. Norton, 1990.

Woodham-Smith, Cecil. *Queen Victoria.* New York: Donald Fine, Inc., 1972.

WASHINGTON SOURCES

Bourne, M. A. *First Family: George Washington and His Intimate Relations.* New York: W. W. Norton, 1982.

Desmond, Alice Curtis. *George Washington's Mother.* New York: Dodd, Mead, & Co., 1962.

Mitchell, S. W. *The Youth of Washington.* New York: Century Company, 1904.

Moore, C. *The Family Life of George Washington.* Boston: Houghton Mifflin, 1926.

WRIGHT BROTHERS SOURCES

Crouch, Tom D. *The Bishop's Boys: A Life of Wilbur and Orville Wright.* New York: W. W. Norton, 1989.

Freedman, Russell. *The Wright Brothers: How They Invented the Airplane*. New York: Holiday House, 1991.

Goulder, Grace. *Ohio Scenes and Citizens*. Cleveland: World, 1964.

Howard, Fred. *Wilbur and Orville: A Biography of the Wright Brothers*. New York: Alfred A. Knopf, 1987.

Kelly, Fred C. *The Wright Brothers: A Biography*. New York: Dover, 1989.

Kinnane, Adrian. "The Crucible of Flight." Unpublished manuscript. George Washington University, Meyer Treatment Center.

———. "A House United: Morality and Invention in the Wright Brothers' Home." *Psychohistory Review*. (1988).

McMahon, John R. *The Wright Brothers: Fathers of Flight*. Boston: Little, Brown, 1930.

Miller, Ivonnette Wright. *Wright Reminiscences*. Dayton, Ohio: Privately printed, 1978.

Renstrom, Arthur G. *Wilbur and Orville Wright: A Chronology Commemorating the One Hundredth Anniversary of the Birth of Orville Wright*. Washington, D.C.: Library of Congress, 1975.

Reynolds, Quenton. *The Wright Brothers*. New York: Random House, 1950.

Walsh, John Evangelist. *One Day at Kitty Hawk: The Untold Story of the Wright Brothers and the Airplane*. New York: Crowell, 1975.

ACKNOWLEDGMENTS

Thanks are due to many people for their support as this book evolved. Randy Gerson was a helpful friend and collaborator in developing the concept; I am grateful for our work together. I am also deeply indebted to my mother, Helen McGoldrick, to whom the book is dedicated for her belief in me and her encouragement throughout the years I was developing the book. I am also very grateful to my sisters, Neale and Morna, for their ideas, suggestions, and honest feedback, and to Neale for her help with the genograms—and willingness to respond at a moment's notice to any problem I was having in my work. I am grateful to my husband and my son for their love and support over all the years it has taken to write this book. My nephews Guy and Hugh Livingston came through for me on many occasions when their support was most needed. My aunt Mildred provided moral support, as she always has for my endeavors. I was most fortunate during the writing of this book to reconnect with Selma Burke, a mentor and inspiration since my childhood, and she has become another important part of my personal going home journey. My friend Kathy Milea believed in the book and my ability to write it from the start and generously read manuscript drafts, making invaluable suggestions over the years. Many other friends offered direct and indirect support throughout the eight years of writing this book. Carol Anderson, Froma Walsh, Betty Carter, Nydia Preto, Meyer Rothberg, Rhea

Almeida, Paulette Hines, Tom Johnson, Nancy Boyd Franklin, Michael Rohrbaugh, Robert Green, Rich Simon, Jette Sinkjaer Simon, Nollaig Byrne, Imelda McCarthy, Celia Falicov, Gerald Grow, John Folwarski, Janey Hart, Jane Sufian, Charlotte Fremon Danielson, Joyce Richardson, Ann Dunston, Evan Imber Black, Jo-Ann Krestan, Claudia Bepko, Elaine Pinderhughes, Ann Hartman, Joan Laird, and Donna Mayer were all important resources for me, though they may not all have realized the role they were playing. My son, John, went from birth to fourth grade as the book progressed. Our marvelous nanny and researcher, Meg Tischio, was a generous, patient, and tireless resource, helping with the research for the book, with the manuscript itself, and in innumerable ways on the home front. My administrative assistants, Jeaninne Stone and Peggy Senanayake, have also offered invaluable direct and indirect support on the manuscript and by fielding other aspects of my life, which made it possible for me to focus my attention on this book. I am deeply grateful to both of them for what they have meant to me. My trainees and clients have been a wellspring of insights and have inspired me by their courage in dealing with the hard issues in their families. Mary Scanlon, medical librarian for Robert Wood Johnson Medical School, was more than generous in helping with references. Finally, my editors at Norton, Carol Houck Smith and Susan Barrows Munro, have worked with me through all the ups and downs of this book. I am grateful for their interest in the project and their help in bringing it to fruition.

INDEX

italicized page numbers refer to illustrations